DATE DUE

AG 20 '93			
JA 7 94			
DE 15 95			
AG 1 01			

DEMCO 38-296

HEAD TO HEAD

HEAD TO HEAD

THE COMING ECONOMIC BATTLE
AMONG JAPAN, EUROPE, AND AMERICA

Lester Thurow

WILLIAM MORROW AND COMPANY, INC.
New York

Library of Congress Cataloging-in-Publication Data

Thurow, Lester.
    Head to head: the coming economic battle among Japan, Europe, and
America / Lester C. Thurow.
        p.   cm.
    Includes bibliographical references and index.
    ISBN 0-688-11150-5
    1. Economic history—1990– 2. Economic forecasting. 3. Japan—
Economic policy—1989– 4. European Economic Community countries—
Economic policy. 5. United States—Economic policy—1981–
6. International economic relations. I. Title.
HC59.T5157   1992
337.52—dc20   91-33300
                                                                                      CIP

Printed in the United States of America

3 4 5 6 7 8 9 10

BOOK DESIGN BY PAUL CHEVANNES

To those at Bretton Woods and elsewhere who in the aftermath of World War II constructed the most productive economy the world has ever seen. May this generation of world leaders be as successful.

ACKNOWLEDGMENTS

The arguments in this book have been honed at too many presentations (inside and outside MIT) to be named, but everyone who offered feedback has my thanks. Without their help, this book would not be what it is. Those (Sandra Del Boca, Michael Cusumano, Ronald Dore, Takashi Iwamura, Robert McKersie) who gave me written comments on drafts of the manuscript have my particular thanks. Members of the MIT-Sloan community were also willing to put up with a certain absenteeism on the part of their dean as I completed this manuscript. Their patience was appreciated. Ryan Matreyek and Torben Thurow helped with data collection and fact checking.

CONTENTS

Chapter 1

THE BEAR IN THE WOODS IS GONE

There is a bear in the woods. For some
people, the bear is easy to see. Others
don't see it at all. Some people say the
bear is tame. Others say it is vicious and
dangerous. Since no one can really be
sure who's right, isn't it smart to be as
strong as the bear—if there is a bear.
—Reagan TV advertisement, fall 1984

Most of the last half century has been devoted to worrying
about the Soviet bear in the woods. Democracy and capitalism
faced off against dictatorship and communism. In the late
1940s it looked as if the Soviet bear, helped by the newly tri-
umphant Red Chinese dragon, wished to conquer the world.
Aid to Greece and Turkey, NATO, rearming Japan and West
Germany, and the Korean War were all efforts at containing
the bears and dragons in the woods.

In the 1950s the Soviet bear's military power seemed to be
matched by its economic and technological capabilities. The
Russian Sputnik flew; the American equivalent did not. In the
1950s the Soviet Union was growing faster than the United
States. If economic trends were projected forward, the Soviet
gross national product (GNP) would pass that of the United
States in 1984—a year with ominous literary overtones. Con-
tainment was not a problem limited to Eastern Europe. In the
Third World, communism, based on the economic success of

11

the USSR, was widely seen as the only model for economic development. Communist Cuba, just ninety miles from the United States, was the wave of the future. When Nikita Khrushchev banged his shoe on the table at the United Nations and threatened to bury the industrial democracies militarily, technologically, and economically, everyone took him seriously. It looked like it was happening.

John F. Kennedy's 1960 campaign for the presidency revolved around getting the country moving again—on all fronts—militarily, technically, and economically. With the construction of the Berlin Wall and the Cuban Missile Crisis, occurring shortly after his election, the Bear loomed ever larger in the early 1960s. At middecade President Lyndon Johnson spotted a North Vietnamese offspring of the Red Chinese dragon in the jungles of Vietnam. For the next ten years the dragon's offspring got most of America's attention and resources.

Two oil shocks and the discovery that the Chinese dragon was a friendly dragon—if not an ally, at least not an enemy—temporarily diverted attention away from the Soviet bear in the mid-1970s. But with a Soviet military buildup in the 1970s (now in dispute as to whether it really occurred), the American humiliation in Iran, and the USSR's invasion of Afghanistan, the bear was back—bigger, badder, and more dangerous than ever. In response to the glimpse of this enormous bear in the woods, President Ronald Reagan doubled America's military budget in the first half of the 1980s. A huge high-tech Star Wars program would be necessary to control the bear and his "evil empire."

Suddenly, the bear disappeared. The Berlin Wall came down, East Germany and West Germany were united, democracy and capitalism arrived in the formerly communist countries of Middle Europe, the Red Army withdrew to the east, the Warsaw Pact was abrogated, the Soviet Union split asunder, and communism ended in Europe, its birthplace. Democracy and capitalism had won. Together they had beaten dictatorship and communism.

In many ways the retreat of communism is just as mysterious as Genghis Khan's abandonment of his conquest of Europe 770 years earlier. While it was clear that the 1950s vision of the Soviet Union as an economic superpower was wrong, the USSR was not, if the CIA is to be believed, an economic basket case in the 1970s and early 1980s. As Gorbachev came to power, the CIA's Directorate of Intelligence was estimating that the USSR had grown at a rate of 2.1 percent from 1975 to 1985—a rate slightly slower than America's 2.9 percent over the same period—but nothing that dictated radical reforms were necessary.[1] In the mid-1980s the USSR was doing even better. In 1983 a 3.3 percent growth rate was recorded, and in 1986 an even better performance, 4.1 percent, was achieved. There were no signs of collapse. Quite the contrary, this was the period when plans for President Reagan's Star Wars program topped the American political agenda. The economic problems that are now highly visible all arose under Mikhail Gorbachev and explain why he is so unpopular at home.

The USSR's inability to deliver civilian consumption goods probably guaranteed that communism could not have lasted forever, but if the intellectual will had been there it could have continued for a long time. Just as he was about to conquer Europe, Genghis Khan turned around and disappeared into central Asia. In many ways the sudden disappearance of communism is no less mysterious.

By undercutting the authority of the old central-planning system that had been in place, Gorbachev created a situation where it was not possible to return to the past. What happened was much more fundamental than his opening the door to change. Once the door was open a crack, the old system was not so much ripped up by Gorbachev as it was dismantled by thousands of Soviet citizens who simply became unwilling to cooperate with it. When their voluntary cooperation vanished, the old system vanished. Even if the leaders of the abortive 1991 coup had succeeded, they could not have restored old-fashioned communism any more than Genghis Khan could once again sweep out of the Mongolian steppes.

Everyone from the far right to the far left in the former Soviet Union understood that the old system had come to the end of the line. Intellectually, this is why the 1991 coup failed. Its leaders had no program to offer to persuade other members of the Army and KGB to join them. If the issue was just personal survival, jumping on the Yeltsin bandwagon was a better option for personal success, which is exactly what the head of the Soviet Air Force did. With the Army and the KGB divided, no coup could succeed.

In many ways the coup and its failure are favorable developments. It is now crystal clear that there is no possibility that the former Soviet Union will go back to the status quo ante. It is no longer a military superpower. Its economy is not strong enough to permit it to regain its previous military status. The Soviet Army no longer sits in the middle of Europe. The Soviet Union of the past seventy years is now only a historical subject. No matter how many or how few countries emerge from the remains of the Soviet Union, no matter who rules, and no matter what system of government triumphs, the USSR is gone.

A sudden unexpected victory creates psychological problems for the victor. Its populace wants to tell glorious tales about how victory was achieved. In America, after the fall of the Berlin Wall, there was a flurry of talk about the "end of history."[2,3] The American system would be adopted everywhere and last forever. To worry about boredom at the end of history, however, is not a problem any human being will ever have to solve. History is far from over. A new competitive phase is even now under way.

In 1945 there were two military superpowers, the United States and the Soviet Union, contending for supremacy and one economic superpower, the United States, that stood alone. In 1992 there is one military superpower, the United States, standing alone, and three economic superpowers, the United States, Japan, and Europe, centered on Germany, jousting for economic supremacy. Without a pause, the contest has shifted from being a military contest to being an economic contest.

THE NEW GAME

When systems fail, the need for change is obvious. Communism failed. That part of the world controlled by communism will change as a result. From it will emerge new players in the world economy. The transition from communism to capitalism is going to be difficult. Some of the new players from the Second World will join the First World; others will join the Third World.

Failure requires change, but so does success. If economies are successful, they slowly alter the circumstances under which they operate. Success generates new conditions, and these new conditions often require different institutions and altered operating procedures if success is to continue. So it is in the world of the successful market economies. In the past half century the world has shifted from being a single polar economic world revolving around the United States to a tripolar world built upon Japan, the European Community, and the United States. In Europe an economic giant, the European Community, is in the process of being created. For the first time in modern history, an oriental tiger, Japan, has emerged as a competitor fully equal to any in Europe or North America.

Because of their different histories and present circumstances, both of these new players are going to be infusing the capitalistic economic game with strategies very different from those found in the Anglo-Saxon world. They will force the economic leaders of the nineteenth and twentieth centuries, the United Kingdom and the United States, to alter their modes of playing the economic game. The United Kingdom's traditional procedures will essentially disappear as it is absorbed into the European Community. Sharp changes will be forced upon the United States as for the first time in a long time it confronts economic and technological equals.

Today's rules for the international economic game, the GATT (General Agreement on Tariffs and Trade)–Bretton Woods system, were written after World War II and built on the realities that then existed. They were designed to help most of the industrial world rebuild from the destruction of World War II and to catch up with the United States. They succeeded. But their very success altered the nature of the system. Rules, procedures, and institutions designed for a unipolar world don't work in a multipolar world. As a result the system that governed the world economy in the last half of the twentieth century will not be the system governing the world economy in the first half of the twenty-first century. A new system of quasi trading blocks employing managed trade will emerge.

While economic success slowly undermined the post–World War II economic system, new technologies were blowing up the old strategies for economic success. The green revolution and the materials-science revolution have reduced the importance of natural resources in economic development. Having natural resources did not now make one rich; not having natural resources did not now stop one from being rich.

A telecommunications-computer-transportation-logistics revolution has permitted global sourcing and the development of a world capital market. Both have made it easier for poor countries to export to rich countries and for rich countries to source abroad in poor countries. Effectively, everyone now has access to the same world capital market. More equal access to capital has reduced the edge that being born in a rich country used to give.

In the future sustainable competitive advantage will depend more on new process technologies and less on new product technologies. New industries of the future such as biotechnology depend upon brainpower. Man-made comparative advantage replaces the comparative advantage of Mother Nature (natural-resources endowments) or history (capital endowments).

Objectively, the changes necessary to be successful in the formerly communistic world are much larger and more difficult to manage than those that will be required in the capitalistic world. Subjectively, the required changes may be more difficult in the capitalistic world. If change is required by success rather than failure, there is an instinctive human inclination to think that emerging problems can be solved by going back to the "ancient Roman virtues." It is difficult to admit that the world has changed and that one's ancient Roman virtues are no longer virtues. It is very hard to recognize that new realities force the creation of new virtues—new procedures, new rules, and new institutions.

Nowhere are the necessary changes going to be harder to make than in the United States, for in the past century it has been the most successful economy in the world. After World

War II the United States did not have economic competitors. It stood alone with effortless economic superiority, by far the world's strongest economy, playing a game designed to fit its strengths. In the next century the United States will be just one of a number of equal players playing a game where the rules increasingly will be written by others. Among the capitalistic economies it will have to make the largest changes. Those changes will be very difficult psychologically—even if objectively they would not look large to an outside observer who did not have to carry the heavy baggage of a successful history.

Looking forward, the next half century will be a competitive-cooperative three-way economic game among Japan, Europe, and the United States. In jockeying for competitive advantage, they will force each other to adjust. To mutually prosper, they will have to cooperate to create a world economy that works and a global environment that allows them to survive and to enjoy what they produce.

THE PROBLEMS OF CAPITALISM

While most of the problems of capitalism are those of success, there are some failures. If one looks at the growth rate of the non-communist world, it slowed from 4.9 percent per year in the 1960s to 3.8 percent per year in the 1970s, and then again fell to 2.9 percent per year in the 1980s.[4] In the 1980s per capita growth in the gross national product (GNP) was only 40 percent of what it had been in the 1960s (1.1 percent versus 2.8 percent per year), and much of the Third World had falling real per capita incomes over the decade.

Capitalism has its virtues and vices. It is a wonderful machine for producing abundant goods and services, but it is hard to get started. Third World failures far outnumber First World successes. The Second World, the formerly communist world, is finding it very hard to get capitalism started. Free markets also tend to produce levels of income inequality that are politically incompatible with democratic government. Witness rising inequality and homelessness in the United States, and note the need for large social-welfare income-transfer payment systems in every major industrial country.

Left to itself, unfettered capitalism has a tendency to drift into either financial instability or monopoly. Tulip mania, the South Sea Bubble, numerous nineteenth-century financial panics, and the stock-market collapse of 1929 were all forerunners of the current mess in America's deregulated financial markets. The current consolidations in the U.S. airline industry are not unlike the great monopolistic trusts of the last half of the nineteenth century.

If government had not come to the rescue, finance capitalism, as it is practiced in the United States, would now be collapsing. Most of America's savings and loan banks (S&Ls) are in government receivership. Large numbers of commercial banks have not yet gone broke but are broke in the sense that they could not be liquidated to pay off their depositors if that should have to be done. The ultimate cost may not end up being as big as that for the S&Ls, but it is going to require a lot of the taxpayer money. If the banking system had not been bailed out by government, panic would have set in as individuals lost their savings accounts, and a repeat of the Great Depression would probably now be under way.

Paradoxically, as Eastern Europe privatizes, America nationalizes. With the collapse of much of its banking sector, by early 1991 the American government had been forced to take over two hundred billion dollars in private assets and was expected to end up owning three hundred billion dollars in private assets before the hemorrhaging stopped.[5] A government corporation, the Resolution Trust Corporation, has become by far the largest owner of property in America. To these totals must be added the large sums that will be needed by the Pension Benefit Guaranty Corporation, the government fund that guarantees pensions, to fulfill its obligations to protect private pension funds. Pension funds hold 30 percent of those dubious junk bonds, and the bankruptcies that are flowing from the financial excesses of the 1980s will require billions in government aid to insure that the private pensions that have been promised are in fact paid. The pension funds of the airlines that were already in bankruptcy by mid-1991 will require more than two billion dollars in taxpayer money all by themselves.[6]

The same problems afflict the insurance sector. Here the guarantees have been given by state governments. Forty-seven states guarantee life-insurance policies, most up to $300,000 per person. In early 1991 the states of California and New York took over the management of Executive Life, a company with thirteen billion dollars in assets, two thirds of which were invested in junk bonds.[7] By midyear three other large insurance companies (First Capital Life, Monarch Life, and Mutual Benefit Life) were under state jurisdiction. To prevent the feared bankruptcy of an out-of-state holding company from bringing down an in-state insurance subsidiary, Massachusetts stepped in to start running an insurance company that had not yet gone broke.

In the industrial sector America has just seen the tip of the iceberg of the corporations that have loaded up with too much debt and gone broke because of the merger and takeover wars. Airlines and large retailing firms lead the parade into bankruptcy, but there is a lot of the parade yet to come. With these industrial bankruptcies will come the need for even more government (taxpayer) help (unemployment insurance for those who end up unemployed, deposit insurance to cover the banks that go broke because they have lent to companies that go broke, and pension insurance to pay the pensions of those who were owed pensions by bankrupt corporations). Unfettered Anglo-Saxon capitalism is finding it difficult to cope with the present and may not be the unstoppable wave of the future that pundits on the political right like to extol.

MILITARY AND ECONOMIC POWER

If this were a book about military power, the book would focus almost entirely upon the United States. The rough military parity between the Soviet Union and the United States in the last half of the twentieth century has disappeared. At least at the beginning of the twenty-first century, there is only one military superpower—the United States. As the War in the Gulf showed, only the United States can move a vast modern army halfway around the world in a few months and impose its military might on what was then the fourth-largest army in the world. Militarily, the United States is going to be the dominant power in the first half of the twenty-first century in a way in which it was not the dominant power in the second half of the twentieth century.

Those in Japan or Germany who argue that the United States can't be an independent military superpower since it will have "to depend on other countries for meeting an over-whelming proportion of its war costs,"[8] or those who think that if "Japan sold chips to the Soviet Union and stopped sell-ing them to the U.S., this would upset the entire military bal-ance,"[9] are simply misreading the Gulf War and the present state of technological competition. When it comes to high-end sophisticated military technology, chips or otherwise, Japan is not a world leader. It leads in low-cost, low-performance civil-ian semiconductor chips. The United States is not a hobbled giant that will need technological aid to employ military force in the next century.

The costs of the War in the Gulf could easily have been paid entirely by the United States. Those costs were very small in comparison with a GNP approaching $6,000 billion per year. Financial aid was requested from those countries that did not provide soldiers, not to pay for the war but to convince the American public that the war was an *allied,* and not just an American, effort. For Americans to die defending the oil sup-plies of Germany and Japan without any Japanese or German contribution was simply politically unacceptable. The Ameri-can public's backlash would have destroyed existing alliances. Given that much of the equipment and ammunition used up in the Gulf War came out of America's military inventories and does not need to be replaced, America made a profit on the War in the Gulf. Financially, it came out of the war stronger than it went in.

But military power does not lead to economic power. Quite the reverse, if a country is to be a military superpower (that is, use up a lot of human and economic resources on military activities—a form of public consumption), it must be willing to be self-disciplined enough to cut its private consumption to levels that insure it is not cutting back on the investments needed to keep civilian productivity growing. Spartan self-dis-cipline is necessary if a country is to have both sustainable military and economic superpower status. An economic superpower must make large investments in civilian research and development (R&D), plant and equipment, public infrastructure, and human skills to remain an economic superpower. A military superpower must make large investments in military R&D, military equipment, military infrastructure, and military training to remain a military superpower. If a nation wishes to be both, it must make both sorts of investments. If a country is satisfied with only one of the two forms of power, economic or military, much less self-discipline is necessary. If a country is interested in neither economic nor military power in the future, no self-discipline is the surest route for having neither.

A country can be a military superpower for a long time, even as its economic might wanes. Economic rot at the core leads to military weakness at the periphery, but the time lags are sometimes very long. Rome won most of the battles with the barbarians on its borders during its centuries of decline. But eventually, problems at the center of the Empire led it to withdraw from the periphery. The Romans were never militarily defeated in the British Isles. One day they just left. Eventually, the Romans moved the center of their Empire from Rome to Constantinople, where they were not finally defeated by the Turks until many centuries after the fall of Rome itself. While Rome was in the economic dark ages, Roman military power was still alive and well in Byzantium.

Similarly, after the Mongol conquest in the thirteenth century, China was never again completely conquered by its neighbors. For hundreds of years China simply sat behind its Great Wall growing weaker and weaker until it had essentially rotted away at the core and the nineteenth-century colonial powers could establish spheres of influence. Throughout those seven centuries China was always the greatest military power in the Orient. But eventually there came a day when that just wasn't good enough.

History is clear. While military power can sometimes outlast economic power for centuries, eventually military power depends upon having a successful economic base. America's success in the War in the Gulf proves that it is, and will be, a military superpower in the century to come. But its success in the Gulf in no way guarantees that it will be an economic superpower in the twenty-first century.

CREATING ECONOMIC COMPETITORS

At the end of World War II, an intense debate raged as to what should be done about the Japanese and German economies. There were those that argued for the Roman solution—sow the fields of Carthage with salt and permanently destroy its economy. Because the German defeat occurred a few months earlier than that of Japan, systematic deindustrialization was to some extent actually practiced in Germany—particularly in East Germany by the Russians. But in the end what many at the time viewed as an extremely naive American approach prevailed. If countries could be made rich, they would be democratic. If their richness depended upon selling in the American market, they would be forced to be allies of the United States. These naive beliefs underlay the inception of the Marshall Plan for those countries, both friend and foe, devastated by World War II. It is important to remember that the Marshall Plan was also offered to the Soviet Union and the communist countries of Middle Europe. The offer was turned down by Marshal Stalin.

The same ideas lead to foreign aid for poor Third World countries—a new concept that had never before been tried. Prior to World War II the world was dominated by colonial empires where the purpose of colonies was to make the home country rich. While historians argue over whether colonies contributed to home-country wealth (they may have cost more than they were worth), there is no argument as to what the colonial powers were trying to do. They were trying to take wealth out of their colonies to make themselves rich.

Although there has been a mixed record of economic development since World War II, the successes have vastly outnumbered the failures. With foreign aid and an open, easily accessed American market, most Third World countries grew from 1950 to 1980 as they had never grown before in all of human history. With the exception of perhaps a dozen countries, mostly in Africa, in 1980 inflation-corrected per capita standards of living were everywhere else much higher than they had been in 1950.

While the ultimate post–World War II goal was for countries to become just as wealthy as the United States, probably no one believed that this was really possible Naive or not, what was then put in place—the GATT–Bretton Woods trading system, the Marshall Plan, the European Coal and Steel Community—worked far better than anyone then could have believed. Only forty-five years later there are several countries just as wealthy as America. Some of the Third World is on the verge of making it into the First World. Europe is integrating. The communist command economies are moving toward capitalism and democracy in Europe. The wildest dreams of the naive dreamers of the late 1940s (Truman, Marshall, and Monnet) are being fulfilled.

Building upon the economic muscle of Germany, Western Europe is patiently engineering an economic giant. If this bioengineering can continue with the eventual addition of Middle and Eastern Europe, the House of Europe could eventually create an economy more than twice as large as Japan and the United States combined. In the Pacific a Japanese economic tiger arose from the ashes of World War II. Emulation led to the birth of four little capitalistic dragons (Korea, Taiwan, Hong Kong, and Singapore) on the Pacific Rim.

From everyone's perspective, replacing a military confrontation with an economic contest is a step forward. No one gets killed; vast resources don't have to be devoted to negative-sum activities. The winner builds the world's best products and enjoys the world's highest standard of living. The loser gets to buy some of those best products—but not as many as the winner. Relative to the military confrontations of the past century, both the winners and the losers are winners in the economic game ahead. Being aggressively invaded by well-made Japanese or German products from firms that intend to conquer American markets is not at all equivalent to the threat of a military invasion from the Soviet Union or mainland China. Nor does it hark back to the German and Japanese military invasions of World War II.

Quite the contrary, the competition revolves around the following questions: Who can make the best products? Who expands their standards of living most rapidly? Who has the best-educated and best-skilled work force in the world? Who is the world's leader in investment—plant and equipment, research and development (R&D), infrastructure? Who organizes best? Whose institutions—government, education, business—are world leaders in efficiency? To be forced by one's economic competitors to do all of these things is a good thing—not a bad thing.

Military competitions are ultimately wasteful. Resources must be devoted to activities that at best (unused), do not contribute to future human welfare, and at worst (used), are destructive to human welfare. Economic competitions are exactly the opposite. Governments are forced to focus on how they can most efficiently make life better for their citizens. "Economic warfare" is not at all equivalent to "military warfare" despite the use of the word *warfare* in both terms. If the world can reduce its spending on armaments, there is a peace dividend to be had in both the developed and the underdeveloped world.[10]

From an American perspective, it is also important to remember that being just one of a number of wealthy countries in a wealthy world is far better than being the only wealthy country in a poor world—even if Americans are some times envious of those newly wealthy neighbors, and even if those newly wealthy neighbors sometimes force Americans to rethink how they live.

In the economic contest that lies ahead, the world is not divided into friend and foe. The game is simultaneously competitive and cooperative. One can remain friends and allies, yet still want to win.

THE TWENTY-FIRST CENTURY

The nineteenth century is remembered as the century of Great Britain. It was the dominant economic power. The twentieth century will be remembered as the century of the United States. It was, and is, the dominant economic power. In terms of the calendar, the twenty-first century has not yet quite begun, but a future economic historian looking backward will date the end of the twentieth century slightly early. Just as the fall of the Berlin Wall in November of 1989 marked the end of the old contest between capitalism and communism, so the integration of the European Common Market, on

Jan. 1, 1993, will mark the beginning of a new economic contest in a new century at the start of the third millennium.[11] At
that moment, for the first time in more than a century, the
United States will become the second largest economy in the
world. This reality will become the symbol for the start of
the competition that determines who will own the twenty-first
century.

Chapter 2

A NEW ECONOMIC GAME

In the spring of 1991 British prime minister Margaret Thatcher lost her job. She had not lost an election. It was not obvious that she would. She lost her job because she insisted on playing the old twentieth-century economic game. She simply would not recognize that the world had changed and that she would have to change with it. She would not play the twenty-first century's economic game. Having lost touch with reality, she had to be pushed aside by those who were previously her allies.

Her downfall arose over the issue of European integration. Her stated purpose was to preserve the powers of the Bank of England to control money supplies and set British interest rates. She saw losing these powers as "the greatest abdication of national and parliamentary sovereignty in our history."[1] She did not understand that these economic powers were no longer within her national political power. In the new world economy what Mrs. Thatcher wanted to do could not be done—even though it had always been done in the past.

As of January 1, 1993, any European bank will be able to place an office in any other European city without government permission. When this happens, everyone will borrow in the country where interest rates were lowest and lend in the country where interest rates were highest—making interest rates the same everywhere in Europe. Mrs. Thatcher's only real choice was to join the European Monetary System (EMS) and have the power to appoint some of the members of a new European central bank, or refuse to do so and watch the German Bundesbank, in the absence of any British votes, gradually become the effective central bank for Europe. To retain any economic power over interest rates for the United Kingdom, she had to participate.

If England did not stay in the Community and did not join the EMS, the financial capital of Europe would move from London to Frankfurt.[2] Finance, Britain's most important industry, would almost certainly be lost. Even with England's full participation in the European Community (EC), with Germany as Europe's leading economic power, it is going to be difficult to keep Europe's financial capital in London. The City of London simply cannot afford the handicap of being outside the European Monetary Union. As a result, a conservative financial community had to dump a conservative prime minister.

In the end Mrs. Thatcher lost her job because she could not come to grips with the new economic realities. She didn't like European integration, but she could neither leave the European Community (Britain could not prosper without being a member) nor stop its further integration (if necessary, the other members would integrate without Britain). Like King Canute, she could not hold back the tides of world history. Mrs. Thatcher may end up in the history books as the most famous leader to lose her job because she could not adjust her thinking to new world realities, but she will be joined by many others.

NEW COMPETITORS

Looking backward, future historians will see the twentieth century as a century of niche competition and the twenty-first century as a century of head-to-head competition. In 1950 the United States had a per capita GNP four times that of West Germany and fifteen times that of Japan. What were high-wage products from the Japanese perspective were low-wage products in West Germany. What were high-wage products in West Germany were low-wage products in America. As a result, imports from West Germany or Japan were not seen as threatening the good jobs that Americans wanted. Conversely, America's exports did not threaten good jobs in West Germany or Japan. The United States exported agricultural products that they could not grow, raw materials that they did not have, and high-tech products, such as civilian jet airliners, that they could not build.

The 1990s start from a very different place. In broad terms there are now three relatively equal contenders—Japan; the European Community, centered around its most powerful country, Germany; and the United States. Measured in terms of external purchasing power (how much can be bought if one's income is spent abroad), the per capita GNPs of Japan and Germany are slightly larger than that of the United States. The exact amount depends upon the precise value of the dollar, mark, and yen when the measurements are made. Measured in terms of internal purchasing power (how much can be bought if one's income is spent at home), America's per capita GNP is higher than that of West Germany or Japan.[3] The precise amount depends upon whether the measurements include social services (the Germans get many more than Americans) and leisure (in Germany scheduled hours of annual work are about 10 percent less than that in America, Germans are absent from work ten days more per year, and many fewer German women are in the paid labor force), or only private goods and services.[4,5,6,7]

Consumer standards of living are one aspect of success, but production abilities are another. Depending upon the industry under consideration, leadership can now be found in Germany, Japan, and the United States. The United States no longer leads in everything. In some areas, such as automobiles, it is a follower, and in others, such as consumer electronics, it is not even a player.

Where American firms used to dwarf their competitors,

they now find themselves increasingly on the small side. In 1970, 64 of the world's 100 largest industrial corporations were found in the United States, 26 were found in Europe, and only 8 in Japan. By 1988 only 42 of the 100 largest were located in the United States, 33 were located in Europe, and 15 were located in Japan. In the chemical industry the three biggest firms are all found in Germany. Each is at least one third bigger than Du Pont—America's largest chemical company.[8] Outside manufacturing, the same trends exist. In 1970, 19 of the world's 50 largest banks were North American, 16 were European, and 11 were Japanese. By 1988 only 5 were North American, 17 were European, and 24 were Japanese.[9] In 1990 there were no American banks in the top 20.[10] In the service sector 9 of the 10 largest firms are now Japanese.[11]

But starting from approximately the same level of economic development, each country or region now wants exactly the same industries to insure that its citizens have the highest standards of living in the twenty-first century. Ask Japan, Germany, and the United States to name those industries that they think are necessary to give their citizens a world-class standard of living in the first half of the twenty-first century, and they will return remarkably similar lists—microelectronics, biotechnology, the new materials-science industries, telecommunications, civilian aviation, robotics plus machine tools, and computers plus software.[12]

What was an era of niche competition in the last half of the twentieth century will become an era of head-to-head competition in the first half of the twenty-first century. Niche competition is win-win. Everyone has a place where they can excel; no one is going to be driven out of business. Head-to-head competition is win-lose. Not everyone will get those seven key industries. Some will win; some will lose.

The shift to head-to-head competition can be seen in the language of current economic discourse. In the Japanese, but not the American, version of the book *The Japan That Can Say No*, Mr. Ishihara states that the superpower military warfare of the twentieth century will be replaced by economic warfare in the twenty-first century, and that Japan will be the winner of the twenty-first century's economic wars.[13] In the American version he talks about "the Pacific age." Nomura Securities sees a world where "competition in the marketplace could well become extremely intense."[14]

Similar views exist in Germany. On German television in February 1990, Chancellor Helmut Kohl of West Germany issued his counterdeclaration of economic war: "The 1990s will be the decade of the Europeans and not that of the Japanese."[15] Implicitly, Chancellor Kohl sees an America already out of the game. The same point has been bluntly put by the prime minister of France, Edith Cresson: "There is a world economic war on."[16] The rotating head of the EEC and foreign minister of Italy, Gianni De Michelis, thinks that "all this points to Europe recovering its role as the core of the world economy. The next ten years will make evident Japan's big short comings."[17]

Today's tough talk is merely a prelude to tomorrow's tough economic competition. Conflicts in economic self-interest will also be sharper than they otherwise would have been because of the disappearance of the Soviet military bear. In the next half century no one has to moderate economic positions to preserve the military alliances that were necessary to contain the USSR. In the past half century military needs prevented economic conflicts from getting out of hand. From now on, economic cooperation will have to stand on its own, and economic arrangements will not be held together with military glue.

On one level a prediction that economic warfare will replace military warfare is good news. Vigorous competition may spur economic growth. There is nothing morally wrong with an aggressive invasion of well-made, superbly marketed German or Japanese products. Being bought is not the same thing as being militarily occupied. At the same time the military metaphor is fundamentally incorrect. The economic game that will be played in the twenty-first century will have cooperative as well as competitive elements. As we shall later see, a cooperative macroeconomic locomotive will have to be built to prevent the cycles that are inherent in capitalism. The world's common environment will require global cooperation if it is to be livable for anyone.

Economics abhors a vacuum no less than Mother Nature.

The economic competition between communism and capitalism is over, but another competition between two different forms of capitalism is already under way. Using a distinction first made by George C. Lodge, a Harvard Business School professor, the individualistic Anglo-Saxon British-American form of capitalism is going to face off against the communitarian German and Japanese variants of capitalism.[18] The Japanese variant of capitalism will be examined in detail in Chapter 4, but the essential difference between the two forms of capitalism is their stress on communitarian versus individualistic values as the route to economic success[19]—the "I" of America or of the United Kingdom versus "Das Volk" and "Japan Inc."

America and Britain trumpet individualistic values: the brilliant entrepreneur, Nobel Prize winners, large wage differentials, individual responsibility for skills, easy to fire and easy to quit, profit maximization, and hostile mergers and takeovers—their hero is the Lone Ranger. In contrast, Germany and Japan trumpet communitarian values: business groups, social responsibility for skills, teamwork, firm loyalty, industry strategies, and active industrial policies that promote growth. Anglo-Saxon firms are profit maximizers; Japanese business firms play a game that might better be known as "strategic conquest." Americans believe in "consumer economics"; Japanese believe in "producer economics."

In the Anglo-Saxon variant of capitalism, the individual is supposed to have a personal economic strategy for success, and the business firm is supposed to have an economic strategy that is a reflection of the wishes of its individual shareholders. Since shareholders want income to maximize their lifetime consumption, their firms must be profit maximizers. For the profit-maximizing firm, customer and employee relations are merely a means to the end of higher profits for the shareholders. Wages are to be beaten down where possible, and when not needed, employees are to be laid off. Lower wages equal higher profits. Workers in the Anglo-Saxon system are expected to change employers whenever opportunities arise to earn higher wages elsewhere. They owe their employer nothing. In contrast, many Japanese firms still refer to voluntary quits as "treason."[20]

In communitarian capitalism individual and firm strategies also exist but are built on quite different foundations. The individual does not play as an individual. One joins a team and is then successful as part of that company team. The key decision in an individual's personal strategy is to join the *right* team. From then on their own personal success or failure will be closely bound up with the success or failure of the firm for which they work. In the Anglo-Saxon world, company loyalty is somewhat suspect. The individual succeeds as an individual—not as a member of a team.

In both Germany and Japan, job switching is a far less prevalent phenomenon than it is in the United States or Great Britain. Labor-force turnover is bad in communitarian capitalism, since no one will plant apple trees (make sacrifices for the good of the company) if they do not expect to be around when the apples are harvested. In contrast, turnover rates are viewed positively in America and Great Britain. Firms are getting rid of unneeded labor when they fire workers, and individuals are moving to higher wage (higher productivity) opportunities when they quit. Job switching, voluntary or involuntary, is almost a synonym for efficiency.

The communitarian business firm has a very different set of stakeholders who must be consulted when its strategies are being set. In Japanese business firms employees are seen as the number one stakeholder, customers number two, and the shareholders a distant number three. Since the employee is the prime stakeholder, higher employee wages are a central goal of the firm in Japan. Profits will be sacrificed to maintain either wages or employment. Dividend payouts to the shareholders are low.

Communitarian societies expect companies to invest in the skills of their work forces. In the United States and Great Britain, skills are an individual responsibility. Firms exist to promote efficiency by hiring skills at the lowest possible wage rates. Labor is not a member of the team. It is just another factor of production to be rented when it is needed, and laid off when it is not.

Beyond personal and firm strategies, communitarian capitalism believes in having strategies at two additional levels. Business groups such as the Mitsui group or the Deutsche

Bank group are expected to have collective strategies. Companies should be financially interlocked and work together to strengthen each other's activities. The Japanese break up into vertical *keiretsu* made up of suppliers, producers, and retailers, and horizontal *keiretsu* made up of firms in different industries. At the top of the pyramid of Japanese business groups are the major former *zaibatsu* groups: Mitsui group (23 member firms), Mitsubishi group (28 member firms), Sumitomo group (21 member firms), Fuji group (29 member firms), Sanwa group (39 member firms), Dai-Ichi Kangyo group (45 member firms).[21] The members of each of these groups will own a controlling block of shares in other firms in the group. In addition each member firm would have a secondary group of smaller customers and suppliers, its *keiretsu*, organized around it. Hitachi counts 688 firms in its family; Toyota, 175 primary members and 4,000 secondary members.[22,23]

Similar patterns exist in Germany. The Deutsche Bank directly owns 10 percent or more of the shares in 70 companies: 28 percent of Germany's largest company, Daimler-Benz; 10 percent of Europe's largest reinsurance company, Munich Rai; 25 percent of Europe's largest department-store chain, Karstady; 30 percent of Germany's largest construction company, Philipp Holzmann; and 21 percent of Europe's largest sugar producer, Sudzucker. Indirectly, it controls many more shares that don't have to be publicly disclosed through its trust department. Deutsche Bank executives sit on four hundred corporate boards.[24] Outside of Germany, it owns 4 percent of the shares in Italy's Fiat. Similar if smaller empires exist at the other universal banks. Among the one hundred largest industrial corporations in Germany, the large universal banks own 10 to 25 percent of the shares in 48 of the largest 100 firms, 25 to 50 percent of the shares in 43 others, and over 50 percent of the shares in 9 of the 100 biggest firms.[25]

When the Arabs threatened to buy a controlling interest in Mercedes-Benz a few years ago, Deutsche Bank intervened on behalf of the German economy to buy up the shares that were for sale. This type of intervention protects the managers of Mercedes-Benz from the raids of financial Vikings. It frees managers from the tyranny of the stock market, with its emphasis on quarterly profits. Bank ownership helps firms plan corporate strategies and helps them raise the money to carry out these strategies. But the bank may also fire the managers of Mercedes-Benz if the car maker slips in the auto market. Managers are prevented from engaging in self-serving activities such as poison pills or golden parachutes that do not enhance the company's long-term prospects.

In March 1990 the two biggest business groups in the world (the Mitsubishi group from Japan and the Daimler Benz-Deutsche Bank group from Germany) held a secret meeting in Singapore to talk about a global alliance.[26] Among other things, both were interested in expanding their market share in civilian aircraft production. From an American perspective everything about that Singapore meeting was criminally illegal. It violated both antitrust and banking laws. In the United States banks cannot own industrial firms and businesses cannot sit down behind closed doors to plan joint strategies. Those doing so get thrown into jail for extended periods of time. Yet in today's world Americans cannot force the rest of the world to play the economic game as Americans think it should be played. The game will be played under international, not American rules.

Both Europe and Japan believe that government has a role to play in economic growth. Airbus Industries, a civilian aircraft manufacturer owned by the British, French, German, and Spanish governments, is an expression of a pan-European strategy. It was designed to break the American monopoly and get Europe back into civilian aircraft manufacturing. Today it is a success, as it has captured 20 percent of the aircraft market and announced plans to double production and capture one third of the worldwide market by the mid-1990s.

But that success came at a high price. An earlier effort, the Concorde, was a technical success but an expensive economic failure. Airbus Industries itself required twenty-six billion dollars in government investments and a captive market in the form of government-owned airlines to become successful. Only twenty-eight planes were built in 1986, but two hundred planes will be built in 1993. McDonnell Douglas's market share has been reduced from 30 to 15 percent. In 1990 Boeing's market share of new orders dropped to 45 percent—the first time in decades it had been below 50 percent. If 747's are not included (Airbus Industries has no plane in this market niche), Airbus Industries actually outsold Boeing.[27] In this industry a greater European share can only mean a smaller market share for Boeing and the demise of McDonnell Douglas.

There are now a number of similar pan-European strategic efforts (Jessi, Eureka, Esprit, Vision 1250) under way.[28] Each is designed to help European firms compete in some major industry.[29] European governments spend from 1.75 percent (Great Britain) to 5.5 percent (Italy) of their GNP in aiding their industries.[30] If the United States were to spend what Germany spends (2.5 percent of GNP), it would be spending more than $140 billion to help its industries in 1991. In the economy that grew the fastest in Europe in the 1980s, that of Spain, government-owned firms produce at least half of the GDP.[31] In France and Italy the state sector accounts for one-third of GNP.[32]

Germany, the dominant European economic power, sees itself as having a *"social-market"* economy and not just a "market" economy. Codetermination is required to broaden the ranks of corporate stakeholders beyond that of the traditional capitalistic owners to include workers. German governments (state and federal) own more shares in more industries (airlines, autos, steel, chemicals, electric power, transportation—some outright, some partially) than any noncommunist country on the face of the globe. Public investments such as Airbus Industries are not controversial political issues. Privatization is not sweeping across Germany as it did across Great Britain.

Government is believed to have an important role in insuring that everyone has the skills necessary to participate in the market. Germany's socially financed apprenticeship system is the envy of the world. Social-welfare policies are seen as a necessary part of a market economy. Unfettered capitalism is believed to generate levels of income inequality that are unacceptable.

In contrast, in the United States social-welfare programs are seen as regrettable necessities, since people will not provide for their own futures (old age, unemployment, ill health), but there are continual reminders that the higher taxes necessary to pay for social-welfare benefits will reduce work incentives for those paying taxes and that the benefits will undercut work incentives for those receiving them. In the ideal Anglo-Saxon market economy, social-welfare policies would not be necessary.

In Japan industry representatives working with the Ministry of International Trade and Industry present "visions" of where the economy should be going. In the past these visions served as guides to the allocation of scarce foreign exchange or capital flows. Today they are used to guide R&D funding. Key industries are targeted. What the Japanese know as "administrative guidance" is a way of life.

Like the European policy in aircraft, the Japanese strategy in semiconductor chips was also lengthy and expensive. The government-financed very-large-integrated-circuit-chip-research project was just part of a much larger effort. In the end a combination of patience, large investments, and American mistakes (a reluctance to expand capacity during cyclical downturns) succeeded in breaking the dominance of American semiconductor firms.

In America's economic theology, government has no role in investment funding and a *legitimate* one only in basic R&D. These rules are sometimes violated in practice, but the theology is clear. In the Anglo-Saxon view governments should protect private-property rights, then step back, get out of the way, and let individuals do their thing. Profit maximization will lead capitalism in the right directions.

These different conceptions of capitalism flow from very different histories. The Industrial Revolution began in Great Britain. In the formative years of British capitalism during the nineteenth century, it did not have to play catch-up with anyone. It was the leader. It was the most powerful country in the world. The United States similarly had a quick start in the Industrial Revolution. Situated between two great oceans, the United States did not feel militarily threatened by Britain's early economic lead. In the last quarter of the nineteenth century, when it was moving faster than Great Britain, Americans could see that they were going to catch up without deliberate government efforts to throw more coal into America's economic steam engines.

By way of contrast, nineteenth-century Germany had to

catch up with Great Britain if it was not to be run over in the
wars of Europe. "The rulers of German states were expected
by their subjects to take an active part in fostering the economic growth of their territories."[33] To have its rightful place
at the European table, Prussia had to have a modern industrial economy. German capitalism needed help to catch up.
Similarly, the Japanese system did not occur by accident. Ad-
miral Perry arrived in the mid-1800s and, with a few cannon
balls, forced Japan to begin trading with the rest of the world.
But the mid-nineteenth century was the height of colonialism.
If Japan did not quickly develop, it would become a colony of
someone—the British, the French, the Dutch, the Germans,
or the Americans. Economic development was part of national
defense—perhaps a more important part than the army itself.
A modern army could not be built without a modern
economy.

In both Germany and Japan economic strategies were important elements in military strategies for remaining politically
independent. Governments pushed actively to insure that the
economic combustion did indeed take place. They had to up
the intensity of that combustion so that the economic gaps
and, hence, military gaps, between themselves and their potential enemies could be cut in the shortest possible time. In
these circumstances it was not surprising that business firms
were organized along military lines or that the line between
public and private disappeared. Government and industry
had to work together to design the national economic strategies necessary for national independence. In a very real sense
business firms become the front line of national defense. Military strategies and economic strategies were woven so closely
together that they could not be separated.

American history is very different. Government's first significant economic act (the establishment of the Interstate Commerce Commission) prevented the railroads from using their
monopoly power to set freight rates so high as to rip off everyone else. A few decades later, its second significant act (the
passage of antitrust laws) prevented Mr. Rockefeller from using his control over the supply of lighting oil to extract monopoly rents. The third major source of government economic
activity flowed from the collapse of capitalism in the 1930s.

Government had to pick up capitalism's mess. As a result adversarial relations between government and the private sector and deep suspicions of each other's motives are deeply embedded in American history.

While very different histories have led to very different systems, today those very different systems face off in the same world economy. Let me suggest that the military metaphors now so widely used should be replaced by the language of football. Despite its competitive element—the desire to win—football also has a cooperative element. Everyone has to agree on the rules of the game, the referees, and how to split the proceeds. One can want to win yet still remain friends both during and after the game. But what the rest of the world knows as football is known in America as soccer. What Americans like about American football—frequent time-outs, lots of huddles, and unlimited substitutions—is not found in world football. It has no time-outs, no huddles, and very limited substitutions. It is a faster game. So too is the economic game ahead. All sides will call themselves capitalists, but participants will be playing two very different games.

NEW SOURCES OF STRATEGIC ADVANTAGE

Historically, individuals, firms, and countries became rich if they possessed more natural resources, were born rich and enjoyed the advantages of having more capital (plant and equipment) per person, employed superior technologies, or had more skills than their competitors. Putting some combination of these four factors together with reasonable management was the route to success.

In the nineteenth century natural resources (coal) and technology (the invention of the steam engine, the spinning jenny, and the Bessemer steel furnace) gave the United Kingdom the edge. Having gotten rich first, higher incomes allowed the British to save more than those in poorer lands. With more savings, more could be invested in plant and equipment. More capital led to higher productivity and, hence, to higher wages. With more income, more could be saved. Being rich, it was easy to stay rich—a virtuous circle.

Historians trace much of America's economic success to cheap, plentiful, well-located raw materials and farm land.[34] America did not become rich because it worked harder or saved more than its neighbors. A small population lived in a very large, resource-rich environment. Natural resources were combined with the first compulsory public K–12 education system and the first system of mass higher education in the world. Together they gave America an economic edge. While Americans may not have worked harder, they were better skilled and worked smarter. Once rich, America also found it easy to stay rich.

New technologies and new institutions are combining to substantially alter these four traditional sources of competitive advantage. Natural resources essentially drop out of the competitive equation. Being born rich becomes much less of an advantage than it used to be. Technology gets turned upside down. New product technologies become secondary; new process technologies become primary. And in the twenty-first century, the education and skills of the work force will end up being the dominant competitive weapon.

Natural Resources

With the exception of a few very lightly populated countries that possess massive amounts of oil, natural resources have essentially ceased to be a major source of competitive advantage. Only 3 percent of the American population now makes its living in farming, timbering, fishing, and mining.[35] Many among this three percent are part-time marginal farmers who earn most of their family income away from the farm. In the next century those earning their living from natural resources will be even smaller.

The green revolution worked in both the developed and the developing world. A very small number of farmers grow more food than those who have money to pay for it want to eat. The growth in farm productivity easily outpaces the demand for more food. The biotech revolution on the horizon can only speed up the process. Simply reducing today's huge farm surpluses will require many fewer farmers tomorrow—something on the order of five million fewer in the developed world. In the nineteenth century, Russia was the world's biggest agricultural exporter. If Middle and Eastern Europe return to being efficient producers, a huge importing area will become a huge exporting area. The numbers that must leave farming could easily double.

Families will have to leave farming, but land will also have to be taken out of production if supplies and demands are to be balanced. What has to occur is similar to what happened in New England in the nineteenth century, when Iowa and Ohio came into production. New England farmers were driven out of business, land values collapsed, and farms in northern New England were abandoned as worthless. Increased production in the Ukraine may well do the same to farmers and land values in North and South Dakota.

The green revolution is being matched by a materials-science revolution, where less and less natural resources are being used per unit of GNP. America uses less steel in 1990 than it did in 1960, while its GNP is two and one half times as large.[36] Reductions in usage have brought about sharp reductions in raw-material prices. After correcting for inflation, raw-material prices in 1990 were 30 percent below where they were in 1980—almost 40 percent below where they were in 1970.[37] The materials-science revolution now under way is going to accelerate in the years ahead, and further reductions in the use of almost all scarce natural resources per unit of GNP are to be expected. Traditional raw-material suppliers in the Third World will find ever-smaller markets for their ever-cheaper resources.

In the twenty-first century a lack of natural resources may in fact be an advantage. The Japanese have the world's best steel industry, though they have neither iron ore nor coal. To some extent they are the best precisely because they do not have iron ore or coal. They are not locked into poor-quality, high-cost local sources of supply. There is no need to buy low-quality British coal or American iron ore. They can buy wherever quality and price are best.

For all practical purposes natural resources have dropped out of the competitive equation. Having them is not the way to become rich. Not having them is not a barrier to becoming rich. Japan doesn't have them and is rich; Argentina has them and is not rich.

Capital

Since it is much easier for the rich to save, living in a rich country has traditionally meant that workers would automatically work with more plant and equipment per capita than those born in poor countries. Working with more capital led to higher productivity, which resulted in wages automatically being higher. Being born in a rich country almost insured that one would die in a rich country.

In the twenty-first century being born rich becomes less of a competitive advantage. Advances in telecommunications, computers, and air transportation have led to a logistics revolution where global sourcing is possible. Multinational companies bring First World capital availability with them when they build production facilities in Third World countries. Those same factors have created a world capital market where a Thai entrepreneur can borrow money to build facilities that are just as capital intensive as those built in a rich country such as Japan—especially if he has sales contracts with retailers in the First World. Today's Korean consumer-electronics factories don't look much different from those found in Japan, despite the fact that Japan has a per capita GNP six times that of Korea.

For those in the highly indebted Third World or Second World, "country risk" can intervene to lock them out of the world capital market. A good business firm with a good project in Brazil won't get a loan. With existing Brazilian debt, no lender can be confident that a Brazilian borrower will be allowed to acquire the dollars needed to pay interest and repay principal from the Brazilian Central Bank. Small companies and those that live in unstable economies with high country risk still don't have the same access as large companies and those that live in stable economies, but the differences in access to capital have sharply narrowed.

A world capital market has arisen partly because of institutional changes (deregulation of financial markets) and partly because of technological developments. In the 1950s an Italian who wanted to move money into Switzerland had to fill her backpack with lira and walk across the Alps. Today she can move her money on a personal computer. When money can be moved on a PC, there is no such thing as governments stopping money from flowing around the world. The last of the post–World War II capital controls are now being abolished (Italy did so in early 1990; France and Japan still have some controls left), but even those that are not abolished will have little impact. Transactions will simply move electronically to someplace on the globe where the offending regulations are not in force.

In principle, once adjustments are made for expected swings in foreign-exchange rates, inflation rates, and local default risks, a world capital market should insure roughly equal access—similar real interest rates and capital availabilities wherever one is geographically located. Wealthy countries will still save more, but their savings will flow into a world capital market where they will be allocated to the regions generating the highest returns.

But there also is a major mystery in the world's capital markets. Among major countries where there was no country risk, the predicted equalization of capital costs did not occur in the 1980s, despite the existence of what everyone took to be a world capital market. Contrary to what theory would have predicted, local savings rates and local investments were highly correlated—high local savings led to high local investments.[38] In 1989, real interest rates (the prime lending rate minus the producer price index) were 6 percent in the United States and 2.9 percent in Japan.[39] Using stock-market price-earnings multiples, the cost of equity capital was less than 1 percent in Japan but over 9 percent in the United States. When taxes and depreciation are factored into the equation, the corporate cost of capital for a twenty-year investment in plant and equipment in the United States was 60 percent above that in either Germany or Japan.[40,41]

In the early 1990s these differentials narrowed substantially as Japan deliberately raised interest rates to stop land speculation and Germany deliberately raised interest rates to attract the capital necessary to rebuild eastern Germany. But no one is sure whether the predicted long-term equalization of interest rates has at last occurred or whether the narrowing was simply a product of reversible short-run monetary policies in Germany and Japan.[42] Will the gaps open up once again when current government policies in Germany and Japan are reversed? No one knows.

The existence of persistent interest-rate differentials and the close connection between local savings and local investment pose both an intellectual challenge and a practical problem. Intellectually, the continued existence of these differentials is difficult to explain. One can argue that the world doesn't yet really have a world capital market, but if this is so, questions, to which there are really no good answers, immediately arise, such as: Why not? And what will it take to bring a real world capital market about? What existed in the 1980s certainly looked like a world capital market—as much as $1,000 billion per day flowed through it.

Small interest-rate differentials can be explained (interest rates are not absolutely identical everywhere in America), but the large differentials that actually existed cannot. To this day what was observed in the 1980s remains a genuine mystery. No one has a convincing explanation of how what did happen could have happened.

If local real interest rates continue to be a function of local savings in major countries, there are two practical conclusions. Anyone who is in a capital-intensive business and doesn't have a huge technological advantage over the Japanese should get out! In the long run it is not possible to compete paying a much higher cost of capital unless a firm has some unique advantage. Alternatively, firms that wish to compete with the Japanese in capital-intensive industries have to be willing to work to insure that their home countries save as much as Japan does.

But regardless of how the interest-rate mystery is solved or circumvented at the national level, at the firm level capital availability clearly has become less important in the competitive equation. There will be factories in poor countries that can match the capital intensity of those in rich countries. To some extent these plants will be owned by local firms who have access to world capital markets, and to some extent they will be the offshore production facilities of multinational firms that bring their access (local or international) to capital markets with them. Either way, many fewer workers will be guaranteed high wages in the twenty-first century simply by virtue of the fact that they were born in a rich country.

Technology

In the past comparative advantage was a function of natural-resources endowments and factor proportions (capital-labor ratios). Cotton was grown in the American South because the climate and soil were right. Slavery provided abundant labor. Cotton was spun in New England because it had the capital to harness available waterpower. Each industry had its natural location.

Consider what are commonly believed to be the seven key industries of the next few decades—microelectronics, biotechnology, the new materials industries, civilian aviation, telecommunications, robots plus machine tools, and computers plus software. All are brainpower industries. Each could be located anywhere on the face of the globe. Where they will be located depends upon who can organize the brainpower to capture them. In the century ahead comparative advantage will be man-made.

Since technology lies behind man-made comparative advantage, research and development becomes critical. In the past the economic winners were those who invented new products. The British in the nineteenth century and the Americans in the twentieth century got rich doing so. But in the twenty-first century sustainable competitive advantage will come much more out of newprocess technologies and much less out of newproduct technologies. Reverse engineering has become an art form. New products can easily be reproduced. What used to be primary (inventing new products) becomes secondary, and what used to be secondary (inventing and perfecting new processes) becomes primary.

If R&D spending by private firms is examined, American firms spend two thirds of their money on new products and

one third on new processes. The Japanese do exactly the opposite—one third on new products, two thirds on new processes. Not surprisingly, both sets of firms do well where they
concentrate their talent. While the Americans earn higher
rates of return on new product technologies, Japanese firms
earn higher rates of return on new processes.[43]

Someone, however, is making a mistake.[44] Both strategies
cannot be correct. In this case the someone is the United
States. Its spending patterns are wrong, but they are wrong
because they used to be right. In the early 1960s it was conventional wisdom, and also true, that the rate of return on
investment in new product R&D was almost always higher
than that on new process R&D. A new product gave the inventor a monopoly power to set higher prices and earn higher
profits. With a new product, there were no competitors.

In contrast, a new process left the inventor in a competitive
business. Competitors knew how to make the product, and
they would always lower their prices to match the inventor's
prices as long as they were covering marginal costs in their
old facilities. To make monopoly rents on process technologies, it was necessary to drive one's competitors out of business. To do this, new process technologies had to have
average costs below the marginal costs of old process technologies. Since marginal costs are typically far below average
costs, an enormous (and very unlikely) process breakthrough
was necessary if one were to establish a monopoly position
with better process technologies. Driving one's competitor out
of business was also likely to get one into trouble with the
antitrust laws. It was simply rational to spend most of a firm's
R&D money on new product development.

While Americans focused on product technologies, Japan
and West Germany focused on process technologies. They did
so not because they were smarter than Americans but because
the United States had such a technical lead in the 1950s and
1960s that it was virtually impossible for either Japan or West
Germany to become leaders in the development of new products. They could only hope to compete in existing markets
that Americans were exiting. As a result, Japan and West Germany invested less of their GNP in R&D, and what they did
invest was invested more heavily in process R&D. They had
no choice.

But what was a good American strategy thirty years ago, a focus on new product technologies, is today a poor strategy. Levels of technical sophistication in Germany, Japan, and the United States are now very different, and reverse engineering has become a highly developed art form. The nature of the change can be seen in the economic history of three leading new products introduced into the mass consumer market in the past two decades—the video camera and recorder, the fax, and the CD player. Americans invented the video camera and recorder and the fax; Europeans (the Dutch) invented the CD player. But measured in terms of sales, employment, and profits, all three have become Japanese products.

The moral of the story is clear. Those who can make a product cheaper can take it away from the inventor. In today's world it does very little good to invent a new product if the inventor is not the cheapest producer of that product. What necessity forced upon West Germany and Japan thirty years ago happens to be the right long-run R&D strategy today.

This reality will force the United States to alter its R&D spending patterns, but it also requires a much more difficult shift in human-resources allocation. Over time, the pay and promotion curve for managers and engineers in production has fallen behind that in other parts of the firm in the United States. Not being key to a firm's success, production ceased to be the route to the top. Among today's CEOs of *Fortune* 500 companies, 34 percent come from marketing, 25 percent from finance, 24 percent from general management, and only 4 percent from production.[45] Noticing this fact, America's best and brightest have not gone into processes. Reversing this allocation of talent is now very difficult, since what has come to be seen as a second-class activity (production) has to be made into a first-class activity. Traditional salary scales and promotion practices have to be disrupted.

If process technologies lie at the heart of the competitive equation, it is also necessary to have CEOs who understand process technologies. The firm's central competitive weapon cannot remain a black box where CEOs rely on the advice of the experts. Large investments in revolutionary technologies will only be made quickly if the man or woman at the top understands them. Yet American CEOs are much less likely to have technical backgrounds than those in either Japan or Europe. Seventy percent there do; 30 percent in the United States do.[46] This difference in educational background is not unrelated to the fact that in industry after industry, American firms have been slow to adopt revolutionary new process technologies such as flexible manufacturing stations, just-in-time inventories, or statistical quality control.

The American steel industry illustrates what happens when technological breakthroughs have to be digested by managers who are not technologically literate. Twenty-five years ago, the American steel industry failed to make the massive investments in oxygen furnaces, continuous casting, and computer controls that their foreign competitors were making. Americans built their first oxygen furnaces and continuous casters six to seven years after the first ones were built elsewhere in the world, and the American steel industry has been playing an unsuccessful game of catch-up ever since. Not understanding the technology revolution that was under way, and not wanting to bet their companies (these investments would have taken billions in today's dollars) upon the advice of the "experts," America's CEOs waited to see what would happen. But by the time it was clear that oxygen furnaces and continuous casters would work, America's foreign competitors had spent three years building their new facilities and three years operating them, and the American steel companies were six to seven years behind. Being far behind, the firms not surprisingly saw their market shares erode. While the time lags in other industries steel are not as long, the Japanese on average are faster at adopting new technologies.[47]

The management of technology is usually seen as something of relevance to manufacturing but not to the rest of the economy. Here again, what was historically true is no longer true. In the twenty-first century there will be high-tech and low-tech products, but most products and services will be produced with high-tech processes. The automobile is a low-tech product; the robots that make it are high-tech. Gaining an edge in high-tech processes will be important in almost every industry, and being masters of process technologies will become central to being rich as an individual, being successful as a firm, or in generating a high per capita GNP as a country.

The new information and telecommunication technologies that are being developed are going to make most service industries into high-tech process industries. In 1991 American financial firms spent seven and a half billion dollars installing what were essentially high-tech financial assembly lines.[48] These computer systems are not management-information systems; they are financial production lines. Using automatic teller machines (ATMs) to deal with their customers, banks are probably more automated than any other industry. Electronic fund transfer systems will eliminate the need for traditional checks. Those financial firms whose computer-telecommunications systems allow them to code information, move information around the world, and decode information faster than their competitors win—not some of the time, but all of the time. Automated computer systems now trade over half of the shares traded on the New York Stock Exchange. Artificial intelligence is being embedded in even better trading systems than those now in use. Financial firms become high-tech manufacturing firms processing money and pieces of paper.

In retailing, those who survive will have the inventory-control systems that best reduce costs. Retail stores will be directly linked to suppliers to minimize the time lags between the customer's purchase of some particular item and the restocking of that item. Just-in-time inventories and just-in-time production are the name of the game. The goal will be a seamless web where merchandise is built only shortly before it is delivered and sold.

Even now, American retailing firms such as The Limited, a clothing retailer, are converting retailing into a high-tech competition. The Limited was the first to use high-definition TV across international boundaries so that it would not have to waste time sending buyers to Hong Kong. If the Limited's inventory-control, telecommunication, and CAD-CAM (computer-aided design/computer-aided manufacturing) systems allow it to know what women are buying, and put precisely those clothes back on the rack within twenty-eight days while their competitors take six months, they win, and their slower competitors lose.

In air transportation today's key competitive weapon is the

computerized reservation system. These systems allow airlines to analyze demand and vary prices over time and over different routes to exploit those demands (charging high prices to business travelers who must go; charging low prices to tourists who will only travel if the price is right) so as to achieve load factors and profits in ways that would have been inconceivable in the era before the computer. In the aftermath of airline deregulation, the effective use of hub-and-spoke route systems (also impossible without the computer) and computerized reservation systems allowed America's major airlines to run their new competitors out of business, despite the fact that the new airlines had lower operating costs per passenger-seat mile. The technology of subsonic aircraft is forty years old. World-class reservation systems are on the cutting edge of technology.

In the United States there has been a lot of worry about the postindustrial age and the possibility that a low-wage service sector would swallow the entire economy. As Chapter 5 will show, these worries are misplaced. The end of the postindustrial era is probably already at hand.[49] Services grew rapidly in the 1980s, but they will probably not grow faster than the rest of the economy in the 1990s. But even if they were to continue growing, no country should worry about deindustrialization and attempt to hold down the growth of its service sector. The right strategy is to grab those parts of the service sector that generate high-wage jobs and to invent new technologies for low-wage services so that they can join the high-wage service sector. While service wages are two thirds of those in manufacturing in the United States, they range from 85 to 93 percent of those in manufacturing in both Germany and Japan.[50] Technology does not dictate that services must be a low-wage sector. Most services can be converted from low to high wages if they are infused with the right new technologies.

The importance of man-made comparative advantage and the accelerating technological competition that flows from it can be seen in national spending on R&D. In the past fifteen years Japan and Germany have pushed their spending to American levels—slightly less than 3 percent of GNP. Japan has announced plans for further spending increases in the

1990s, and the Europeans are rapidly developing pan-European, partially government financed R&D consortiums such as Eureka, Jessi, and Esprit.

American R&D spending patterns are currently in flux. The end of the Cold War and cutbacks in military spending will undoubtedly lead to less military R&D. Private R&D spending is also falling, at least in the short run, because of the high debt burdens incurred in the takeover wars of the 1980s—although it is difficult to be sure because of the strong cyclical element in American R&D spending. While others are beefing up R&D spending, America seems to be cutting back.

In the twenty-first century man-made comparative advantage, with an emphasis on process technologies, will be the starting point for economic competition. Many parts of the world are going to develop strategies to capture what they see as the key industries of the future. As in chess, the economic player who is planning his game five moves ahead loses to the player that is thinking six moves ahead. The words of the world chess champion, Gary Kasparov, have a certain relevance for economics in the era ahead. A competitor "must find the best position for a piece, to fight for the open line, to have a strong center, to attack the opponent's king. Material must be compared against time. Material and time must be evaluated against quality. It takes imagination. At the highest level, chess is a talent to control unrelated things. It is like controlling chaos."[51]

Skills

While technology creates man-made comparative advantage, seizing that man-made comparative advantage requires a work force skilled from top to bottom. The skills of the labor force are going to be the key competitive weapon in the twenty-first century. Brainpower will create new technologies, but skilled labor will be the arms and legs that allow one to employ—to be the low-cost masters of—the new product and process technologies that are being generated. In the century ahead natural resources, capital, and new-product technologies are going to rapidly move around the world. People will move—but more slowly than anything else. Skilled people become the only sustainable competitive advantage.

If the route to success is inventing new products, the education of the smartest 25 percent of the labor force is critical. Someone in that top group will invent the new products of tomorrow. If the route to success is being the cheapest and best producer of products, new or old, the education of the bottom 50 percent of the population moves to center stage. This part of the population must staff those new processes. If the bottom 50 percent cannot learn what must be learned, new high-tech processes cannot be employed.

Firms have to be able to use new computer-based CAD-CAM technologies, employ statistical quality control, manage just-in-time inventories, and operate flexible manufacturing systems. Information technologies have to be integrated into the entire production process, from initial designs through marketing to final sales and supporting services such as maintenance. To do this requires the office, the factory, the retail store, and the repair service to have average workers with levels of education and skill that they have never had to have in the past. To employ statistical quality control, every production worker must be taught some simple operations research. To learn what must be learned, every worker must have a level of basic mathematics that is far beyond that achieved by most American high school graduates. Without statistical quality control, today's high-density semiconductor chips cannot be built. They can be invented, but they cannot be built.

In a global economy where goods can be sourced in low-wage Third World countries, the effective supply of unskilled workers has expanded enormously. As a consequence, wages must fall for the unskilled who live in rich countries. Quite simply, supply and demand require it. In a global economy a worker has two things to offer—skills or the willingness to work for low wages. Since products can be built anywhere, the unskilled who live in rich societies must work for the wages of the equally unskilled who live in poor societies. If they won't work for such wages, unskilled jobs simply move to poor countries.[52]

What economists know as "factor price equalization" demands wage equalization. Economic activity won't be put in any geographic location unless that location is the least-cost location for producing that particular product. If American productivity isn't higher than Korean productivity, Americans cannot be paid wages higher than those paid to Koreans ($3.57 per hour in manufacturing in 1989).[53] In a global market for labor, Korean wages will rise and American wages will fall until wage differentials mirror productivity differentials.[54]

What theory predicts, reality delivers. Between 1973 and 1990 America's real per capita GNP rose 28 percent, yet the real hourly wages for nonsupervisory workers (about two thirds of the total work force) fell 12 percent, and real weekly wages fell 18 percent.[55] Weekly wages fell faster than hourly wages because firms shifted to part-time workers who did not have to be paid fringe benefits such as health insurance.[56] In the late 1980s and early 1990s, real hourly wages were declining at 1 percent per year. The lower the education level, the bigger the decline in real earnings. Living in a country with a rising per capita GNP did those Americans without skills no good in the last twenty years.

In an isolated national economy, President Kennedy could talk in 1960 about how a rising economic tide would raise all boats. In an American economy floating in a world economy, his famous dictum no longer holds. The general economic tides (the per capita GNP) have been rising, but a majority of the boats (individual wages) have been sinking.

Several factors have kept this decline from happening elsewhere. In countries such as Japan or Germany, the bottom two thirds of the work force is better skilled. Their skills contributed to higher rates of productivity growth and validated higher wages. Stronger unions and much higher legal minimum wages have also played a role—essentially redistributing wage gains from the skilled to the unskilled. But they have also been much less open to manufactured imports from the low-wage Third World than has the United States. Their workers simply were not subject to the same downward wage pressures.[57]

If sustainable competitive advantage swirls around workforce skills, Anglo-Saxon firms have a problem. Human-resource management is not traditionally seen as central to the competitive survival of the firm in America or Great Britain.

Skill acquisition is an individual responsibility, and business firms exist to beat wages down. Labor is simply another factor of production to be hired—rented at the lowest possible cost—much as one buys raw materials or equipment. Workers are not members of the team. Adversarial labor-management relations are part of the system.

The lack of importance attached to human-resource management can be seen in the corporate pecking order. In an American firm the chief financial officer (CFO), is almost always second in the pecking order. The post of head of human resource management is usually a specialized, off-at-the-edge-of-the-corporation job, and the executive who holds it is never consulted on major strategic decisions and has no chance to move up to chief executive officer (CEO). By way of contrast, in Japan the head of human resource management is usually the second most important person after the CEO. To become CEO, it is a job that one must have held.

While American firms often talk about the vast amounts spent on training their work forces, in fact, they invest less in the skills of their workers than do either Japanese or German firms. What they do invest is also more highly concentrated on professional and managerial employees. The more limited investments that are made in average workers are also much more narrowly focused on the specific skills necessary to do the next job rather than on the basic background skills that make it possible to absorb new technologies.[58]

As a result, problems emerge when new breakthrough technologies arrive. If American workers, for example, take much longer to learn to operate new flexible manufacturing stations than those in Germany (as they do), the effective costs of buying those flexible manufacturing stations is lower in Germany than it is in the United States. More time is required before equipment is up and running at capacity, and the need for extensive retraining generates costs and creates bottlenecks that limit the speed with which new equipment can be employed. The result is less American investment and a slower pace of technical change.

In Germany there is an extensive training system for the non–college bound. The non–college bound enter a dual school-industry apprenticeship system at age fifteen to sixteen. At the end of three years, after passing written and practical examinations, they become journeymen with known skill levels. After another three years of work and additional courses in business management, law, and technology, a journeyman can become a master—a credential necessary to open one's own business.[59] Outside observers often cite this training system as the key ingredients in German economic success. The Germans are not the best educated at the top (America, with its superb graduate schools, is far better at this level), nor are they the best educated at the very bottom (the Japanese win there), but they are the world's very best over a broad range of midlevel, noncollege skills.

In the end the skills of the bottom half of the population affect the wages of the top half. If the bottom half can't effectively staff the processes that have to be operated, the management and professional jobs that go with these processes disappear. This effect can be seen in something near and dear to my heart. American economics professors make two to three times as much money as British economics professors but 20 to 30 percent less than German economics professors. We do so not because we know more economics than the British and less economics than the Germans but because we play on a more productive team than the British and a less productive team than the Germans. The quality of my team makes a difference to my income.

NEW RULES FOR PLAYING THE GAME[60]

The late 1920s and early 1930s began with a series of worldwide financial crashes that ultimately spiraled downward into the Great Depression. As GNPs fell, the dominant countries each created trading blocks (the Japanese Co-Prosperity Sphere, the British Empire, the French Union, Germany plus eastern Europe, America with its Monroe Doctrine) to minimize imports and preserve jobs. If only one country had kept imports out, limiting imports would have helped it avoid the Great Depression, but with everyone restricting trade, the downward pressures were simply magnified. In the aggregate, fewer imports must equal fewer exports. Eventually, those economic blocks evolved into military blocks, and World War II began.

In the aftermath of World War II, the GATT–Bretton Woods trading system was built to prevent a repetition of these events. Trade restrictions and tariff barriers were gradually reduced in a series of trading rounds such as the Kennedy round or the Tokyo round. Under the rules, each country had to treat all other countries in exactly the same way—the most-favored-nation principle. The best deal (the lowest tariffs, the easiest access, the fewest restrictions) given to anyone must be given to everyone—effectively prohibiting trading blocks.

This system has been described as "unilateral global Keynesianism."[61] It was unilateral in that the United States was "single-handedly prepared to direct and maintain the system." The dollar was the medium of exchange and the standard of value. America was the manager of the system. It practiced "global Keynesianism" (tightening monetary and fiscal policies when inflation threatened; loosening monetary and fiscal policies when recession threatened) so that it could be an economic locomotive for the rest of the world. It provided a "market of first resort" where countries could export relatively easily and the United States did not insist on strict reciprocity in its commercial dealings with other countries. The system was also very Anglo-Saxon—a universal rule-driven system as opposed to a deal-driven system.

America performed these functions not because it was altruistic, although it might have been, but because, as the world's biggest economy, it had more to gain from an open global economy than anyone else. America believed that it could not be prosperous unless the world was prosperous and everyone had equal access to raw materials and markets.

History will record that the GATT–Bretton Woods trading system was one of the world's all-time great successes. In the forty years after it was adopted, the world economy grew faster than it had grown in all of human history. That growth was also much more widely shared. With the exception of a handful of countries, mostly in Africa, everyone had much higher real per capita incomes in 1990 than they had had in 1945. Where the United States was once much richer than the rest of the world, by the late 1980s it had become just one of a number of approximately equally wealthy countries. As America's position shifted from one of effortless economic superiority to one of equality, America's share of the world's GNP necessarily fell from far more than half of the world's total in the 1940s to 22–23 percent of the total in the late 1980s.[62]

This success makes evolution along the previous track impossible. Economic arrangements that work in a unipolar world simply do not work in a multipolar world.

In the first three decades after World War II, everyone played a win-win economic game. Imports that looked small to the United States (3 to 5 percent of GNP) provided large markets to the rest of the world because of America's great wealth and giant size. Export opportunities were abundant for anyone who wanted to sell in the U.S. market, and the jobs that were associated with these exports were high-wage jobs by the standards of the exporting countries. Viewed from the American perspective, these imports were not threatening. Foreign market shares were small, and import penetration came in what were in America labor-intensive, low-wage industries that were being phased out anyway.

These imports were just an expression of what came to be known as the "product cycle." America would invent a new high-tech product and learn to mass produce it. Gradually, the product would shift to being a mid-tech product best produced in mid-wage countries such as Japan or Europe, from whence it would eventually move as a low-tech product to low-wage countries in the Third World.

Balancing America's trading accounts was not a problem. America could grow farm products that the rest of the world could not grow, supply raw materials such as oil that the rest of the world did not have, and manufacture unique high-tech products such as the Boeing 707 that the rest of the world could not build. America's exports did not compete with products from the rest of the world. They filled gaps that the rest of the world could not fill. In the jargon of today's strategic planners, each country had a noncompetitive niche where it could be a winner. America grew rapidly; the rest of the world grew even more rapidly.

Because of its size, America served as a locomotive for the world economy. When the system was established, memories of the Great Depression were still sharp. Whenever the world sank into a recession, to prevent it from becoming a depression the United States would use its fiscal and monetary policies to stimulate demand—benefiting both American and foreign producers. Foreign exports to America would rise, pulling the exporting countries out of their economic slump. With higher export earnings, these countries would buy more unique American products.

But with success, the American locomotive gradually grew too small to pull the rest of the world. The last gasp of the old macroeconomic locomotive was seen in the aftermath of the 1981–1982 recession. American macroeconomic stimulus, starting in the fall of 1982, pulled the industrial world out of its sharpest post–World War II recession. In 1983 and 1984 most of the growth in both Europe and Japan could be traced to exports to the American market. But for the first time the United States found itself burdened with a large trade deficit as a consequence. It's exports did not automatically rise to balance its imports.

America's effortless exports were a thing of the past. The green revolution in the developed and underdeveloped world had sharply curtailed foreign markets for American farm products. America had gradually shifted from being a large exporter of raw materials, such as oil, to being a large importer. The unique high-tech products that the rest of the world could not build had disappeared in a world of technical parity. They could be gotten many other places. What in the past had been a temporary cyclical trade deficit became a permanent structural trade deficit.

A successful noncompetitive niche-export environment had evolved gradually into an intensely competitive head-to-head export environment. Head-to-head competition is never win-win; at best it is win-lose, and everyone can see it as potentially lose-lose.[63] In America, with imports $162 billion greater than exports in 1987, politically there were simply many more American losers than winners.[64] Abroad, the elimination of America's trade deficit (the loss of all of those exports) threatened the jobs of millions of workers.

The nature of the problem can be seen in the maneuvering over high-definition television (HDTV). Europe, Japan, and the United States are all deliberately setting different technical standards for HDTV to insure that producers from the other regions cannot dominate their market.[65] The spirit of GATT would call for common standards to set a level playing field. But no one wants a level playing field. Everyone wants an edge.

In response, slowly but surely, trade is increasingly being managed by governments. Nontariff import barriers are rising everywhere. In the United States the percentage of American imports subject to nontariff restrictions has doubled to 25 percent in the past decade.[66] At the leading edge of technology, the Japanese-American semiconductor pact effectively turns semiconductor chips into a managed sector, and at the lagging edge of technology, the ever-expanding multifiber agreement keeps textiles in the managed sector. Autos, an intermediate technology, have for more than a decade been in the managed sector. The door to the market of first resort is slowly but surely closing.

The trends are clear. America makes special arrangements with Canada and is negotiating special arrangements with Mexico. Europe talks about associate memberships in the European Community for the remaining nonmember countries in Western Europe and some of Middle Europe. Migration pressures from North Africa are leading it to a Mexican-style agreement with the countries of North Africa whereby it will become Europe's preferential low-wage manufacturing area. Bilateral negotiations, prohibited under GATT and leading to principles very different from that of most favored nation, are under way everywhere.

Most of them are held under the cover of setting up a "common market." Technically, the common market escape clause from the most-favored-nation principle is only supposed to be used if the ultimate objective of the common market is a real political union. Europeans can argue that this is the case in Europe, but in North America there is not even a pretense that the Canadian, Mexican, and American economic talks are a prelude to political union. The Structural Impediment Talks between Japan and America didn't even bother with this legal "fig leaf." The world has forgotten what it learned in the 1920s. Bilateral negotiations cannot lead to a stable trading system.

To work, a multipolar, integrated, open world economy requires fiscal and monetary coordination among the major countries—Germany, Japan, and the United States. A common locomotive is needed, and it can only exist if the major countries stimulate or restrict their economies in unison. There is no doubt that coordination can work. The world witnessed a demonstration of its effectiveness in 1988. In 1988 almost every developed country grew faster than it had in 1987, faster than it was predicted to grow in November 1987. The coordinating event was, of course, the stock market crash of October 1987. In the aftermath of that crash, every government thought that its economy would tumble into a recession, and all took prompt actions to stimulate their economies. In concert, the stimulation worked—forward momentum was almost instantaneous.

In normal times, however, coordination has proved illusive. Within two days in February 1991, the U.S. Federal Reserve Board announced that it was lowering interest rates, while the German Bundesbank announced that it was raising interest rates. In early 1991 America had a recession and wanted to stimulate demand; it needed lower interest rates. Germany had a boom and wanted to cut back on consumer demands. Higher interest rates were necessary to attract capital to pay for investments in eastern Germany. No agreement was possible.

Coordination is one of those words that is easy to say but hard to do. It means that each country must occasionally take actions that it does not want to take. The reasons for the resistance to coordination are easy to understand. In February 1991 Germany and America would have had to agree on whether the world's major problem was recession or inflation. Coordination would have required the United States to balance its budget to allow the world to move to lower real interest rates. The world needs more savings to handle the investment demands of the Second World and Third World and to repair the damage in Kuwait. America should not be the world's biggest borrower. But Americans neither want to raise taxes nor cut government services. That is what they voted for in November 1988, when they elected a Republican read-my-lips, no-new-taxes president and a Democratic no-cuts-in-government-services Congress.

If American budget balancing is not to depress world aggregate demand and instigate a recession, coordination requires Germany to grow much faster over an extended period of time. In the 1980s, West Germany was unwilling to do so. It faced negative demography and a falling German labor force in the 1990s. It did not want to grow faster and suck in hundreds of thousands of guest workers. All of those desires were reversed at the end of the decade because of events in East Germany, but the shifts in German policies were not brought about by desires to build an efficient world locomotive. The German interest in growth arose because of the desperate need to bring east German income levels up to those of western Germany just as soon as possible to prevent everyone in eastern Germany from moving to western Germany.

While the events in eastern Germany provide a window of opportunity to reduce the world's structural trade imbalances (the German trade surplus will fall from 135 billion marks in 1990 to about 30 billion marks in 1991), fortunate circumstances are not a permanent substitute for deliberate macroeconomic coordination.[67] They give the world economy a little breathing room and the prospect of faster growth in the 1990s, but in the long run, accidental coordination is not a good substitute for planned coordination.

If the 1991 Anglo-Saxon recession were to spread to the rest of the world, the United States could not do in 1992 what it did a decade earlier. It entered the recession with an already large trade deficit—not the surplus of 1981. Instead of being the world's largest net creditor, which could borrow at will, it would be the world's largest net debtor and a shaky credit risk. It could not compound its already large internal government deficit with further tax cuts or increased expenditures. It simply could not set its macroeconomic policies to grow faster than the rest of the world so as to provide an export market to pull everyone else back to prosperity.

The need to construct a new macroeconomic locomotive has gotten a lot of attention, if not much action, but a market of first resort is no less important. All of the successful developing countries in the past half century have gone through a phase where they sent most of their exports to the United States. The United States has effectively been the open market of first resort on which any country that wished to join the industrial world focused its attention during the takeoff phase of economic growth. Between 1981 and 1986, 42 percent of Korea's growth and 74 percent of Taiwan's growth could be traced to exports to the American market.[68] While America represents only 23 percent of world GNP, in 1987 it took 48 percent of the manufactured exports from all of the Third World countries combined.[69] In contrast, the European Economic Community (EEC) took 29 percent and Japan, 12 percent. Yet the aggregate EEC GNP is larger than that of the United States, and Japan's GNP is only 40 percent smaller. Earlier, during the dollar-shortage era of the 1950s, Europe was equally dependent upon access to the U.S. market for its success. The United States has been the market where successful developing countries earned the foreign exchange they needed to grow.

The American market cannot forever absorb most of the exports from the Third World. At some point in the future, the United States will have to generate a trade surplus to pay interest on its accumulated international debts. When it does so, it will cut back on its foreign purchases and go through a period where its market is effectively closed to developing countries.

The system also needs a manager if it is to work.[70] That need can be seen in the failure of the Uruguay round of GATT trade negotiations to meet their deadlines. Freer trade in agricultural products heads the Uruguay negotiating list, but this is an area where little progress is possible, since millions of farmers and the land they now farm would have to leave farming.[71] The world can simply produce more than those who have money to pay for it want to eat. No government is going to sign an agreement that forces large numbers of its farmers and much of its land to leave agriculture.

Services are second on the Uruguay negotiating list, but they are just not worth fighting about.[72] Less than 10 percent of America's exports are real services (returns on American investments abroad are counted as service exports in the official statistics) and real services have not been growing in importance in recent years. Service industries can be owned by foreigners, but most services have to be produced where they are consumed. Leaving travel and license fees aside, America's 1990 service exports to foreigners amounted to only twenty-seven billion dollars.[73] Financial services were seen as a boom area, but U.S. exports never exceeded five billion dollars.

Although Third World countries firmly believe the opposite, they might even be the big beneficiaries from freer trade in services. With modern telecommunications, American computer-software factories have, for example, been opened up in India, and the Caribbean is increasingly being used for processing insurance forms. The developed world's clerical functions could well move to the Third World with freer trade in services. But the Third World doesn't see it that way. These countries think their future growth industries, the services, will be captured by companies from the First World.

With the United States opting out of its leadership role to look after its own narrow self-interests, bilateral negotiations (the Japanese-American Structural Impediment Talks) and special bilateral trade agreements (United States-Canada and United States-Mexico) have replaced multilateral negotiations as the place where real concessions are made. But this automatically leads to a trading-block mentality. The semiconductor agreement between the United States and Japan guarantees the United States more than 20 percent of the Japanese market, but no provision is made for the Europeans.[74] Outsiders do not have equal access, and the special privileges given to one are not given to all.

Everyone is now unilaterally judging their own trade disputes—no one more so than the United States. One of the GATT–Bretton Woods institutions, the International Trade Organization, was never created. The need to do what it was designed to do—judge trade disputes and enforce decisions resolving those disputes—has only become more obvious in recent years. Increasingly, countries are making themselves judges of their own trade disputes. When this happens, multilateralism ceases to have any real meaning.

To make an open world economy work, everyone must feel
that they have an equal chance to win—what is known as "a
level playing field" in America; "reciprocity" in Europe; or
"equal opportunity, not equal outcomes," in Japan. But if the
economic game is to be seen as fair, there must be broadly
similar taxes, regulations, and private modes of operation.
"Economic life-style variables" such as fringe benefits must be
harmonized. German firms cannot give three years leave to
new mothers unless the rest of the world is willing to match
its generosity.[75]

In theory, exchange-rate differences could compensate for
differences in microeconomic systems. Those countries less
open to imports or with lower social-welfare payments would
have higher currency values than they would have had if their
systems had been more open or more generous. But in fact,
currency values don't automatically handicap the players in
the required manner. Currency values are often dominated by
other factors, such as capital flows.

Even if exchange rates did work as theory predicts, they
would not solve the problem. The players in the market
would every day see an unfair game and would not notice the
offsetting changes in currency values. Consider the Japanese
business groups (Mitsui, Mitsubishi, etc.) and their interlocking ownership. They hold monthly meetings to plot strategy in both the Japanese and American markets. American
CEOs holding such a meeting would find themselves all in jail
regardless of whether they were talking about the Japanese or
the American market. The opportunity to work out common
strategies of conquest in home or foreign markets cannot be
permitted to only one side, even if a lower value of the dollar
would theoretically compensate the American side for its inability to form such strategic alliances. If distribution systems
are owned or controlled by producers in one country (Japan)
but open in another (Holland), one set of exporters finds it
much easier to get his products on store shelves than another.
Philips, a Dutch firm, not surprisingly complains that it does
not have equal access to the Japanese market for its consumer
products.

In the real economic world the game must be roughly similar to be seen as fair. Complicated opaque compensatory factors are not a satisfactory political answer, even if they are a theoretical economic answer.

In an open world economy the high minimum wages of Europe are threatened by the low minimum wages of the United States. Long European vacations (thirty days in Germany) are not viable given short vacations in the Pacific Rim (eleven days in Japan).[76] Production simply moves to those parts of the world where such benefits don't have to be paid, thereby forcing the benefits to be eliminated. Benefits that are now hidden in prices have to become overt in wages. Economists think markets become more efficient when hidden benefits become visible benefits, but average voters have very different preferences.

In an open world economy, everyone, not just unskilled American workers, has to be willing to live with factor price equalization. The capitalist who is willing to work for the lowest rate of return in the world sets the maximum rate of return for everyone else. If the Japanese capitalist will accept a 3 percent return, Americans cannot have 15 percent.

The GATT–Bretton Woods trading system is dead. It died not in failure but at the normal end of a very successful life. Logically, a new Bretton Woods conference should now be under way. But politically, it cannot be called. Such a conference can only occur if there is a dominant political power that can force everyone to agree. In 1944 the United States was such a power (Germany and Japan were not even represented). Today there is no such power. If the Uruguay round cannot succeed, much more fundamental negotiations certainly could not succeed.

The required economic changes cannot, however, wait for the right political moment to call such a conference. Success is forcing the rules of the game to change, even if no one formally writes a new set of rules. In this case the rules of the new game will be informally written in Europe. Those who control the world's largest market get to write the rules. That is as it always has been. When the United States had the world's largest market, it got to write the rules. As the Europeans negotiate the rules for their internal common market and decide how outsiders relate to that market, they will effectively be writing the rules for world trade in the next century. Everyone else will gradually adopt Europe's rules as the world's de facto operating system.

The Europeans are going to write the rules for a system of "managed trade" and "quasi trading blocks" (see Chapter 3). Management agreements, such as those now governing semiconductors, will spread, and the countries within any one block, such as Canada within the American market, will get special trading privileges not given to outsiders. I will call the blocks quasi trading blocks to distinguish them from the trading blocks of the 1930s. The quasi trading blocks of the 1990s will attempt to manage trade, but they will not attempt to reduce or eliminate it as the trading blocks of the 1930s did.

NEW OPPORTUNITIES

At temperatures near absolute zero, and now at much higher temperatures in some ceramic materials, superconductivity occurs. The rules that govern the propagation of electricity suddenly change. Old constants are no longer constant. New rules suddenly apply. Resistance disappears, and electrical devices that could not previously be built can now be built, but the currents that are unleashed are difficult to control.

Much the same is happening in the world economy. New players, technologies, and rules are coming together to generate an economic form of superconductivity. Old constants will have to be discarded. Suddenly, new rules will emerge in a very different game. Potentially, much more productive economies can be built, but controlling the currents that will be unleashed will be equally difficult.

Chapter 3

THE HOUSE OF EUROPE: CATALYST FOR CHANGE

Two events make Europe the focal point of attention in the 1990s.[1] In Western Europe, at the stroke of midnight on December 31, 1992, the European Community (EC) integrates, and with that integration instantly becomes by far the world's largest economic market—380 million people now that the members of the European Free Trade Association (EFTA) have effectively been added to the 337 million inside the EC.[2] In Middle and Eastern Europe communism has dissolved and is being replaced by capitalism. In both Eastern and Western Europe something is being attempted that has never before been done—move from central planning to a free market, and voluntary integrate a very large, linguistically heterogeneous market of former military enemies.

Most of the Third World watches the events in Europe with some ambivalence. The ex-communist economies have low wages, well-educated populations, and a convenient location next to the world's largest market. Some of Middle and Eastern Europe will certainly be offered associate memberships in the newly integrated European Community with the prospects of full membership at a later date. Their special access will effectively close Europe's markets for mid- and low-income countries elsewhere in the world that don't have such special access. Capital and managerial talent will be drained away from other developing areas.

Japan and America worry that the economic integration of Europe will make it harder for them to sell their products in Europe. Even if Europe does not become an economic fortress, its markets will be harder to penetrate.[3] An American firm and a German firm that were equally competitive in Italy before integration will find that in 1993 the German firm has an advantage. The barriers facing German products will have gone down, while the barriers facing American products will remain unchanged. Similarly, if an Italian and Japanese firm were equally competitive in Germany before integration, then after 1992 the Italian firm will have an edge.

Outsiders also understand that their losses will surely be larger than this irreducible minimum. In building the House of Europe, economic gains not shared with outsiders are the glue necessary to politically weld together a set of disparate countries. To work, this economic glue must be a powerful glue, and it can only be powerful if there is a large gap between how insiders and outsiders are treated.

The British are the best example of what the economic glue must do and why it must be very strong. Originally, the British refused to join the European Community. They believed that entry would require them to give up too much national sovereignty. But Britain eventually reversed its decision and joined when it became clear that the economic handicaps of staying out would be so large that it could not afford to pay the economic price that insular national sovereignty would require. When the other members of the EC decided to move ahead on monetary union, a British prime minister who refused to go along had to be fired. She was fired because the costs to the British of not going along were simply too great to be paid. It was cheaper to find a new prime minister.

The British regularly object to the use of the word *federalism* in EC planning documents, but just as they had to reverse their earlier refusal to join, so will they stay, even if Europe becomes a federation. Britain will stay in the EC not because the EC agrees to replace the word *federalism* with the word *confederation* in its planning documents, but because it cannot afford to give up the economic gains that will accrue to inside members and cannot afford to pay the price that outsiders will have to pay.[4] Symbolically, the British have already recognized this reality at Heathrow Airport in London. The special passport lines that used to exist for members of the European Economic Community have disappeared, to be replaced by special lines for members of the European Community. Implicitly, the British have accepted the fact that they did not just join an economic free trade zone—the ultimate long-run goal is political union.

When talking to each other, Europeans understand that if they did not gain some special privileges relative to the rest of the world, there would be no reason to integrate. As Umberto Agnelli, the president of Fiat, Europe's largest industrial company, has said, "The single market must first offer an advantage to European companies. This is a message we must insist upon without hesitation."[5] Similarly, the EEC commissioner for external relations, Willy de Clerc, states, "We see no reason why the benefit of our internal liberalization should be extended unilaterally to third countries."[6] Insiders simply must make big gains relative to outsiders, or countries will eventually start to drop out of the European Community.

Realistically, outsiders have to face the fact that European integration will hurt them. It wouldn't work if it didn't.

The federation of Europe will take a long time. It has already taken almost forty years just to get to the point where border controls can be abolished. Another century may well be necessary to complete economic and political integration. Progress will be erratic—two steps forward, one step back, one step to the left, one step to the right.

It is easy to make a long list of difficult issues that will have to be resolved. The list can easily be used to argue that real European integration will never occur. But the formation of the House of Europe is now unstoppable. First, the opportunities to create an integrated House of Europe are just too good to pass up. An opportunity as good as this one hasn't

existed since the fall of the Roman Empire. Second, the need
to compete against the Americans and the Japanese in a global
economy almost demands that the House of Europe be built.
If it isn't, the individual countries of Europe will find themselves economically marginalized between two much bigger,
more aggressive economies. Third, enough integration has
now occurred to make it very difficult for anyone to withdraw. Fourth, an internal dynamic has been set up whereby
each step forward essentially forces the participants to take
further steps forward.

The ever-tighter degree of economic integration that is required by steps taken in the past is neatly illustrated in a sequence that began with the decision to build a European
Exchange Rate System (ERS) to prevent the destabilizing effects
of large currency fluctuations—a step taken to insure that business firms could make large investments without the risk that
sudden large currency swings would make them worthless. But
once the ERS was in place, it was obvious that if it were to work,
monetary policies would have to be harmonized. If one country
were to print money much faster than the rest of Europe, the
value of its currency could not be stabilized. As a result, the existence of the ERS essentially forced the Europeans to think
about a European Monetary System (EMS), the details of which
are now under active development.

But once monetary policies are linked, it becomes necessary
to start talking about a European central bank if one does not
want the German Bundesbank to become the de facto central
bank for Europe. Since each country will want to have some
influence on monetary policies, and since this influence is
only to be had if there is a European central bank, it is only
a question of time until a European central bank comes into
existence. Vague discussions are now under way.

But if common monetary policies are adopted, then limits
must be placed on government fiscal deficits if the deficits of
individual countries are not to absorb the capital funds that
other member states want to put into private investment in
plant and equipment. Monetary coordination forces fiscal coordination. Similarly once markets are opened to flows of
goods across national boundaries in 1993, business firms from
different European countries will require a level playing field

where each faces approximately the same taxes and social charges. If taxes were not equalized, production would simply move to the country where taxes were lowest, and the lowest-spending country would essentially force everyone else to adjust to their expenditure patterns. To prevent this from happening, the harmonization of taxes and social charges is now being negotiated in Brussels.

To equalize taxes, countries must agree upon common spending patterns. With similar taxes and similar spending patterns, national governments lose many of their traditional economic powers. In this circumstance, giving more political power to a European parliament doesn't seem like such a radical change.

Political integration will lag economic integration, but economic integration inevitably forces political integration. Quick, collective foreign-policy decisions will be the most difficult of all—witness Europe's problems in coming to grips with the Persian Gulf War or the civil war in Yugoslavia. But the House of Europe will be built.

Adding Middle and Eastern Europe to the House of Europe is also going to be a slow process, although several countries have already signaled their desires to join. The short run economic prospects for rapid growth in the ex-communist countries were grossly exaggerated when communism first started to disappear. The transition from central planning to the market is going to be much slower and much more painful than was originally imagined. The human and physical infrastructure of capitalism will have to be built—both will take a long time.

To start a capitalistic economy, there must be some initial distribution of resources—property rights. All of those things now technically owned by the state have to be given or sold to someone. Who is to get them? What is the fair way to distribute existing economic resources? Neither the theory nor history of Western capitalism provides any answers. There is no *right* initial distribution of property in a market economy. Market economies can adjust to any initial distribution of property rights—no matter how equal or unequal. Historically, Western capitalism sometimes began by taking the distribution of property rights that came out of feudalism (Britain), and sometimes began by having a revolution to alter the feudal distribution of property rights (France). Lacking theoretical or historical guidelines for handing out property, Middle and Eastern Europe will spend a lot of time figuring out how to do it. Yet markets cannot start until it is clear who owns what. Who has the right to sell what? Who can collect rent from whom?

Some countries will solve their problems faster than other countries, but the transition will occur. The transition will occur because everyone in Middle and Eastern Europe understands that communism is dead and that they cannot go back to the old system. They have no alternative but to try something different. They may fail in their efforts and end up joining the Third World, but they have to change.

EURO-PESSIMISM TO EURO-OPTIMISM

The 1980s opened with Euro-pessimism. The pessimists were right! Western Europe, Middle Europe, and the USSR were all located at the bottom of the world's tables for industrial growth in the decade of the 1980s (see Table 3.1). Western Europe did better in the second half of the decade than it did in the first half of the decade, but at the beginning of the 1990s, the economies of Middle and Eastern Europe were in an advanced state of decay, if not collapse, with many experiencing sharp economic declines.

TABLE 3.1
Industrial Growth Rates 1980s
(in percent)

Country	1979–1989
Japan	4.6
U.S.	2.6
EEC	2.0
EFTA	1.8
USSR	2.2
Middle Europe	1.1

SOURCE: Council of Economic Advisers, *Economic Report of the President 1990* (Washington, D.C.: GPO), p. 419.

Western Europe grew slowly in the 1980s because the West Germans wanted to grow slowly (1.8 percent per year over the decade). The announced reason was the fear of inflation, but the real reason was demography. The Germans knew that their labor force would shrink sharply in the 1990s. If Germany grew rapidly in the 1980s, it would be forced to import large numbers of guest workers in the 1990s. Most Germans thought that there were already too many foreigners, and they did not want more.

With West Germany deliberately setting its monetary and fiscal policies to grow slowly, it was impossible for the rest of Europe to grow rapidly.[7] If governments tried to stimulate their economies, as the French did at the beginning of the decade, they simply produced large trade deficits that could not be financed. The restrictive macroeconomic policies of Germany effectively forced everyone else in Western Europe to adopt similar policies. The result was slow growth and very high unemployment—over 10 percent for much of the decade, and over 20 percent in Ireland and Spain.

But the events in East Germany in 1989 dramatically changed German demography. Instead of facing a shrinking labor force in the 1990s, Germany has 9 million new workers (16.5 million new people) that need to be brought up to western German income levels just as fast as possible. It is also facing an inflow of millions of ethnic Germans from Middle and Eastern Europe. All of these millions want German standards of living quickly, and they can get it by moving to western Germany. If Germany does not want to see eastern Germany depopulated, it has no choice but to adopt policies that can only be described as "full speed ahead."[8]

Any obstacles that stand in the way of this goal will simply be bulldozed out of the way. Thus far, the costs of integration have been many multiples above those originally estimated. But there has been no thought of going slower. The extra costs are simply paid. The German central bank urged caution in the conversion of East to West German marks, and the traditional German interest in low inflation would properly have called for caution, but this traditional interest was completely jettisoned to accomplish what German political leaders saw as a far more important task—the economic integration of their country. In the end the conversion was done generously (one-to-one) to raise East German living standards rapidly, but at the price of some inflationary risk.

The same interest in speed can be seen in the way that inflation was measured in the newly enlarged Germany.[9] Increases in East German prices up to the levels of West Germany simply weren't statistically counted as inflation. The West Germans explain that East German price increases should not be counted as inflation, since the East Germans were given West German marks. But this argument is no different than maintaining that any inflation covered by indexing should not be counted as inflation, since it does not represent a real fall in purchasing power. As this slight-of-hand measurement indicates, inflationary risks were, and will be, taken in Germany. In mid-1991 Germany did in fact have the highest rate of inflation among major industrial countries.

With "full speed ahead" the economic order of the day, Germany's current-account surplus, the world's largest in 1989, was headed towards an annual deficit in 1992.[10] From 1989 to mid-1991 European Community exports to Germany grew 30 percent; Germany's trade surplus with the rest of the EC fell by more than seventy million deutsche marks.[11] Dramatic growth opportunities opened up for the rest of Europe.

As German macroeconomic policies shift from deceleration to acceleration, the macroeconomic policies in the rest of Western Europe can shift with them.[12] Most Western European countries have high levels of unemployment but also have the infrastructure and managers to quickly absorb that unemployment if demand for goods and services were only rising fast enough. With very different macroeconomic policies in place, all of Western Europe should grow very rapidly in the next five years as it moves from underemployment to full employment. In the second half of the 1990s, investment opportunities in the rest of Middle and Eastern Europe should be ready to play the locomotive role for an enlarged European Community, but in the first half of the decade, the action will be in Western Europe.

The 1990s open with Euro-optimism. The optimism is deserved—not because Eastern Europe will grow rapidly, and not because of the growth dividend from integration efficiencies in the EC—but because an engine for economic growth has been found in the dramatic shifts in German macroeconomic policies. Policies that had been set to restrict growth will be set to accelerate growth. Germany will become an economic locomotive for the rest of Europe. And if the EC does not become too much of an economic fortress, the trade created by this growth should compensate the rest of the world for the inevitable trade losses that it will suffer in the aftermath of 1992.

WRITING THE TRADING RULES FOR THE TWENTY-FIRST CENTURY

The world has outgrown the GATT–Bretton Woods trading system and must build a new system based on the realities of a tripolar economic world. Irresistible forces cannot be resisted. If the pressures cannot be relieved in logical ways (a new Bretton Woods conference), they will be relieved in other ways. Since a new Bretton Woods conference cannot be held without a dominant power to force agreements, the European negotiations at Brussels will become the de facto new Bretton Woods conference. As the European Community harmonizes its internal rules and regulations, decides the conditions of access for outsiders, and offers associate memberships to other European nations such as Switzerland or Czechoslovakia, it will effectively be writing the rules of international trade for the next century. Whatever rules it adopts, others will learn to play by those rules.

It is an old axiom of history that the rules of trade are written by those who control access to the world's largest market. Everyone else needs access to that market and has no choice but to play by the rules of the game. It was always thus. Britain wrote the rules of world trade in the nineteenth century. The United States did it in the twentieth century. As the world's largest market, the House of Europe will be writing the rules of world trade in the twenty-first century, and the rest of the world will simply have to learn to play their economic game.

Europe will be blamed for destroying GATT, but in fact no

one on either side of the Atlantic or the Pacific is willing to do what would have to be done save the current system. Given the reality of three roughly equal regions, no one could expect to play by their own traditional rules and practices more than one third of the time. Everyone would have to be prepared to give up two thirds of their economic way of life. It is not just the Europeans who are unprepared to do so.

GATT bled to death from the wounds described in the previous chapter, but European integration will provide the official death certificate. Legally, common markets are permitted if they lead to political unions. While the European Community meets this requirement, a common market as big as the EC violates the most-favored-nation spirit of GATT (any trading privilege given to one nation should be given to all nations) even if it does not violate the letter of the law. But more importantly, there are no GATT provisions allowing for associate memberships in common markets. If associate memberships are permitted for Middle European countries and for countries such as Switzerland, GATT effectively ceases to exist. External third parties are not being treated equally in any sense whatsoever. Yet it is clear that the European Community will give associate memberships to countries such as Hungary and Switzerland. They will do so because it makes sense to do so. Each of us would do so if we were European. The chance to build the House of Europe is too good to pass up, regardless of the rules written in the past.

With judicious expansion, there is no reason why the House of Europe could not be by far the largest and most prosperous economic region in the world. Europe has 850 million well-educated people, and none of its existing countries, with the possible exception of Albania, is really poor. Imagine what could occur if the high-tech science capabilities of the former Soviet Union were paired with the world-class production capabilities of the Germans. With natural gas from the new Commonwealth, Europe could be energy self-sufficient and not have to worry about Persian Gulf oil and the political instabilities of that region.

If building the House of Europe is the positive side of the equation, preventing migration is the negative side of the equation. Middle and Eastern Europeans will not stay for long on their side of the border and earn one tenth of what those in Western Europe earn. Easterners have to be given special privileges in the markets of Western Europe to accelerate their economic growth or they will start moving. The Europeans also have something comparable to America's Mexican problem in North Africa. They need to make it into Europe's low-wage offshore manufacturing area if millions of North Africans are not to move into southern Europe.[13] But associate memberships or preferred access for the countries of the European Free Trade Association (EFTA), Eastern Europe, and North Africa automatically create a trading block. All outsiders will not be treated alike. Some (those in Europe or near Europe) will be treated more equally than others.

This combination of positive and negative motivations will lead the Europeans to write the rules for a system of quasi trading blocks with managed trade. Trade will be much freer within the blocks, but trade between the blocks will be managed by governments.

Any hard-nosed analysis of the Brussels negotiations quickly leads to this conclusion. History tells us that an economic union has to keep outsiders out, since this is the glue that holds the disparate insiders together. In the one hundred years after it was formed, the American common market was very restrictive on outside access. This issue was in fact one of the major causes of the American Civil War, which began in 1861. The North was attempting to keep the South from buying cheap British manufactured products.

Political analysis leads to the same conclusion. Europeans talk as if they all will be winners in 1993, but beneath the present euphoria there is an undercurrent of concern. Each company and each geographic region is asking its experts to determine whether it is likely to be a winner or a loser after 1992. Looking at market shares in the United States and comparing them with those in Europe reveals that most European firms are going to lose market share to a few new giants, and that many firms are going to be driven out of business entirely.[14] As a result, some of those consultant reports will come back with the conclusion that the firms commissioning the report will be winners, but a much larger number will come back with the message that the firms will be losers.

Similarly, the geographic distribution of economic activity in the United States reveals that some regions of Europe will be big losers. Some American states are sparsely populated, and the poorest states have per capita incomes only one third that of richest. Two thirds of America's three thousand counties are losing population. Ireland may become the North Dakota of Europe. In a common market with free labor mobility, workers must move to the most dynamic areas (Germany); economic activity seldom moves to where the unemployed are currently located (Ireland).

Those who feel that they will be hurt in the economic integration (the Spanish banks feel threatened by the German banks) will go to their governments for protection. Their governments, however, cannot give them the direct protection they seek if integration is to go forward. In lieu of direct protection from insiders, their governments will offer them protection from outside competitors. Less competition from American and Japanese banks will be offered to the Spanish banks to compensate them for more competition from the German banks. It doesn't take deep political insight to know that compensation is always easier to give if the costs can be imposed on outsiders, and in this case they can.

What logic would lead one to suspect, current developments confirm. In most of the proposed European Community trading rules that have thus far been drafted, the access of outsiders is at least slightly restricted. Insurance is to become more difficult for foreigners to sell; America's market share in TV programs and movies is to be held to less than 50 percent.[15]

It does not take a European automotive genius to note that on neutral turf, the American market, the Japanese have scored what in boxing terms would be a TKO.[16] Across the board, European car manufacturers either have been driven out of the U.S. market or are rapidly losing market shares.

What the Japanese have done in America they can do, are doing, and will do in Europe if given a chance. In those European markets that were open to them, the Japanese were selling more than 30 percent of the cars purchased in 1990.[17] In some markets, such as Ireland and Norway, the Japanese market share was above 40 percent.

The Japanese can assemble a luxury car with only one quarter of the labor that is required in Europe.[18] They can put new models into production faster and their cars have fewer defects. Is it any surprise that the president of Fiat calls for measures that keep the Japanese under control? "Nothing could be more Japanese and less 'global' than a big Japanese company even if it operates on all five continents. The decision-makers are Japanese, the stockholders are Japanese, the organization and the R&D are Japanese as is the 'conquistador' mentality underlying its industrial and commercial strategies. . . . To leave Europe wide open to extra-European competition during this period would produce the mistakes that the Americans made and for which they are now suffering the consequences."[19]

No one enters a competitive game that they expect to lose, especially at home. The result is draft regulations calling for the Japanese to be limited to a 16 percent market share in the year 2000, regardless of whether the car is imported from Japan or built in Europe. But if the Europeans are to manage their auto trade with Japan, they must manage it with America. The Japanese are building more production capacity in the United States than they can possibly use in America. What are they going to do with it? The obvious answer, as Honda is now attempting to do, is to export some of those American built cars to Europe.[20] What looks like a Japanese-versus-European fight quickly becomes an American-versus-European fight.

The French and the Italians may have been the most vociferous advocates of limits on the Japanese, but everyone else (the Germans in particular) hides behind their stubbornness, since no one thinks that they could win a fair-market game with the Japanese.[21] Germany is simply not the bastion of free trade that it is often made out to be in the United States. In a *New York Times* article entitled "Greetings from Fortress Germany," it is described as follows: "Although less pervasive than in Japan, protectionism in Germany is often just as deep-rooted and effective. The telecommunication, banking, insurance, electrical utility, and chemical industries, for example, operate as virtual cartels. It is almost impossible for a foreign company to enter those markets without a German partner.

Other barriers include restrictive laws, massive Government subsidies, and the rigid protocols of a clannish, old-boy network that dominates the economy."[22] Implicitly, most of Europe harks back to the words of Sir Joseph Chamberlain in 1906: "You cannot go on watching with indifference the disappearance of your principal industries."[23]

If the history of the European Community teaches any lesson, it teaches outsiders to expect the worst. Agriculture is the one place where Europe has already completed its economic integration. In the process it produced a highly restrictive market. Why should the results in agriculture be unique? Won't the same political forces produce the same results in other industries? The obvious answer is yes! Even 65 percent of the members of the British Parliament agree.[24] They agree because that is what is happening. Nineteen bilateral agreements shield European textile producers. Sixty percent of European Community imports come from countries who have entered into preferential agreements with the EC.[25]

When foreigners charge "Fortress Europe," the European Community's official answer is that it only requires "market opening measures extended internationally on a firm basis of clear reciprocity".[26] Translated into clear English, that bureaucratic jargon means that if rest of the world wishes to be treated equally in Europe, it must change its rules so that they are identical to those that will exist in Europe after unification. Since the rest of the world will find it difficult (and sometimes impossible) to change its rules and regulations to conform to those in Europe, although Fortress Europe and reciprocity sound very different, they are, in fact, identical.

Consider the ability of foreign banks to enter or expand in the Common Market. Under the doctrine of reciprocity, Europe can keep American banks out of Europe or stop those that are already in Europe from expanding on the grounds that many American states do not permit interstate banking. If a European bank does not have access to all of America, then an American bank cannot have access to all of Europe. Similarly, America does not allow banks to own shares in industrial firms. If European banks are not to have that privilege in America, then American banks cannot have that privilege in Europe. Sir Leon Brittan, the EC commissioner for finance,[27] has stated that

Americans must repeal their state laws limiting branch banking and their national laws prohibiting banks from owning industrial firms if they are to have unfettered access in Europe. When he states these requirements for equal access, he knows full well that they are unlikely to be met.

What are reciprocal subsidies? Europeans argue that direct subsidies to Airbus Industries are equivalent to indirect American subsidies that come via the Defense Department, despite the fact that Boeing has had no contracts for military airplanes for many years (it does have missile contracts). Sometimes they are, of course, right. The Defense Department investment in Sematech (a government-backed consortium formed to improve semiconductor production capabilities) has no military purpose. It is clearly a civilian industrial policy designed to combat the Japanese that is disguised as a military program.

How will Europe deal with Japan, where the whole distinction between public and private has little meaning? Are Japanese participation bonds (loans that are often forgiven if efforts to enter targeted areas such as aircraft manufacturing fail) investments equivalent to European state ownership—or are they subsidies not to be permitted? Is holding down the real rate of interest paid on postal savings accounts in Japan a violation of reciprocity or merely a legitimate policy to raise savings and stimulate economic growth?

In my trips to Europe I hear over and over again from private businessmen and public officials the phrase "We are not going to let the Japanese do in Europe what they have already done in the United States." What many have been saying privately for a long time, the prime minister of France, Edith Cresson, now says publicly. "Japan is an adversary that doesn't play by the rules and has an absolute desire to conquer the world. You have to be naive or blind not to recognize that."[28] "The Japanese have a strategy of world conquest. They have finished their job in the United States. Now they are about to devour Europe."[29]

The Japanese are not blind to these realities. In their words Europe is headed "in the direction of an exclusionary and protectionist trading block."[30] The Europeans "are determined to protect their national markets in severe 'dog eat dog' competition. Europe really means it."[31] The Japanese are right. Europe does mean it!

In the long run, regionalism may well be a positive development for the world. Free trade within regions and managed trade between regions may well be the long-run route to freer world trade. Jumping in one big leap from national economies to a world economy is simply too big a leap to make. It is necessary to take smaller intermediate steps first, and quasi trading blocks combined with managed trade may be just such a necessary intermediate step.[32]

Because of their effects in the 1930s, to speak of trading blocks is to be accused of being a pessimist, but they need not be a disaster. Interblock trade will be managed by governments, but trade management is not necessarily a synonym for trade reduction or elimination. In fact, world trade in the next half century is apt to grow even faster than it did in the last half century. Any decline in trade between blocks will be more than offset by more trade within the blocks.

The inefficiencies of managed trade are also not as high as some economic descriptions of free-trade virtues would lead one to believe. It is possible to show theoretically that free trade maximizes national incomes, but only if one is willing to make a number of highly restrictive assumptions. An enumeration of these assumptions quickly dispels the notion that the choice between free trade and managed trade is a choice between heaven and hell.

The theory of free trade admits that there will be sharp income-distribution changes within each participating country. Average incomes will go up with free trade, but there may be millions of losers in each country. The theory simply maintains that the losses of the losers will simply be smaller than the winnings of the winners. The theory assumes that the winners will compensate the losers, so that everyone in each country has an incentive to move toward free trade, but in fact such compensation is almost never paid. Without such compensation there are individuals who should rationally oppose free trade as antithetical to their economic self-interest. In a Mexican-American free-trade agreement, for example, skilled Americans win and unskilled Americans lose, since the supply of unskilled labor effectively expands, and, relatively speaking, the supply of skilled labor shrinks.[33]

Average incomes must rise under free trade since unemployment is assumed not to exist. Workers fired in any industry losing market share to imports quickly find work elsewhere. In reality, significant time lags exist. Regions that lose their dominant industries have high unemployment rates for long periods of time. Contrary to the theory of free trade, there are large unemployment costs in simply letting someone else capture your home markets. When unemployment is factored into the analysis, there is no guarantee that average incomes will rise by moving to a system of free trade. The issue becomes an empirical one of how much unemployment is created in the transition.

In addition, the theory assumes that the costs of making structural shifts from one industry to another are zero. In reality, these costs are often large. Old plant and equipment must be scrapped; new plant and equipment must be built. If new industries are built in different regions, public infrastructure must be abandoned and rebuilt. The theory also assigns no value to the costs of tearing up of human communities, since friends and neighbors have no value in economic calculus. In some cases the costs of free trade may well be higher than the benefits of free trade.

In the theory of free trade, individuals are assumed to be paid wages based upon their individual skills, not upon the industry in which they work. When they lose their job in an old industry, on average, they receive the same wages in their new employment. In reality, floor sweepers in textile factories are not paid the same wages as those in auto factories. Displaced American auto, steel, and machine-tool workers did not find jobs with equal wages.

In the theory of free trade, trading accounts are also assumed to balance in relatively short periods of time. Yet the 1980s prove that free trade is not quickly self-equilibrating as the theory assumes. But persistent deficits mean that a country must sell off the assets that determine its future standard of living—Brooks Brothers, Firestone Tire & Rubber, Rockefeller Center. Income streams that would have gone to Americans now go abroad. Countries may not want to raise their present consumption at the cost of lowering their future consumption.

If each block manages its macroeconomic coordination better than the world is now managing its macroeconomic coordination, then faster growth within the blocks may lead to more trade and swamp the hypothetical gains that flow from a more open, but slower growing, world economy. Germany might worry, for example, more about European growth if it knew that the United States was not worrying about European growth. The United States might be much more willing to do something about Latin American debt if it saw Latin America as part of its trading block.

How the rest of the world responds to Europe's quasi trading block is not clear. The former U.S. ambassador to Japan, Mike Mansfield, has publicly called for a U.S.-Japanese common market. Given the great differences in the economic systems of these two countries, the establishment of an American-Japanese common market would be difficult. Like Europe, America and Japan would have to harmonize their systems of government and their traditional ways of doing business. But the cultural gap between Japan and the United States is simply much bigger than the gap between France and Germany.

If the world splits into three blocks, the nature of the split is not obvious. The Japanese Ministry of International Trade and Industry talks about an East Asian regional order but sees most of the potential gains for Japan in China and eastern Russia.[34] In doing so, it is not thinking of a common market of manufacturing equals but one with raw-materials suppliers (Russia) and potentially large markets (China) for Japanese manufactured goods.

Unless Japan is willing to become a major net importer of manufactured goods from the Pacific Rim, a trading block made up of Japan, Taiwan, Korea, Singapore and some of the other developing nations of Southeast Asia would look more like the old Japanese Co-Prosperity Sphere than it would like a common market of equals. These countries would simply be assigned low-wage Japanese manufacturing tasks. Politically, to be a trading block of equals, mainland China would have to belong. But it is impossible to have a real common market with open labor mobility between poor and rich countries. Too many people move. And Japan is the country in the world that would find it hardest to accept any large number of immigrants.

In the Americas similar problems exist. While there are a lot of people in Latin America, the GNPs of the constituent states are small. Economically, Latin America adds nothing of significance to North America. Also, no one knows how to attach a poor country to a common market of wealthy countries. The Europeans haven't even dared to try with Turkey, and its per capita GNP is closer to that of the poorest country in the Common Market than any part of Latin America is to the poorest state in the United States.

Economic geography may well end up being more important than physical geography. Singapore, Korea, and Taiwan are much more integrated with the United States than they are with Japan.[35] With modern technology, there is no reason why trading blocks have to involve contiguous countries. There are lots of potential opportunities for creative or surprising alliances.

During the transition from the GATT–Bretton Woods system to a system of quasi trading blocks with managed trade, there is apt to be a great deal of uncertainty. While it will be clear that the old GATT–Bretton Woods system no longer exists, the exact parameters of a new system combining quasi trading blocks with managed trade will be murky.

THE TRANSITION FROM COMMUNISM TO CAPITALISM[36]

In the transition from communism to capitalism, Middle and Eastern Europe start with some advantages.[37] No country is truly poor by Third World standards. Before the fall of the Berlin Wall, the economies of Middle Europe and Eastern Europe were thought to have per capita GNPs that ranged between thirty-five hundred and ten thousand. Among the republics that used to make up the USSR, Tajikistan is the poorest and Russia, the richest, with per capita production about 45 percent below and 19 percent above that of the Soviet average respectively.[38] This put all of them in the same income range as the little tigers of the Pacific Rim (see Table 3.2).

After the nations of Middle and Eastern Europe have had a chance to look at their economies in more detail, estimates have been lowered. Goods were even more inferior and shortages more widespread than had been previously believed. A lot of what was produced never reached the consumer because of distribution inefficiencies.[39]

There may also be a scandal lurking in these changing estimates. The high estimates were always CIA estimates. Were the Western intelligence agencies such as the CIA deliberately exaggerating the performance of the communist economies to increase Western military budgets? If not, were they then grossly incompetent, wasting billions on faulty estimates?

TABLE 3.2
1989 Per Capita GNPs in the Command Economies
(in thousands of dollars)

	Average*	High†	Low†
East Germany	9,679	13,000	4,000
USSR	8,802	9,000	2,000
Czechoslovakia	7,878	10,000	4,000
Hungary	6,108	9,000	3,000
Bulgaria	5,710	7,500	2,000
Yugoslavia	5,464	6,500	3,000
Poland	4,565	7,500	2,000
Romania	3,445	6,500	1,500

SOURCE: Central Intelligence Agency, *International Herald Tribune*, May 17, 1990. "Grossly Deceptive Product," *The Economist*, p. 71.
*CIA, *Tribune*, May 17, 1990
†"Deceptive Product," *Economist*, p. 71.

In sharp contrast to their economic performances, the communist countries did not run world-class K–12 education systems. Most of their universities did not turn out a particularly high-quality product, but they did turn out a very large supply of engineers. The exception is the former Soviet Union, which has a world-class science establishment. With an educated citizenry, Middle and Eastern Europe should be fast learners when it comes to acquiring modern industrial skills. The human capital exists to support very rapid growth.

Monetary wages are low (East German wages were one tenth of those in West Germany), but real wages are much higher, since many necessities that must be purchased in capitalistic societies were provided free or almost free under communism.[40,41] The average Russian spends only 1 percent of his family income on housing. Basic necessities such as bread are very cheap—thirteen kopecks (one half of one U.S. cent) per kilo. In a market economy these and other necessities will rise to the levels found in other market economies (housing costs 30 to 40 percent of family income in most market economies; a kilo of bread costs about two dollars in the United States), and cash wages will have to rise to cover these new cash costs. As a consequence, the Second World will not be in competition with the Third World for the very low-wage, low-skill jobs in industries such as textiles. They will be competing with mid-wage developing countries.

The transition from communism to capitalism will be difficult, since to go up, one must first go down.[42] Successful market economies may generate higher standards of living than those that were generated under communism, but communism must be dismantled before market economies can be built. During this transition phase, average incomes will be lower—much lower—than they were under communism. One year after integration, eastern Germany's industrial production was 40 percent below where it had been.[43] Two years later, it is 80 percent below where it had been.[44,45] Fifty percent of the labor force is expected to end up either unemployed or working short-time. Western Germans wonder where they will find the "starter motor" for eastern Germany's growth and keep looking for signs that the economy of eastern Germany has finally bottomed out.[46]

In Poland's economy 1990 average family incomes were 40 percent below the peak attained under communism. No one has yet forecasted production upturns in 1991.[47] In 1990 and

1991 GDPs fell 16 percent in Poland, Czechoslovakia, Hungary, Romania, and Bulgaria, with industrial production plunging 28 percent.[48] Bridging the chaos between communism and capitalism is going to try the economic fortitude and the political patience of even the most masochistic.[49,50] In the fall of 1991 Romanian miners were threatening to bring down the government because of falling standards of living. Even in eastern Germany, where money was plentiful, where managers could be imported in large numbers from the west and where there was no argument about the system (East Germany simply adopted West German laws), the economy was not expected to hit bottom until mid-1992.

The problems are going to be particularly difficult in what was the USSR. The system cannot be blamed on outsiders and has been in place much longer. Practices and attitudes are deeply rooted. The government cannot collect taxes; the country is too big to get significant aid from the outside; there are no managers who understand capitalism; and there are huge differences of opinion over what should be the characteristics of the new system. There is no agreement as to what to do or how to do it. The Russian Republic announces that prices will be deregulated, while the mayor of Moscow announces that rationing will be instituted. Just letting the market work may take too long, yet active government involvement to speed up the transition is resisted, given everyone's memory of communism.

Two painful transitions are simultaneously under way. All of the problems of shifting from communism to capitalism exist, but the economy also needs to be torn apart and reassembled to allow a whole set of new countries to emerge. This is particularly difficult in the former Soviet Union, since part of the old communist strategy was to hold the republics together by making them economically dependent upon each other. If Polish incomes fell 40 percent, incomes in the newly independent republics are going to fall much more. A 25 percent decline had taken place even before the USSR dissolved in the summer of 1991.[51]

As the joke goes in the ex-communist world, the difference between capitalism and communism is as follows: "In communism your pockets are full of money, but there is nothing in the stores to buy. In capitalism the stores are full, but you have no money in your pockets." In the next few winters, that joke isn't going to be funny.

The ex-communist economies are often talked about as if they were a homogeneous group, but they differ greatly in their prospects. Eastern Germany is a special case all by itself.[52,53,54] It starts as the wealthiest country of Middle Europe and the one with the oldest industrial traditions. Western Germany will buy eastern Germany the private and public infrastructure that capitalism needs to function. Two hundred billion dollars have already been allocated to rebuild infrastructure (electric power, transportation), and seventy billion dollars set aside to clean up the environment.[55] Thirty-three billion dollars is to be invested to build a world-class telephone system.[56] A multibillion-dollar Unity Fund will pay for transition costs such as unemployment insurance for those who lose their jobs in the shift to a market economy.[57] In 1992 the Bonn government was spending sixty-four billion dollars to aid eastern Germany.[58] There are those who argue that it will cost up to ten times the current estimates of future annual aid to eastern Germany, and today they look more nearly right.[59,60,61] But western Germany is going to buy whatever has to be bought. It has no choice.

More important even than the money, it is socially acceptable to flood eastern Germany with western German managers to get the development process started. In the rest of Middle and Eastern Europe, the necessary outside business managers don't exist, and even if they did, it would be politically unacceptable to use them.

But even with a wealthy big brother, eastern Germany is caught in a tough economic trap. If eastern Germans are to be paid wages equal to those in western Germany, productivity in eastern Germany has to equal that in the west. To get equal productivity, massive investments ($1,000 billion according to the International Monetary Fund) must be made in plant and equipment, and these investments take time even if the money is available. Yet eastern Germans expect to instantly make what western Germans make. If they don't, those eastern Germans with skills will simply move west, stripping eastern Germany of the skilled workers it needs to be successful in the long run.

Recent events bear out this scenario. After being set at one third of the wage level in western Germany immediately after integration, eastern wages in the following year promptly rose 50 to 80 percent in many industries.[62] But at these wage levels (about two thirds of those in the west), investments have not led to profits in eastern Germany and have been slow in coming.

In the end, Germany will succeed. Rapid development will occur in the east. If necessary, public investment will replace private investment. There is no doubt about eastern Germany's long-run success. The only questions are those of method and timing.

The rest of the ex-communist economies are a much more complicated story in that economic prospects differ greatly from country to country and from region to region. Realistically, some of these countries will leave the Second World to join the First World, and other will eventually be seen as part of the Third World. If one were ranking prospects for development in Middle Europe, the Czech part of Czechoslovakia would be the most likely prospect for development after east Germany. Hungary would come next, with Poland following. Slovakia, Romania, Bulgaria, and Albania would be the least likely prospects. Among the countries that used to make up Yugoslavia, Slovenia would be at the top. Border and ethnic problems make success among the other regions unlikely.[63,64,65]

Yugoslavia and the USSR may not be the only countries that do not remain one country. The Slovaks and the Czechs may end up in divorce court. Romania has a large Hungarian minority. Bulgaria has a large Turkish minority. Both minorities want more independence.

The countries that are emerging from the remains of the USSR in Eastern Europe are a very peculiar mixture with demonstrated competence in many high-tech fields such as space exploration but great backwardness in other areas such as distribution.[66, 67] A study by the Deutsche Bank in Germany ranked the different republic's economic potential on a scale of 1 to 30, with the Ukraine getting the highest score, a 27, and Tajikistan getting the lowest, a 6 (see Table 3.3).

TABLE 3.3
Economic Potential of the Republics of the Commonwealth
of Independent States*
(scale: 1 to 30)

Ukraine	27
Russia	24
Kazakhstan	19
Baltic States	18
Georgia	17
Belarus*	14
Azerbaijan	13
Uzbekistan	12
Moldova*	11
Armenia	10
Turkmenistan*	10
Kirghizia	8
Tajikistan*	6

SOURCE: Deutsche Bank. "Deutsche Bank Report," *The New York Times*, September 5, 1991, p. A13.
*Revised from source to reflect new name.

The political and social problems are enormous in the new Commonwealth of Independent States. Before the USSR broke up, much of the decline in its GNP could be traced to the ethnic and border disputes in Lithuania, Armenia, Azerbaijan, and Tajikistan, and the consequent refusal to ship products to each other. Internal markets effectively ceased to function as different groups refused to trade with each other. With real countries emerging from the remains of the USSR, these problems can only get worse. Moreover, some of these new countries (Russia, the Ukraine, and Kazakhstan, at the very minimum) are going to be instant nuclear military powers.[68]

Disentangling the former USSR economically may not be as deadly as disentangling it socially and militarily, but it will be at least as complicated. While no area is ever completely self-sufficient, the old Soviet republics are much less self-sufficient than would be the case if the fifty American states were to break up into fifty separate nations. Stalin believed that the secret to economic success was to be found in economies of scale. As a result, the Soviets built giant factories much bigger than those built in market economies. In one survey of almost six thousand products, 77 percent of the products made in the former USSR were found to be produced in one—and only one—factory.[69] Each of the newly independent republics has far too much production capacity in a few areas and no production capacity in most areas. Initially, none of them will have the capacity to build even the semblance of an economy. Two of the republics (Russia and Turkmenistan) could shut down everyone else by cutting off energy supplies.

While it makes sense for the republics to continue trading with each other, it will be difficult to do so. Those who generate products such as oil that can be sold on world markets for hard currencies will want to do so. They won't want to trade with other republics for shoddy goods. But most of the republics will find themselves saddled with products that cannot be sold on world markets, since their quality is not up to world standards. Retooling to make world-quality products will take years.

Each republic also finds that its citizens don't want to trade with each other. Farmers, for example, have started to horde what they produce. By refusing to sell his grain in the fall, a farmer knows that he can get a much higher price in the winter, when people are really hungry. In the fall of 1991 less than one third of the normal supplies were sitting in state granaries. The state was buying grain at three hundred rubles a ton, but farmers were asking for twelve hundred rubles a ton.[70] There are lots of historical examples where hoarding has created famines, even though there was enough for everyone to eat if food had been carefully rationed.

The problem is made more complicated with the emergence of different countries with different currencies. What type of money should the farmer accept for his food? The Soviet ruble may not be the money used in his country in the future. If he takes it, he may be taking something that will become worthless. As a result, farmers only want to trade their crops for something they can use.

But without clear ownership rights, who sells what to whom? Technically, the grain the farmer is trying to sell does not belong to him. It belongs to the state—everyone. But the state has no effective way for taking it away from him. Basically, the farmer has appropriated the grain for his own use. Others might call it stealing.

But the same is true of urban products that the farmer might want. Who owns the products created in a state factory? Technically, the state, but here again it cannot collect what it owns. Urban products will effectively be appropriated by the workers in the factories that produce them and traded for what they need—food. But what about those unlucky enough to work in places that do not generate products that can be appropriated and traded for necessities—the police and the army for example. They don't have products to trade, but they do have guns. Perhaps they will just take what they need.

The word *autarchy* has two meanings. The most common is rule by an absolute sovereign, a despot. The less common meaning is self-rule, where every man has become his own ruler. For at least a while, those who live in the remains of the USSR are essentially going to be moving from the first form of autarchy to the second. Unfortunately, neither works.

The possible solutions to the border and ethnic problems of Middle and Eastern Europe are three in number: (1) Everyone could agree to put aside their historic border and ethnic problems and concentrate on economic growth. Unfortunately, history teaches us that human nature makes this rational solution unlikely. (2) Borders could be rectified without turmoil and warfare to produce ethnically homogeneous countries. Again, sensible, but an even more unlikely solution if history and human nature are any guide. (3) Everyone could very rapidly envision joining the European Community where the EC was seen as a collection of regions or peoples rather than historic states. The Hungarians living in Romania would agree to technically continue living in Romania, since the important decisions would be made in Brussels and not Bucharest. Essentially, everyone would agree to live in the House of Europe to avoid having to live in the house of their hated neighbors.

Conventional wisdom holds that the events of Eastern Europe will slow down the process of political and economic integration in the European Community. The truth is apt to be exactly the opposite. If the Western Europeans want peace on their eastern frontiers, they will have to speed up their own integration and offer early associate memberships in the EC to quiet ethnic problems in Middle and Eastern Europe.

Migration points in the same direction. While the willingness to move to improve one's standard of living will not be as high in the rest of the ex-communist economies as it is in eastern Germany, the long-run propensity to migrate will be very high if living standards don't rapidly improve in the next five years. Unless Western Europeans are willing to build a Berlin Wall in reverse, which they aren't, migration will force Western Europe to work to insure the success of the reforms in Middle and Eastern Europe. Western Europeans will be forced to establish a development fund for the rest of the ex-communist economies equivalent to Germany's funds for eastern Germany if they don't want millions of easterners moving west. Given the need to bring the East up to Western living standards as cheaply as possible, some associate status in the European Community will seem a quite natural part of the strategy.

The next five years, however, are apt to be a repetition of what happened in Western Europe after World War II. From 1945 to 1948 everyone waited for spontaneous capitalistic economic combustion to happen. It didn't. In 1948 the British economy was falling apart. When that reality became apparent, the Marshall Plan was initiated by the United States. For ten years, seventeen billion dollars per year (in today's dollars) was pumped into Western Europe and Japan to create the human and physical infrastructure of a market economy. Aid amounted to $410 per capita, or about 10 percent of the recipients' GNPs.[71] Outside public aid proved to be necessary to jump start the engines of private market capitalism. Experience teaches us that even in a relatively wealthy country with established markets, deregulation does not work quickly. New Zealand did more deregulation than anyone else in the developed world in the 1980s, yet it also had no growth between 1985 and 1991.[72]

Logically, the history of the post–World War II recovery and the investments that Germany thinks will be necessary to insure the success of a market economy in eastern Germany should make it completely clear that the rest of the ex-communist economies cannot succeed in moving to the market without outside help. But no one wants to pay the taxes necessary to create the investment funds that are necessary. It is far easier to pretend that markets really can spontaneously combust without help. Unfortunately, the failure will probably have to be real, as opposed to predictable, before the developed world, and Western Europe in particular, are willing to act.[73]

Physical Infrastructure

The ex-communist economies start off without the physical infrastructure that is necessary to run market economies. Telephone systems, for example, are rudimentary. Since plant managers were given all of the information they needed to know to fulfill their five-year plans in their five-year plans, nothing had to be bought or sold. Telephones weren't needed. Market economies need them. Materials have to be bought and sold; information has to be acquired. Market economies also require decentralized truck-transportation systems rather than the highly centralized rail-transportation systems that now exist. But neither the roads nor the trucks now exist.

Given the environmental damage of brown coal, electrical generating plants and nuclear plants that are not up to Western safety standards will require massive investments in electrical power systems to correct health and safety problems even before one can think of building the plants that will be necessary to service an expanding modern industrial economy. The Germans have already decided to close down six of eleven nuclear plants in eastern Germany. But where is the money to come from to build the new plants?

If a factory that was the sole producer of a particular product were denationalized, the new owner would be an immediate monopolist with no competition and thus would have the power to set monopoly prices. To have a competitive market, new factories must be built, yet the funds to do so don't exist, and even if they did, the new factories could not be built overnight.

Rural dwellers don't want to become capitalistic farmers,

because they don't know where they would buy tractors, gasoline, and seeds, or how they could transport and sell their crops once they had them. Potential sellers of farm supplies and buyers of farm output don't want to go into business until there are some farmers to sell to or buy from. Both sit waiting for the other to make the first move. But the party to take the initial plunge would incur substantial costs and would also face the risk that others might not follow. As a result, no one wants to be first to go into business.

Human Infrastructure

While Middle and Eastern Europe have an educated work force, market economies require additional human attributes. There are open questions about motivation. As any visitor could attest, no one worked hard in the factories of the ex-communist countries. They did not work hard for the reasons expressed in a Soviet joke: "We pretend to work. They pretend to pay us." If work doesn't pay off, why should one work?

While work may now start to pay off, those in the ex-communist economies have had a lifetime to get used to not working hard. Will they start working hard once the right incentives are in place—once their standard of living can improve if they do work hard? No one knows for sure. I suspect that the answer is yes, since individuals are going to be hungry for the goods found in capitalist societies and willing to work to get them—but I may be wrong.

Initiative is a more important concern.[74] Markets require individuals willing to take risks. After a lifetime of being told what to do and what not to do, initiative may be a hard attribute to recapture. Russian immigrants to the United States find it difficult to get apartments. They are used to putting their name on a list and don't know how to search. In the former Soviet Union most citizens seem to be sitting around waiting for the market to happen. The market is viewed as just another economic system that the government will organize, and there is little realization that their personal initiative is required. As stated by one government official, "Most people here think the free market just means the shops will be full and work will be easier. They have no idea what's involved."[75] Those who have studied Soviet managers report that "factory managers have no clear grasp of capitalism's cut and thrust. They refer constantly to cooperation. The idea of competition makes them acutely uncomfortable."[76] But in a market economy the government isn't going to do anything but get out of the way.

To some extent the initiative problem is a knowledge problem. No one really knows in detail what a market entails. This is equally true for the highest leadership, the leading economists, the plant managers, and the average citizen.[77] They all know the word *market*, but they all have very fuzzy ideas as to what it means where practical details are concerned. A study commissioned by the Swedish foreign ministry found "a widespread lack of understanding" of what a market entails even in the Baltic republics.[78] Since none of the citizens of these countries have ever lived in a market economy, this should not come as a surprise. Market behavior isn't instinctive. Some are going to take longer than others to learn it.

Basic attitudes about fairness will have to change. After a lifetime of being told that income inequality is bad, the citizens of the ex-communist economies are going to have to learn to accept a lot more income inequality than they have had.[79] Most people's absolute incomes will go up in the long run, but relative income gaps will widen. Since the bottom 40 percent of the population had a much higher proportion of national income in the ex-communist countries than it will have in the new capitalist countries, that 40 percent is apt to see itself as a big loser. A Hungarian study published midway through Hungary's transition found 10 percent much better off, 30 percent much worse off, and 60 percent much the same.[80]

Negative attitudes toward entrepreneurs are already visible in the formerly communist world, where those who have taken initiative—the newly wealthy—are often despised. In a study of Polish attitudes toward entrepreneurs, they were seen as "a class without culture, one that brings very little to society. It is one based on materialism, shady values and speculation."[81] These new capitalists are seen very much as

Americans view the leaders of the savings and loan industry—unethical rip-off artists who got wealthy employing un-
scrupulous tactics. In public opinion polls the support for
capitalism is very weak in the countries of Eastern Europe. In
the former Soviet Union 79 percent of the people still believe
in government ownership of heavy industry, banks, transportation, and the media.[82] Less than 25 percent supported a shift
to a free-market form of capitalism, and the populace evenly
divided on whether business firms should be allowed to maximize profits. None of these attitudes are surprising if one remembers how every Soviet citizen has been educated in the
past seventy years, but they make the transition to a market
economy very difficult.

Such attitudes are going to be difficult to combat, since at
the beginning of the transition to a market economy, those
who first become rich will not be those that make the products
that the public wants. The quick rich will be the speculators
and arbitragers who take advantage of the imperfections of
the price system left over from communism. Market prices
will be very different than those that existed under communism, and the first successful entrepreneurs will be those
shrewd enough, or lucky enough, to control the assets that
rise most in price. Speculative profits will be huge.

To an economist, these speculators and arbitragers perform
a worthwhile activity (they equalize prices and bring them up
to market levels), but to the average citizen their activities are
going to be seen in a very negative light. What they gain by
selling at higher prices, the average citizen is going to see
himself losing. This is especially true since many of the new
capitalists will be the old *nomenklatura* who have essentially
seized the assets they used to manage as communist officials.[83]

But what should happen to the collaborators—those in
charge under the old system. Often the public does not want
them to be in charge under the new system, but they have
the knowledge and power to give themselves a head start in
the market game. If it is a question of starting up new companies, they know the best assets to buy. Yet millions of people
were involved as collaborators in the old system, and they

cannot all be prevented from taking part in the new system. In eastern Germany this has become a major problem. Who was and who was not an informer?

Shifting from a communist economy to a market economy requires an enormous shift in power. Those who have been giving the commands no longer do so. Those who have been running the factories under the command economy may not be those that do so under the market economy. A very different set of skills will be required, and there is no reason to believe that those that are good at functioning in a command economy are good at functioning in a market economy.

Enormous management problems exist. The plant managers of the ex-communist economies have not in any sense been business people. They were told what to do (given a plan), shipped materials, told whom to hire, what to pay, what to produce, and where to ship what they produced. They never bought anything, they never sold anything, they never set any prices, and they never made any decisions on what to produce. Basically, plant managers were army officers. Converting a military mentality to a market mentality is not easy. Management skills are going to be in very short supply.

Some of the market-management skills such as accounting, finance, and marketing simply don't exist. Those skills weren't needed in a communist economy. Such skills will have to be created, and that is going to take time.

Macroeconomic Management

While the problem does not exist everywhere, in some countries, such as the newly independent states that once made up the USSR, there is an enormous monetary overhang.[84] For years people have received more pay than there were goods to buy. As a result, citizens have accumulated billions of rubles that could not be spent. If something isn't done to sterilize this monetary overhang, Latin American–type hyperinflation could easily break out when prices are freed. Prices in the former Soviet Union, it is estimated, would have to rise 50 percent to sop up their existing monetary overhang.[85]

In the aftermath of a war, a sterilization would occur by forcing everyone to exchange today's rubles for a much smaller quantity of new rubles. But only an external conquering military power could enforce such an exchange. Alternatively, the government could attempt to persuade individuals to trade their money for interest-paying bonds, but few citizens would voluntarily do so since they would see this as just another way to give them something even more worthless than their current rubles.

The best technique for eliminating the monetary overhang would be to sell everyone the apartment or house in which they now live. The Moscow City Council has actually proposed giving everyone their current apartment.[86] It did not succeed in doing so, but it did give every individual the right to 18 square meters (190 square feet). In theory, their space can be sold if they wish. The need to start paying maintenance costs would absorb much of the monetary overhang even if the houses were given away. In one step this would create a nation of property owners; it would create a system with an enormous vested interest in market prices for homes, rather than today's vested interest in rent control (almost free housing); and it would relieve the government of the enormous costs of heating and maintaining the existing housing structure—making the government deficit much more modest. The objection, of course, is that such a policy would build yesterday's inequalities into tomorrow's ownership of housing. The old communist functionaries with the best houses would be the new owners of the best capitalistic housing.

Tax systems have to be built.[87] In the past firms sent their revenues to the government, the government used some of these funds to pay for traditional government services, sent some funds back to the firm to carry on the next year's activities, and invested some of the funds in new activities. But if firms are allowed to keep what they earn, the government is left with no tax system. In the former USSR this problem led to a tenfold increase in the government deficit—from nine billion rubles to ninety billion rubles between 1987 and 1989. Organizing a tax system in a country with no prior tax system and no tax collectors is not a simple task.

Without tax collections, governments can only pay for what

they need to do by printing money to pay their bills. Essentially, inflation is used as a tax system. No one likes it, but there is no choice. There are things that governments have to do (for example, pay the police and army), or they cease being governments. Just before it broke up, the old Soviet government was printing money at a very rapid rate, and inflation was approaching 300 percent per year.[88]

Private savings systems have to be built. Under communism the state did the saving by taking income away from state firms and using it for investment. Without state firms, individuals will have to save. But they have no tradition of doing so.[89] Under communism all of their income could be devoted to current consumption.

As a result, the inflationary pressures of the monetary overhang are apt to be augmented by the monetary printing presses, excessive fiscal stimulus, and little private savings. If these sources of upward price pressure are added to those flowing from the need to bring the prices of basic necessities up to market levels, a period of substantial inflation is to be expected.

The standard Western capitalistic technique for controlling inflation (the use of macroeconomic policies to create a recession so that unemployment goes up, pushing wages and prices down) cannot be employed, because the necessary monetary and fiscal mechanisms aren't in place. Wage and price controls cannot be used, since wages and prices need to be decontrolled to generate the right market signals.

Inflation is apt to create all of the feelings of unfairness that it creates everywhere else. In China inflation was one of the factors that led to the counterrevolution against market reforms in June of 1989. Counterrevolutions are a real danger everywhere since government employees, including the army, are almost sure to be among the groups whose wages fail to keep up with prices. Governments responsible for stopping inflation are almost always the last to raise the wages of their own employees to keep them from falling behind. But those who hold government jobs are powerful everywhere—and particularly powerful in ex-communist societies.

Some of Middle Europe suffers from international debt burdens—Poland ($39 billion), Hungary ($20 billion), Yugoslavia

($18 billion)—just as severe as those plaguing Latin America.[90] These debts were incurred by earlier communist governments. They borrowed foreign funds to finance the importation of Western equipment and technology. The new plants that these were used to build were then to be combined with lower-cost Middle European labor in order to produce Western products that could be exported to pay off the loans. But in general the output of these new plants could not be exported, since the plants were unable to produce goods at Western quality levels.[91] The strategy failed, and the communist countries were left with hard-currency debts they could not repay. These burdens have been passed on to today's non-communist governments.

The USSR borrowed fifty-six billion dollars from the West, but who is responsible for those debts?[92] The Soviet government that borrowed the money no longer exists. Arguments over who owes what to whom were under way even before the USSR disappeared.[93]

These debts are going to prevent growth in Middle and Eastern Europe, just as they prevent growth in Africa and Latin America. If the debts are repaid, the real resources that are necessary for investment at home will be sent abroad. If the debts are not repaid, new investors are not going to invest, since no one invests in places where there is no prospect for repatriating either earnings or capital. Without unpaid outstanding debt, one becomes last in a very long line waiting to get money out. Realistically, these debts will have to be dealt with before economic growth can start. The problem, however, cannot be solved in the context of Middle and Eastern Europe. It will either be solved for all developing Second World and Third World debtors, or it will be solved for none. If Poland were granted relief, Mexico would have every right to demand equal treatment, and if not given equal treatment, it would have the right to unilaterally impose equal treatment.

Before outside private investment will occur in any magnitude, currencies also have to be made convertible.[94] Currency convertibility is necessary to determine the real value of the earnings streams that potentially exist in any of these countries. With the exception of those that have raw materials to export, most of the ex-communist economies have very little that is sellable on world markets. As a result, their currencies would have a very low initial value if they were to be made convertible. Such a low value would make their existing assets, such as land, very cheap for outsiders to buy. Essentially, they would be selling their national patrimony at fire-sale prices. With Middle Europe just having gained its national independence from the USSR, nationalism is running high, and there is going to be great resistance to accepting market currency values.

Finally, there is a great economic mystery. All of the communist economies were believed to have been heavy investors—30 to 40 percent of their GNPs was the common estimate. This, along with heavy military spending, was the common reason given for why their consumption standards did not match what one would have expected, given estimates of their per capita GNPs. Yet when these economies are examined closely by outsiders, little new investment is to be found. Plant and equipment is on average, old, and what does exist has not been well maintained. In the USSR much of the investment may have gone into military or space ventures, but this could not have been the case in Middle Europe. Either internal and external estimates of investment were very wrong, or investment was squandered on high tech or mega-projects that did not work. No one knows the proportions, but it is likely that some of the funds were wasted, some were used in half-finished, never-completed projects, some went into space and military efforts, some went into high-tech efforts that never yielded consumer products, and some never existed in the first place.

STARTING THE MARKET

A market economy requires competition between different owners. This does not mean that the state cannot own some enterprises (German, Italian, Spanish, and French governments own shares in many enterprises), but it does mean that governments cannot own all enterprises. If the government is not to own everything, private property rights must be created.

But how is private property to be created in a society where everything is owned by the state?[95] Where everybody owns everything, in a real sense no one owns anything. The key issue is determining the initial distribution of ownership rights.

Do individuals buy the existing assets from the state? If so, how do they finance their purchases in countries without financial institutions? Even if financial institutions were to be created, what would the borrowers use as security. No one has any existing wealth that can be mortgaged. What track record could a bank look at to determine if a borrower has the ability to earn profits in a market economy and repay her loans? Who is a good credit risk, and who is not? There are no histories of credit worthiness.

If state property is to be sold, what is its fair market value in countries without markets? Are foreigners to be allowed to buy? What about the rights of those that used to own property before it was expropriated by the communists? Do they get back what they used to own? No one is going to buy anything if clear titles cannot be given.

What if assets are simply given away? If workers are to be given shares in the enterprises for which they now work, are these shares to be distributed equally, or are they to be given out in proportion to wages or some other variable that measures that individual's past contributions to society? But even if that problem can be solved, isn't it unfair to give workers shares in the enterprises for which they now work, since some of those enterprises are already known to be unviable and those workers would be given what are already known to be worthless shares? What is to be given to those workers (to the police, for example) who work in areas that in market economies would be the public sector?

How would a new owner, local or foreign, get control of the existing enterprises away from the works councils (the effective owner in most cases) or keep the former communist managers from walking off with the best physical or human assets? Once a legal system is in place, who is going to enforce property rights? How can a new owner know that her property rights will be enforced?

All are important questions; all are unanswered questions; none have axiomatic answers.

Middle and Eastern Europeans are essentially trying to do something the existing capitalistic world never did—start the market game fairly.[96] In the West the game began with one thousand years of your relatives clubbing my relatives. One of us was a duke; the other a serf. The game began unfairly.

Some, the Germans, are trying to go back to the old unfairness—that is, they're giving property back to those that used to own it.[97] But who gets it when several people had it unfairly taken from them, when records were not kept (the communists never planned to give it back), and when years will be needed to resolve property disputes? Over a million applications for a return of property have been made in eastern Germany.[98] What about those that now live abroad? One third of the landowners whose property was seized in Hungary do so. Do they have a claim? Other countries, such as Poland, are offering bonds to old owners in place of getting their property back, but that is just seizure by another name if the bonds cannot be cashed—and the bonds cannot be cashed, since the countries have no resources to cash them.

Capitalism has no answer for how the game can be started fairly, since capitalism wasn't started with a fair distribution of property rights. When the distribution of property rights became too unfair (whatever that means), revolutions intervened to modify existing property rights, or individuals emigrated from the Old World to the New World.

Fast Track Versus Slow Track

Which provides the least painful transition from a command to a market economy—the fast track or the slow track? Both have their disadvantages; neither is without pain. On either track, real incomes will fall before they rise.

The fast track has as its major advantage the fact that prices are quickly decontrolled. This allows the market to give potential enterprises the right signals about what they should or should not do. The disadvantages lie in the major disruptions that occur. Transitional unemployment is apt to be very high and may last for a substantial period of time.

Estimates differ somewhat, but the western German economic think tanks that have looked at eastern Germany closely in 1990 estimated that 40 percent of its industry would have to be shut down, 15 percent was viable as it is, and the other 45 percent would take major investments to make it viable.[99] Those estimates now look optimistic. Whatever the truth in eastern Germany, the rest of Middle and Eastern Europe will be worse, since eastern Germany was the most developed nation in the region and has the funds to rescue the industries that can be rescued.

Those over fifty-five years of age will be hardest hit by unemployment, since no firm will want to invest in giving older workers the skills necessary to function in a modern market economy. Skill investments will properly focus on the young. It should be remembered that in most market economies an unemployed worker over fifty-five years of age is either permanently unemployed or forced to accept reemployment at wages far below what he or she had before being unemployed. That is just the way capitalism works.

Major shifts in the distribution of income will occur. Those unemployed will lose their paychecks. Germany will provide unemployment insurance for eastern Germans, but there are no funds to pay unemployment compensation in the rest of the command economies. A market wage distribution will be both different and less egalitarian than the wage distributions that now exist in the ex-communist economies. Since prices can change far faster than production, and since basic necessities such as bread and housing have the farthest to rise until they reach market levels, most of the work force is apt to suffer large real-income losses in the initial phases of a market economy.

The slow track has the advantage of slowing down and spreading out the sharp shifts in the distribution of income that come with the fast track, but the costs are high. When some prices are controlled and others decontrolled, the market gives misleading signals about the most profitable activities for enterprises to undertake. When China deregulated farming but kept price controls on food necessities such as sugar, farmers not surprisingly quit growing sugar where prices were still controlled and started growing fruit where prices had been decontrolled. The result was an unnecessary sugar shortage and a need to spend scarce hard currencies to import sugar.

Spreading out price increases is also likely to result in permanent inflation as wages chase prices ever upward year after year. A sudden price shock is less likely to become permanent inflation, since the population may be willing to accept a one-time reduction in its real income without attempting to compensate for higher prices with higher wages. But no population will accept price shocks year after year without attempting to raise wages to keep up.

The slow track also leads to widespread opportunities for corruption. Consider two industries that use aluminum—one controlled and one decontrolled. Aluminum prices are kept low in the controlled industry and allowed to rise to market levels in the uncontrolled industry. This creates enormous incentives to move aluminum from one industry to the other. Moving materials from low-value uses to high-value uses is a legitimate activity in a market economy. In a half-regulated economy, it is corruption. Just such corruption played a key role in generating public support for the counterrevolution in China in 1989.

Or suppose that there are two industries, again, one regulated and one deregulated, with lower wages in the regulated industry. Students have to be drafted to go into the low-wage industries, since they produce necessities such as electric power. Not surprisingly, the students all want to go into the unregulated high-wage industries. The state must draft workers, and those drafted are apt to protest. Such labor controls were one of the issues that brought the students into Tiananmen Square in June 1989. The state did not have to shoot them, but it did have to force them to work where they did not want to work.

The slow track guarantees what will be perceived as unfairness. At one time a few years ago, taxi drivers were the highest-paid workers in Budapest. The industry had been deregulated, and they could own their taxicabs while most other industries were still regulated. Others felt cheated. If toothpaste and soap are sold at different lower prices in the Russian state stores than in the free-market stores, but are available in the free-market stores and not in the state stores, Siberian coal miners not surprisingly will feel that they are being cheated.

On the slow track, hoarding becomes a major problem. Since people know that prices are only partly decontrolled and have farther to rise, everyone has an incentive to buy more than they need and hold it for resale or barter. In the Soviet Union hoarding led to rationing for products that had not been rationed since World War II and to rules prohibiting nonresidents living in Moscow or Leningrad from purchasing goods in Moscow or Leningrad. But if Soviet rubles are not good in Moscow, what good are they? A country where citizens cannot spend that country's money anywhere in that country, especially the capital, isn't really a country. And eventually, the USSR ceased to be a country.

Halfway between central planning and the market lies chaos. A communist command economy works because people obey commands. People obey commands for two reasons. They will be promoted if they do obey; they may be sent to Siberia if they don't obey. But during the transition period, neither motive still functions. With glasnost, everyone knows that they will not be sent to Siberia. But with perestroika on the way, they also know that they won't be promoted for obeying commands. The system is about to change to the market, and those issuing today's orders won't be around tomorrow to reward those who obey today.

Central planning may not be the world's most efficient economic system, but it does not work at all if the market is coming but has not yet arrived. The market also does not work if much of the economy is still centrally planned. Managers in the Soviet Union's heavy-engineering plants understood this reality: "The 1991 plans for the manufacture of complex and much needed engineering products are under genuine threat of disruption. The reason is that up to this day, no decision has been taken on the procedure for supplying materials for the proper working of the economy. The old system of fixed quota supplies has been demolished. The new market system has not yet been established."[100]

There is a lot of economic pain on either the fast or the slow track, but based on the limited experiments that have been run, a three-stage process would probably minimize the pain. First, sell or give everyone their existing home in order to give everyone a capitalistic stake in the system, to soak up the monetary overhang, and to reduce the government's deficit. At the same time, decontrol agriculture and fill up the food stores. Hungary and China have proved that agriculture can be decontrolled by itself. Wage shocks and high unemployment are a lot easier to take if the food stores are full. Then, quickly decontrol industrial prices on the fast track. The defects (inflation, corruption, labor controls, unfairness, and hoarding) of the slow track are insurmountable.[101]

Perhaps the difficulties can best be summed up in a letter that I received from a Russian friend in 1990.

Dear Lester,

I spent the last few months, along with some of my colleagues, in preparing the background materials for policy decisions on the transition to a regulated market economy. When the time for action came it turned out that neither the economy nor public opinion is ready for it. It appears to be easier to build communism rather than to return to capitalism.

The economic situation continues to deteriorate. Last year's fall in GDP (in real terms) is about 5 percent. This year's drop in industrial production is already close to 7 percent (18 percent in Azerbaijan, 9 in Armenia, 8 in Georgia, over 5 percent in Tadzhikistan and Lithuania). Many economic links have been disrupted, the country is becoming economically ungovernable and from here it is not too far to political instability too.

The main reason for a continuing slide in economic performance, as I understand it, is that reforms proclaimed in 1987 undermined the old command system without really having found a replacement for it. Nor have they diminished the tremendous waste, the elimination of which would have been in itself a substantial leap forward in the standard of living.

Such a situation is due to the confusion with regard to a basic choice facing the country: What kind of a society do we want to live in? What is the ultimate goal of perestroika? What is the name of the final destination: a renovated socialism or a kind of a Western democracy?

Ambiguities like "regulated market economy" or "a planned socialist market" do not answer the question. But the fact that private property is not mentioned by name because of the alleged "exploitation" (though everyone knows that the biggest exploiter in this country is the state) speaks for itself. Can you imagine a market without private ownership of the means of production? I cannot, but they do not want to listen. They say that the choice made in 1917 is irreversible. But it was done at a time when no one in Russia knew what was socialism, including Lenin himself, who spoke in 1921 of the need to "overhaul all our concepts of socialism." To determine the preference of the Soviet people one has to organize a referendum. Not on the market economy, but on the basic choice facing the nation. And unless and until such a choice is made, the policy of the government will continue to be half hearted, incoherent, indecisive.

Now they want to make a transition to the market economy without pain. Social protection and safe nets are obviously needed. But the policy of indexation, as conceived by the government, is the surest way to transform a suppressed inflation into a permanent self-supporting process. And you cannot make them understand it. The alternative is this: either to continue to sink or to make a jump into the unknown and try to swim to a "bright future." I should not hope. But I do. There is no choice.[102]

But once institutional meltdown has occurred (the condition that existed in the winter of 1991–1992 in the former republics of the USSR), there is no option but to quickly decontrol everything and live with the chaos and privation that will occur. There is no chance to go back and do it right.

BUILDING THE HOUSE OF EUROPE

Europe has a chance to become, but no guarantee that it will become, the world's most rapidly growing region in the 1990s. The Germans have lifted the speed limit on their economic autobahn and when there are no speed limits the Germans like to go very fast. If Europe can put a significant part of Middle and Eastern Europe together with Western Europe in an enlarged Common Market, it can build something that no one else can build—by far the world's biggest, most self-sufficient, market—850 to 900 million people, depending upon whether Turkey is considered a European country. Even if Europe gets only part way along their economic autobahn, they will still be by far the world's largest economy.

As the Europeans write the rules for their economic integration, they will essentially be in charge of writing the traffic rules for the world economy in the twenty-first century. They will be the ones who determine the nature of the vehicles on the economic autobahn and whether the traffic lights show green, red, or yellow for the expansion of world trade.

In the end not all of the ex-communist economies will succeed in getting to their destinations—moving to the market and rapidly raising the living standards of their citizens. The number that does succeed will depend a great deal upon the degree of outside help.

Japan and the United States may choose not to help. Japan may end up saving its resources for that moment when the communist countries of Asia also cease to exist. The United States may convince itself that its economy is too poor to help, despite the fact that its real GNP is four times as large as it was when the Marshall Plan was offered to Europe. It may ignore a region that has never been one of its prime interests.

In the end Western Europe will have no choice but to help. Preventing westward migration, reducing border tensions, and lowering ethnic hatreds all demand economic success in Middle and Eastern Europe. A mixture of altruism and fear of the Russian military bear led to the original Marshall Plan. A mixture of altruism and a fear of chaos on immediate borders will lead to a similar plan for Middle and eastern Europe.

For the House of Europe, the advice given to Macbeth is sound: "If it were done when 'tis done, then 'twere well/It were done quickly."

Chapter 4

JAPAN: THE CHALLENGE OF PRODUCER ECONOMICS

> The Master in the art of living makes little distinction between his work and his play, his labor and his leisure, his mind and his body, his education and his recreation, his love and his religion. He hardly knows which is which. He simply pursues his vision of excellence in whatever he does, leaving others to decide whether he is working or playing. To him he is always doing both.
>
> —Zen Buddhist text

If the world economy were a canvas waiting for a Brueghel painting, the Europeans would be setting the broad outlines of the composition as they write the rules for world trade, as they create the world's largest economy, and as they shift from communism to capitalism. But the Japanese would be painting the interesting small detailed vignettes that make a Brueghel so interesting. In this particular Brueghel the sharp-eyed observer would note that in the Japanese vignettes water was everywhere running uphill.

Anyone who believes in gravity and watches water run uphill has a fundamental problem. Facts are very difficult to deal with when they conflict with both theory and previous experience. Before changing their beliefs, most human beings will spend long periods of time pretending that the facts that conflict with their theories don't exist, hoping that such facts will somehow magically go away, or denying that the facts conflict with their theoretical views of the world in any important

113

way. Only if facts are very painful and very persistent (i.e., they produce a crisis) will humans deal with fundamental inconsistencies in their worldviews.

Japanese business firms create just such a series of painful and persistent facts. Practices such as age-based seniority wages that don't take individual merit into account should make Japanese business firms inefficient, yet when facing American or European competition they always seem to win. Their market share always goes up, never down. Inexorably, they defeat the pride of American and European industry. What are handicaps for others (higher-valued currencies) are strengths for them.

Are the Japanese just better as individuals—playing the same game but just doing it better by working harder, saving more, and being smarter than everyone else—or does their success spring from having organized a different system, playing the game differently? Is Japan just better, or is it exceptional? If it is exceptional, and I believe it is, it is going to force major changes in how capitalism is played around the world. The communitarian Japanese business firms' modes of play are quite different from those of the Anglo-Saxons, and their success is going to put enormous economic pressure on the rest of the industrial world to change.

ALWAYS WINNERS!

Consider the outcome of the last twenty years of economic competition in the auto industry. In the early 1970s, General Motors, the colossus of the auto industry, towered above every other industrial firm. Nothing was comparable. It was regularly voted the best-managed firm in America. Autos were an unassailable bastion of American economic strength.

Twenty years later it is an open question whether any American auto firm can survive another twenty years. The Japanese market share, crossing the 30 percent mark in mid-1991, slowly but surely, year by year, continues to grow.[1] Toyota tells its affiliated supplier companies something that would have been unthinkable twenty years earlier: "Toyota is determined to pull past General Motors by the end of the century."[2] It is buckling down to win.

Today the managers of the American auto industry are regularly castigated as incompetents by the very people who twenty years earlier were calling them the best. Were the financial writers of the early 1970s simply stupid? Could they not tell the difference between competence and incompetence? Could decades of the world's best management suddenly have been followed by two decades of the world's worst management?

In the American market, where the Japanese and the Europeans have to play under identical American rules, the European auto industry fared even worse. Fiat, Peugeot, Range Rover/Sterling and Renault have all been completely driven out of the American market by the Japanese. Volkswagen is in the process of being driven out (a market share down from 10 to 1 percent), and when it leaves there will be no European mass manufacturers left in the U.S. market. With the introduction of the Japanese luxury cars (Lexus, Infiniti, Acura) the European luxury carmakers (Mercedes-Benz, Audi, Saab, Volvo, Jaguar, Porsche) are all losing market share and are on the defensive. Are their managers, the pride of Europe, also all suddenly incompetent?

IBM, a firm that in the early 1980s was winning prizes for being the best-managed firm, is now similarly on the defensive. The Japanese press talks about the "Big Three Computer Makers being ready to tackle 'Big Blue.'"[3] They are more than ready. Two of the three already have market shares larger than that of IBM in Japan. The third is also about to surpass the American giant. In 1990 IBM Japan's sales rose 1 percent while the total Japanese market was expanding 10 percent.[4] Yet IBM is number one everywhere else in the world. Why is IBM incompetent in only one country? Other American companies in the computer business are doing no better.

In the 1970s semiconductors were the very bastion of high-tech American entrepreneurial capitalism. The industry was created by Americans; its managers were the best and brightest. Yet in less than two decades the entrepreneurs that had founded and dominated this industry were losing their industry. The Japanese worldwide market share is now larger than that of the Americans—and rising. American firms such as Motorola are locating their new production facilities in Japan.

Those who lost the American semiconductor industry are exactly the same people who created it in the first place. They were not an incompetent second generation of managers. Did each suddenly become senile in their middle age?

Over the past twenty years what has happened in semiconductors and computers has been replicated almost across the board in every high-tech industry. America's trade deficit in office and telecommunication equipment rose sixty-sixfold, a trade surplus in machine tools became a large trade deficit, the deficit in engineering products rose from four billion dollars to sixty-six billion dollars per year.[5] High-tech trade deficits with Japan, but with no other have exploded. Are all of these other high-tech managers also suddenly inferior? The problem is not America's traditional lack of interest in foreign markets and its export incompetence. Its losses in its home markets are larger than its losses abroad.

No industrial country runs a trade surplus in manufactured products with Japan. The world's greatest exporters, the Germans, cannot successfully compete in the Japanese market. The little dragons of the Pacific Rim have similar deficits. Are the world's best exporters suddenly incompetent when it comes to this one market?

In the second half of the 1980s, when the value of the yen and European currencies such as the German mark rose sharply against the dollar, both Japanese and European producers were suddenly handicapped by much higher dollar production costs. When the dollar had risen rapidly in the first half of the decade, American firms rapidly lost market share. When the value of European currencies rose sharply in the last half of the decade, America's trade deficit with Europe rapidly vanished. But a doubling of the value of the yen (a 100 percent increase in Japanese production costs when measured in dollars) did almost nothing to the Japanese market share in the United States. Its bilateral trade surplus still hovered around fifty billion dollars five years later.[6]

Screams of outrage, managed trade with the Japanese in semiconductors agreement, and big increases in the exports of raw materials managed to lower the bilateral surplus with America to forty-two billion dollars in 1991, but the Japanese simply redirected their attention to other markets and in the first half of 1991 its trade surplus with Europe rose 63 percent and its trade surplus with the rest of Asia rose 50 percent. In 1991 its European trade surplus was expected to be bigger than its American trade surplus.

Sharply rising currency values, which should have been a weakness for the Japanese and is a weakness for everyone else, becomes a strength for Japan. All of this is explained by arguing that the rising value of the yen forced Japanese firms to ruthlessly become more efficient. But why didn't the rising value of the dollar in the first half of the 1980s and the rising value of European currencies in the second half of the decade have the same effects on American and European firms? Up is down! What makes Japan more competitive makes Europe and America less competitive.

Japan's propensity to import manufactured goods from other developed countries is one fourth that of the United States and one twelfth that of Germany.[8] Depending upon the particular study, Japanese imports are found to be 25 to 45 percent less than would be expected given Japan's circumstances.[9] Price differentials that should not exist in a global market do exist. The prices of tradable products are 86 percent higher in Japan than the prices of those same goods in the United States.[10] Theoretically, there is a lot of money to be made by buying products in America and selling them in Japan. Yet no one in Japan takes advantage of these huge profit opportunities. Outsiders who try, fail.

Are such data merely random noise to be ignored? If theory tells Americans that water does not run uphill, then it does not run uphill—regardless of what their eyes see. Or are such data painful reflections of a reality that requires changes in beliefs?

PRODUCER ECONOMICS

The profit-maximizing Anglo-Saxon business firm is derived from the rational utility-maximizing individual where more consumption and more leisure are the sole economic elements of human satisfaction. Higher productivity at work is desired since it gives individuals higher incomes to buy more consumption goods and the ability to reduce work effort to obtain more leisure without sacrificing consumption. Work and saving (leisure and consumption forgone) are both disutilities tolerated solely because the future income that flows from these activities provides the economic resources needed for future consumption.

The Anglo-Saxon model is not wrong. Individualism and the desire for consumption and leisure are all parts of human nature. But they are not all of human nature. Business firms can be based on the historical, psychological, and sociological fact that individuals are also social builders who want to belong to empires that expand. Man is a consumer, but he is also a tool-using animal. As a tool-using animal, work is not a disutility. It determines who one is. Belonging, esteem, power, building, winning, and conquering are all human goals just as important as maximizing consumption and leisure. Work is where one achieves such goals. While Anglo-Saxon economics is not built upon these producer drives, "animal spirits" (the intrinsic desire to build) are sometimes invoked to explain human actions by Anglo-Saxon economists.[11]

If one wants to understand Japanese companies, there is more to learn from an analysis of the empire builders than there is to learn from an understanding of the economics of Anglo-Saxon profit maximization.[12,13,14] The Japanese secret is to be found in the fact that they have tapped a universal human desire to build, to belong to an empire, to conquer neighboring empires, and to become the world's leading economic power. Their goal is market-share maximization (strategic conquest) and value-added maximization (a measure that includes profits and wages), not simple profit maximization. Only in the contracting phase of a product's life cycle are profits maximized so that it serves as a cash cow to finance the expansion of new areas of endeavor.

From the perspective of social builders, individuals may rationally decide to have fewer consumption goods in their home environment to have more production goods in their work environment. To them, the ownership and use of investment goods can generate just as much pride of ownership (just as much utility in the language of economics) as consumption goods. A higher standard of living at work may even be more important than a higher standard of living at home. Such behavior is often seen in American farmers who voluntarily choose to have the fanciest tractor in the neighborhood rather than the fanciest car. Anglo-Saxon economic theory says that they should be cost minimizers on their farm and then spend their profits on whatever gives them pleasure in their consumption lives. They, however, think that greater pleasure can be derived from having the best-equipped, most productive farm.

Current observers note that imperial Rome had a very different mix of public and private buildings than would be found in a modern city. Much larger fractions of Roman wealth were put into public buildings, and much smaller fractions were put into the private housing than would be the case today. Today's Americans get the greatest personal utility from having the fanciest homes. Yesterday's Romans got the greatest personal utility from having the fanciest public buildings. Humans were and are the same, but their cultures lead them to express themselves in very different ways when it comes to constructing a city. The Romans had their own unique mix of individualistic and social building instincts.

Those remembered in human history are not the great consumers. They are the conquerors, the builders, the producers—Caesar, Genghis Khan, Rockefeller, Ford. Being part of collective effort, of a powerful group, may in fact be more important to some individuals than having a lot of personal consumption. The very rich, great consumer who inherits her fortune or who wins the lottery may be envied for her standard of living, but she is not respected—and never admired. Sometimes the rich attempt to purchase esteem with conspicuous consumption, but it almost never works. Esteem is not bought. It can only be earned by being part (leader or follower) of a successful production team.

When workers join a business firm, they are looking for some of the same factors that they seek when joining an army. In the end, all armies are essentially voluntary. No one can force anyone to fight and die when they do not want to do so, yet historically there has been no shortage of people willing to fight and die. Armies clearly fulfill some fundamental human needs. Few wars would have been started if all

decisions were based upon the calculus of profit maximization—discounted net present values. The up-front costs of
war almost always exceed the downstream benefits—even for
the winner. But historically, individuals were forming tribes,
building empires, and fighting wars long before they were
talking about maximizing consumption and leisure.

Empires don't exist because there are great individuals who
force their leadership upon resistant followers. Empires exist
because individuals want to be part of a group, want to have
the security that can only be had if one is part of a group,
want to be held in esteem by those above and below them
in the group's pecking order, and want a place to build and
lead—even if they are not the supreme builder or leader that
history will remember.

Individualistic consumer economics is not wrong! It merely
explains only part of what needs to be explained! Man is not
just a consumption-leisure–maximizing machine. He or she is
also a producer. In the language of bumper stickers, humans
may be born to shop but they are also born to build. These
desires to build generate what I will call Japanese "producer
economics" to distinguish it from Anglo-Saxon "consumer
economics."[15]

In the modern world, corporations offer the best opportunities for empire building. The nation-state forbids making war
on the neighboring clan, the days of colonial empires are over,
expanding one's national borders by conquest is rare, and nuclear weapons make conquering the world a goal not worth
pursuing. Even the family now offers fewer opportunities to
exercise leadership and power. The family is no longer the
basic production unit it used to be, when most families were
farm families. Today there are few troops to be led in the family (many of our families are one- or two-person units), and
with multiple earners and little need for family labor, exit (divorce) is much easier than it used to be.

To have power over others requires an institution where
there are strong voluntary incentives to participate and where
exit is not easy. One cannot really lead—exercise control over
others, organize activities where some real degree of personal
self-sacrifice is both demanded and given—unless there are
real rewards and punishments. The modern industrial leader

is not a general who can shoot deserters, but he is a leader who can hand out real punishments and rewards. Individuals can be demoted or fired, banished from the group, deprived of security, belongingness, and the esteem of others. Individuals can be promoted. Economic soldiers can be made into officers; majors can be made into generals. Together, individuals can build something bigger than they could ever dream of building by themselves. Men and women can conquer markets much as they used to conquer neighboring clans.

In doing so, they share in the booty of conquest. Even in friendly takeovers, within a short period of time the top management at the firm being taken over is almost always replaced by managers from the firm doing the takeover. Within a year of the "friendly" American takeovers at Jaguar and Saab, American managers from Ford or General Motors had replaced the local British and Swedish managers.[16,17] If jobs were simply given to the best people, one would expect a random distribution of postmerger job opportunities as firms integrate. But conquering managers are almost always put in charge of the "captured provinces," much as they were in the days of the Roman or British empires.

This reality lies behind the ferocity with which incumbent managements fight hostile takeovers. They are not fighting for lifetime consumption. With golden parachutes, most CEOs would have a higher lifetime income with an unfriendly takeover than they would have had without it. They certainly would have more leisure. But they don't want to surrender leadership and decision-making authority. Consumption and leisure are not substitutes for power.

What is always true is even more true in Japanese corporations. Sixty-nine percent of the senior managers of Japanese subsidiaries in America are Japanese.[18] In contrast, only 20 percent of senior managers of American subsidiaries in Japan are American. American managers working for Japanese firms usually find that there is a promotion ceiling beyond which they cannot go. Even the Japanese Ministry of International Trade and Industry sees the ceiling:

> The perceived exclusion from decision making and strategic planning, the absence of training and management development programs and the apparent lack of career opportunities

discourage even the most loyal and determined (foreign) individuals from long-term commitment to the (Japanese) company. . . . While it is doubtful that the full integration of overseas executives into the management infrastructure of the parent company is possible without some degree of familiarity with the Japanese language, efforts to learn the language were not really appreciated (by Japanese companies). . . . Most Japanese firms recruit U.S. executives or senior managers without regard to the individual's career aspirations, or without a long term plan as to what these individuals may do in the future.[19]

To put it bluntly, Americans aren't part of the Japanese team.[20,21] They hit the "glass ceiling" earlier, and even if they technically hold top positions, they often don't have the decision-making power that they would have in an American firm.[22]

Economic Wolf Packs

In the animal kingdom, some species, such as the American mountain lion, are solitary species—meeting only briefly to mate. Others, such as the African lion, live in prides. Humans are individuals, but they are also herd animals. In herd or pack species the desire for equity (a share of the earnings) is not a perverse human desire that has to be suppressed but a glue that can be used to generate solidarity and a willingness to sacrifice for the welfare of the group. Without this willingness, no army, and no company, can really expect to win. At the same time, the wolf pack has to sort out the alpha wolves—to establish its hierarchy.

From the perspective of the Japanese business firm, tapping into these "pack" producer drives is the key to designing better organizational structures. Bonus systems and lifetime employment can be used to generate strong production groups with internal and external solidarity. Inefficient seniority-based wages become effective instruments to promote group solidarity.

In the Anglo-Saxon world the business firm exists to provide income-earning opportunities—no more, no less. Worker interest in security is met through individual savings and insurance. No employee should worry about hanging onto her current job. She should understand that her old firm is becoming more efficient if she is fired. This increased efficiency raises her real income by lowering the prices she has to pay. She can also always find an alternative job that will pay her a fair market wage—a wage equal to her productive contribution. To offer job security in the Anglo-Saxon view would be to undercut motivation. Individuals work hard because they fear being unemployed—losing consumption privileges. Reduce fear, and everyone will work less hard.

From this perspective it is difficult to make sense of Japanese firms that deliberately give explicit lifetime-employment guarantees as part of their efforts to create more productive labor forces. But viewed from the perspective of a social builder, security is an important attribute of the firm. Empires and nations attach citizens to them by offering external security (freedom from conquest) and internal security (law and order).

Despite what humans often say about themselves— "We like to change!"—humans like stability and order. They hate to be forced to change. Human security is more than a steady income. It is stability and knowing how one's own immediate world functions. Even if changing jobs does not lower an employee's lifetime income, if she or he is well insured during the transition from one job to another, the personal stability of one's environment has disappeared. Old friends and workmates disappear; new ones have to be made. Exactly what one does at work and who one has to know to get promoted all suddenly change when one's job changes. To be fired or laid off is to be tossed out of one's pack. Why should that be any less traumatic to one's feeling of belongingness than being exiled from one's village in days gone by?

Firms that effectively provide security to generate group solidarity obtain employees who are more directed in their focus, more willing to mobilize and prolong their effort to meet firm goals, more willing to sacrifice immediate self-interests, and more interested in achieving the goals of the firm. Japanese business firms recognize that they are in the empire-and army-building business, even if they are only very small firms. The central problem facing any firm is to generate social groups that will become effective production groups that can win, that can conquer market share, that can become number one.

While there is some belief in the value of teams, the Anglo-Saxon–shareholder wealth-maximization view of the firm explicitly denies the legitimacy of the group. Only individual capitalists count. All other humans are simply rented factors of production. To the extent that a CEO subscribes to such a view of the world, he is announcing that his employees are not on his team. They should look out for their own self-interests, just as he has been hired to look out for the self-interests of the shareholders. Can anyone imagine a general going into battle making similar announcements to the troops? They, the soldiers and officers, are merely mercenaries, not members of the team. What general would announce that he reserves the right to surrender if some group that is not on the field of battle (the shareholders) would enjoy more consumption privileges as a result of his surrender? Any such general would not be successful. Historians would say that he does not understand the nature of military combat.

Long ago, nations learned that soldiers who believed in what they were fighting for almost always beat soldiers who are simply paid to fight. But why should the motivations of economic combat be any different? People obey and sacrifice because they wish to join. If there is nothing to join, there is no reason to obey and nothing that merits sacrifice.

COMPETING GAMES

Profit Maximization Versus Strategic Conquest

Profits are important to firms in every form of capitalism. An empire-building firm needs profits to finance the expansion of its empire. Conversely, there are probably few firms that are pure profit maximizers where the desire to build and conquer plays no role. Social instincts cannot be completely submerged in the calculus of income and profit maximization.

While the firms in producer economics and consumer economics both want profits, the role played by profits is very different.[23] In the profit-maximizing firm, profits are the goal—the objective function. In the empire-building firm, profits are the means to the end of a larger empire—a constraint. The goal is market share. A profit-maximizing firm will devote its higher profits to individual consumption; an empire-building firm will devote its higher profits to investment in expanding its empire.

If one thinks of a continuum with profit-maximizing firms at one end and empire-building firms at the other, the exact placement of a nation's business firms on the spectrum would be controversial, but the order of the positions on the continuum is not. American firms would be closer to the profit-maximizing end of the spectrum, whereas Japanese firms would be closer to the empire-building end of the spectrum. In Europe Continental firms such as those in Germany are on the empire-building end of the spectrum (although not as far along it as those in Japan), while British firms are at the profit-maximizing end of the spectrum (perhaps even farther along that continuum than the American firms).

Pushing Consumption Down to Push Investment Up

Army generals always want unlimited quantities of the latest equipment. There is always a better technology. Their interest flows from an asymmetric loss function. One never wants to take a chance on losing. Generals don't make marginal cost-benefit calculations, they want dominance—not sufficiency. To accomplish this objective in wartime, every society organizes itself to push consumption down so that they can push military spending up.

So too in an economy interested in producer economics. It will organize itself to lower consumption and raise investment far beyond what would be happening in an economy interested in maximizing consumption and leisure. In Japan a society has systematically been built to raise investment (plant and equipment, R&D, human skills) at the expense of individual-consumption privileges.

The system starts with company unions, the bonus system, and the annual spring wage offensive to hold down labor's share of national income. Japan's work force gets the lowest share of national income in the five leading industrial countries, and its share is falling. Wages have been rising only half as fast as productivity in the past fifteen years.[24] At the same time, the average Japanese worker enjoys an expense account that is very generous when compared with that of workers in America. Consumption activities that contribute to team building at work are encouraged; consumption activities at home are discouraged.

With lower wages, more income is left with the corporation, but little of that income is given to the shareholders. Future investments are often expensed to lower reported profits. Of those lower after-tax profits only 30 percent are paid out in dividends.[25] In contrast, in the United States 82 percent of after-tax profits were paid out to shareholders as dividends in 1990.[26] In 1989 the average shareholder could expect a dividend yield on their investment in Japanese companies of only 0.43 percent—about as close to zero as it is possible to get.[27] The returns to external shareholders are limited to the capital gains that accrue from rising share prices. After paying wages, essentially everything is reinvested in future growth.

To maximize the income going to businesses, consumer prices are held far above what would prevail in a "free" market. Relative to New York, the Tokyo consumer spends three times as much for rice, beef, and potatoes, two times as much for watches, VCRs, sugar, and taxies, two thirds more for a movie, and one quarter more for airfares.[28] On average, products are 40 percent more expensive in Japan than they are in the United States.[29] Small houses (only 40 percent as large as those in the United States) further limit the ability to buy many large consumer durables, although the Japanese have made the miniaturization of traditionally large consumer durables into an art form.[30]

Further investment funds are then extracted from the average Japanese worker-consumer by forcing him to save a large proportion of his income, yet paying him little on what he does save. For the Japanese passbook saver, real interest rates have been negative for much of the post–World War II period.[31] At the same time, a variety of other factors (very limited consumer credit; large down payments on housing;

rudimentary public and private monthly pensions; and land policies that lead to very high prices for housing, forcing high savings to make the necessary down payments) have persuaded the average Japanese family to save a large fraction of its income despite a negative rate of return on its willingness to forgo current consumption.

The intrinsic rate-of-time preference (the rate at which individuals are willing to give up consumption today to get more consumption tomorrow) may be lower in Japan than it is in the United States (although there is no evidence that this is true), but there is no doubt that the Japanese would save much less if they lived in the American system and that Americans would save much more if they lived in the Japanese system. Much of the observed difference is the result of forced saving.

The system has worked as designed to produce a high-saving, high-investment society. In the last five years of the 1980s, Japan invested 35.6 percent of its GNP while the United States was investing 17 percent.[32] If housing investments are left out (technically investment but really consumption, in the sense that it doesn't make a country more economically powerful in the future) the two-to-one investment gap becomes a three-to-one investment gap.

The results can be seen in the number of robots working in Japan. The Japanese claim they have 275,000 of them, the American Robotic Industry Association says there are only 175,000, but either figure is far above the 37,000 robots working in the United States, a country with twice as many workers.

The system did not come about by accident. Historically, it was deliberately designed to shift resources directly from consumption to investment so as to allow Japan to recover from the destruction of World War II. Studies of the cost of capital (a measure that includes the impact of the tax and depreciation system as well as raw interest rates) show how Japan has systematically organized itself to lower required rates of return on investment. The required rates of return on an R&D project with a ten-year lag in payoff were 8.7 percent in Japan, 20.3 percent in the United States, 14.8 percent in Germany, and 23.7 percent in the United Kingdom.[33] For plant and machinery with a twenty-year lifetime, the required rates of return were 7.2 percent in Japan and 11.2 percent in the United States. The equivalent rates were 7.0 percent in Germany and 9.2 percent in the United Kingdom. These rate differences are evidence of overt, deliberate public policies designed to promote a long-term focus.

In addition, the Japanese system, strongly encouraged by its tax laws, is organized to use much more debt relative to equity—a source of capital that does not depend upon immediate profits. In the late 1950s it was not unusual to see firms with 90 percent debt capital. With higher leverage rates, the same profits can support much more capital investment in Japan than they would be able to support in the United States.

A similar pattern is observed if one looks at single proprietorships in the United States—the American circumstances where it is possible to be an empire builder. Here Americans act very much like the Japanese. Single proprietorships overinvest and earn a below-market rate of return on what they do invest. They also pay themselves lower wages than they could command if they had worked for someone else.[34] For most, personal consumption and leisure would be much higher if they were to sell their businesses and go to work for someone else. Yet they do not do so. To do so would mean to cease being a builder.

While the Japanese system lowers individual consumption far below what it could if the Japanese operated the American system, there has never been a political rebellion by the Japanese voters to change their system. The average Japanese knows what is going on. They publicly refer to themselves as poor people in a rich country. They grumble, but they are willing to put themselves in a voluntary-consumption prison. Urban salary earners put up with higher prices because they see themselves as the beneficiaries (their firms invest the extra earnings to expand their job opportunities), and not just the payers of high charges, as would be the case in the United States. This willingness can only persist if the consumer-voter has goals other than simply maximizing his own consumption. Japan is, after all, a well-educated democracy.

Public-opinion polls confirm these alternative goals. Only 16 percent of Japanese believe that "it is better to consume imported products if they are less expensive."[35] Those are not the statistics that one would find in the United States.

The large Japanese trade surplus is irrational from the perspective of conventional economic analysis. It impoverishes the present (they get to consume less than they produced) and enriches the future (they get the income on today's foreign investments), despite the fact that those who live in the future will be much wealthier than those who live in the present. But it is highly rational if empire building is the goal.

In contrast, the low American savings rate and shorter American time horizons are in accordance with the necessities of maximizing individual consumption. Because of advances in technology and productivity, those who live in the future will be richer than those that live in the present. As a result, the present should not be sacrificed to raise the living standards of the future; the poor (this generation) would be subsidizing the rich (the next generation). Technically, those living in the present should dissave to insure that the poor of the present are not subsidizing the rich of the future. Americans practice what they preach. Domestic saving is at an all-time low, and the trade deficit is at an all-time high. By saving very little and selling off existing American assets to finance a trade deficit that allows them to consume more than they produce, today's Americans gain consumption privileges at the expense of tomorrow's Americans. Instead of investing in the future, today's Americans borrow from the future—very rational behavior if the goal is consumption maximization.

Accepting a Lower Rate of Return on Investment

Empires overinvest relative to profit-maximizing firms, since they plan to last forever. Their aim is future expansion, not maximizing current consumption. No believer in consumer economics would have built the cathedrals that play such an important role in the Kingdom of God, the buildings and roads of Rome, or the monuments of ancient Egypt. All of these projects took too long to complete and required too much up-front capital. Yet humans built them all. In Japan, the generals, the capitalists, have been willing to invest *too much*, but in doing so they are being very human, even though they're not Anglo-Saxon.

If empires invest more, they must be willing to accept lower rates of return on their investments than those who invest less. Studies show that the returns on investment required for American firms to invest in robotics are 50 percent above those of Japanese firms.[36] If Japanese firms had used American required rates of return in their calculations, they would have bought 50 percent fewer robots than they did buy.

Many very successful firms in Japan have in fact made rates of return over the past two decades lower than they could have made by simply investing in government bonds. Honda is a good example. During the fifteen years from 1965 to 1980 when it was getting into the auto-manufacturing business, its rate of return fell from the 9 percent that it had reached when Honda was a motorcycle-manufacturing firm to 3 percent.[37] A 3 percent rate of return is far below what it could have earned if the same money had been invested in government (American or Japanese) bonds. Honda knew that these alternative financial opportunities existed, but Honda did not divert its investments into these higher-rate-of-return, lower-risk investments.

Nissan announced that it did not expect any profits on its new car, the Infiniti, in the first five years.[38] In contrast, 47 percent of all American firms will not invest unless profits start flowing within the first three years. Only 10 percent of Japanese firms set a similar hurdle.[39]

A big part of the Japanese success in coping with the rising value of the yen is found in their willingness to accept lower profits. While they certainly worked to become more efficient, companies such as Matsushita and Hitachi were willing to cut their profits in half in an effort to remain competitive. Matsushita profits as a percent of sales went from over 12 percent in the early 1970s to between 7 and 8 percent at the end of the 1980s. Hitachi's profits fell from the 11 to 12 percent range into the 6 to 7 percent range.[40]

A recent study by the London Business School and *The Economist* magazine rated companies on their ability to earn pure profits (income over and above that needed to pay for the materials, labor, and capital costs of producing output). Among the thirty large companies (sales over one billion ecus [European Currency Units]) with the highest level of pure profits relative to sales, twenty-three were American, four were British, and none were Japanese. Neither were there any Japanese companies among the thirty most profitable smaller companies.[41]

Over time the number of Japanese firms that list higher profits as a company priority has risen, while those that list higher turnover or the pursuit of market share as a goal has fallen, but the time scale of what the Japanese mean by profit maximizing is so long that it isn't what Anglo-Saxons mean by profit maximizing.[42] With a market interest rate of 10 percent, profits earned fifteen years from now are worth only twenty-four cents on the dollar and are very unlikely to cover costs incurred during the previous fifteen years.

Interestingly, the Japanese see the American desire for profits as a major cause of America's weakness in international competition.[43] What they see as a weakness in America tells us something about what they see as a strength in themselves.

Income-seeking shareholders want to maximize the number of bidders for their shares so that they can, when they want, sell out for the highest possible price. At the right price everything is always for sale. To preserve their independence, however, those in producer economics will forgo profitable chances to sell out. After World War II, foreign investments in Japan were severely limited by the Japanese government to protect national economic independence. Majority foreign ownership wasn't allowed, except where something other than money (usually technology) was seen as so valuable that it could be acquired in exchange for the rights to set up majority-owned operations. IBM Japan was started by being willing to cross-license technology with what are now IBM's major foreign competitors.

The result is a huge disparity between foreign direct investment in Japan and Japan's direct investment in the rest of the world. From 1950–1989 foreigners invested $15.7 billion in Japanese facilities, but the Japanese bought $253.9 billion worth of facilities from the rest of the world.[44] From 1985 to

1990 foreigners bought firms that represent 9 percent of the stock-market capitalization in the United States, but foreigners only bought one half of 1 percent of the Japanese stock-market capitalization during the same time period. The Japanese were also buying out existing foreign investments at a faster rate than foreigners were buying in. As a result, direct foreign ownership fell from 2 to 1 percent of the total. The Japanese often buy but seldom sell.[45]

Many of what look like famous foreign corporations, such as McDonald's of Japan, don't have majority foreign ownership. In 1990 there were only 132 majority-owned foreign firms in Japan with sales over $5 million per year.[46] Their sales totaled 616 billion yen, or just 0.2 percent of the Japanese GNP. Foreigners own little and sell even less. The trends are also all moving in the wrong direction. Despite a booming Japanese economy in 1990, 52 of the 132 foreign-owned firms in Japan were experiencing falling sales. Another 20 were failing to grow as fast as the Japanese economy. Effectively, more than half were thus losing market share.

Given price/earnings (P/E) multiples of sixty to eighty on the Tokyo stock exchange in the mid- and late 1980s, profit-maximizing firms should have issued and sold shares until their stock-exchange-P/E multiples were brought back into line with the P/E multiples available on government bonds.[47] By selling their shares and buying government bonds until the two markets were brought back into equilibrium, they could have risklessly made a lot of money. They did not do so. Something stopped them. That something was, of course, independence. If they had issued those shares, they would have diluted their ownership and control, and they would have made themselves vulnerable to takeovers. A majority of their shares might not have been owned by other members of their business group.

Very high P/E multiples mean that Japanese firms can easily buy foreign firms, but that foreign firms can only with great difficulty buy Japanese firms. While the Japanese P/E multiples have come down (they stood at 46 times earnings in late 1991) they are still far above those in Europe and the United States. High P/E multiples are the modern financial equivalent of the medieval moat and wall that hold potential invaders at bay.

By way of contrast, if one examines the American consumer-electronics industry, it is a history of a profit-maximizing strategic retreat into oblivion.[48] When the Japanese attack came in black-and-white TV sets, the Americans simply refused to let their required rates of return fall to Japanese levels and left the market. But in their remaining activities, they continued to earn their demanded 15 percent rate of return. As the attack and willingness to accept lower rates of return came in market segment after market segment (radios, stereos, color TV), American firms systematically retreated until they were out of the consumer-electronics business entirely. But at every point in time, they made their demanded rate of return. Being rational, they would go out of business before they would accept a below-market rate of return.

Fighting for greater market share is irrational to the rational profit maximizer. He would rather surrender than fight. Fighting lowers one's consumption. Since his theories tell him that he can always go to work for the winner, going out of business is the rational thing to do. Nothing is lost by surrender, because the winners will not reserve the highest-paying jobs for their own troops. Individuals are, after all, paid in accordance with their individual marginal productivities. Who one works for is not important. The consumption maximizer is a mercenary who would rather switch than fight. In contrast, empires repel invaders.

Studies of competitiveness indicate that the willingness of Japanese firms to accept lower profits is a big part of their competitive edge vis-à-vis American firms. In industry after industry, among them, semiconductors, Japanese firms are willing to accept much lower rates of return.[49] If all else fails, it is their atomic bomb. When pressed they will drop it. To keep IBM off its turf, Fujitsu won the computer contract for the water-distribution system of Hiroshima City with a bid of just one yen.[50] Such bids serve as a warning to outsiders that they should not waste their time and effort making competitive bids. They will incur costs, and in the end they will lose, however low their bid.

Mutual Support: Business Groups

To lengthen time horizons and accept a lower rate of return, impatient consumption-orientated stockholders must be kept under control. The Japanese or German business groups have been organized to do just that. Seventy-eight percent of the shares listed on the Tokyo stock exchange are owned by *keiretsu* members.[51,52] Because a majority of the shares of each member of the group are owned by other members of the group, no member of the group can be bought by outsiders. Each member of the group is part operating company, part holding company, and part investment trust.[52]

With interlocking ownership, impatient consumption-orientated shareholders can be held at bay. This was shown in T. Boone Pickens's attempt to take over a member of the Toyota *keiretsu*. He became the largest single shareholder, but that did not give him a seat on the board of directors.[54] The greenmail aspects of the case (Pickens was suspected of wanting to be bought out by Toyota at a much higher price rather than wanting to run the company) and the fact that Pickens bought his shares from a Japanese greenmailer and had a contract to sell them back at a fixed price gave the Japanese establishment an excuse to keep Pickens out, but they would have probably done exactly the same even if no taint of greenmail had been present.

Members of the business group gain not by being paid dividends but by getting and giving preferential treatment to each other as preferred suppliers and customers. As stated by a Japanese auto executive talking about suppliers in the American market, "First choice is a *keiretsu* company, second is a Japanese supplier, third is a local (American) company."[55] Direct discrimination against outside suppliers does not occur. The preferential treatment comes in the form of buyers and sellers who are willing to work together to insure that the Japanese *keiretsu* supplier is in fact the best supplier. When the Japanese don't treat American firms equally in buying parts (in Honda's Ohio plant only 16 percent of the parts came from U.S. suppliers in 1989) or selling parts that are in short supply (U.S. electronics companies have charged that they have been denied parts, and their charge has been backed up by the

General Accounting Office of the U.S. government), they are not being unfair. They are simply doing what everyone does—playing ball with those on one's own team.

As a group, *keiretsu* members have the advantages (size and coordination) of being a conglomerate without the disadvantages (excessive centralization) of being a conglomerate.[56] Member companies pressure each other to grow and can coordinate their planning.

Business groups are irrational if the aim is to maximize share prices. Potential buyers are discouraged from buying. Outside owners won't be treated in the same fashion as inside owners with access to inside information. The more buyers there are and the easier it is to buy, the higher the price the seller—the shareholder—will eventually get. But groups are rational if the goal is to lengthen time horizons and maximize investment.

Countries that believe in producer economics are going to make it easy to form business groups. No impatient shareholders pressure business firms to cut back on growth to maximize profits and dividends. Countries that believe in profit maximizing are against business groups (different classes of shareholders aren't treated equally), and these countries make it difficult to form business groups. In the United States, Japanese-style business groups are illegal under the antitrust laws, and in Germany's universal-bank business, groups are illegal under the American banking laws.

Historically, America had bank-centered business groups very similar to those now found in Germany. The House of Morgan was a group that included U.S. Steel, International Harvester, General Electric, and thirty-seven other American firms. Historical analysis shows that firms that were part of the Morgan group had a higher rate of return than firms that were not part of some business group.[57] James J. Hill, the builder of the Great Northern Railroad, even called his fastest train the Empire Builder.

Such groups were made illegal in the 1930s. The public was looking for a personal devil to blame for the Great Depression, much as the public looked for someone to blame for the space shuttle disaster and is now looking for someone to blame for the savings and loan crisis. In the 1930s the public found such a person in the merchant banker J. P. Morgan, Jr., and adopted legislation designed to punish him for his supposed crimes. Everyone now understands that the Great Depression was caused by much more fundamental factors than the speculations of J. P. Morgan, Jr., but the rules that were adopted then still exist.

Even more importantly, in the 1930s laws were passed to limit pension funds and mutual funds to the ownership of only a small fraction of the stock (10 percent) of any one company. Legally, pension funds and mutual funds are not allowed to take real ownership positions and exercise control. They cannot sit on boards of directors and get inside information. Essentially, they are forced to be speculators who can earn money only by buying and selling shares. They cannot be builders or conquerors. When these laws were passed, pension and mutual funds owned only a small fraction of the total number of shares outstanding. But today they own 60 to 70 percent of the shares of most publicly listed companies.[58]

As a result, the United States has organized a system that is the exact opposite of that of Germany and Japan. Those countries have organized a system (business groups) to minimize the influence and power of impatient shareholders, while the United States has organized a system (fund dominance) to maximize the influence of impatient shareholders.

When American businesses talk about working with their customers and suppliers to produce better products, they are indirectly talking about business-group strategies. A group is formed to work together. Unfortunately, it isn't possible in most circumstances to work with one's suppliers or customers without establishing a formal business group. Customers and suppliers in one line of business are often competitors in another, or supplier firms also supply one's competitors. Few firms want their customers or suppliers to take what they have learned from them and to pass it along to one of their competitors. To build confidence and to prevent these fears from being realized, firms have to own substantial numbers of shares in each other so that they can sit on each other's boards of directors as insiders so as to insure that they are not being double-crossed.

Whom Firms Serve

If the executives of profit-maximizing American firms are asked to state the order in which they serve various constituencies, shareholders come first, with customers and employees a distant second and third. Most managers will argue that the sole purpose of the company is to maximize shareholder wealth. Customers and employees are only important to the extent that they contribute to this goal. As recently stated by John Akers, the current chief executive officer (CEO) of IBM, "The average IBM'er has lost sight of the reasons for his company's existence. IBM exists to provide a return on invested capital to the stockholders."[59]

If Japanese firms are asked the same question, the order of duty is reversed—employees first, with customers second, and shareholders third.[60] "The goals of the company will be growth and longevity, with profitability a distant third as a priority. Independent shareholders will rank fairly low on the list of constituencies whose interest management is to represent. . . . Japanese managers are agents of the entire coalition of stakeholders rather than the shareholders or any other single group."[61] If wages are part of the objective, firms become value-added maximizers rather than profit maximizers. As in the case of American law firms, the best firm is not the firm that pays the lowest wages but the firm that pays the highest wages. But to pay those wages it must have the productivity to justify them.

The Treatment of Labor

Differences in the way that workers are viewed can be seen in the takeover and buyout wave in the United States. Company divisions, including the employees, are bought and sold or restructured in a manner reminiscent of kings buying and selling provinces in medieval Europe. As in medieval Europe, the employees are chattel serfs who are not consulted on whether they want to have different masters. Not much corporate loyalty can be expected if one can expect to be treated as a slave and sold to the highest bidder. The buying and selling of provinces ended in Europe with the rise of nation-states that could command nationalistic loyalties. People were bonded to the state, and states where this bond was constructed were simply able to defeat armies and conquer territories where this bond had not been created. Lack of bonding may be no less damaging to the survival ability of business firms.

In contrast, the empire-building firm sees labor as a strategic asset to be nurtured.[62] One wants the highest-quality and best-fed soldiers. A community is to be built in Japan.[63] Money is to be made in the United States.

In America the goal is money. Start with salaries at the top. In keeping with the practice of maximizing consumption, one would expect American CEOs to be paid more than those running similar companies in the world of producer economics. And so they are.[64] In 1990 American CEOs were making 119 times as much as the average worker. Japanese CEOs had a better record in the 1980s (productivity had grown three times as fast), yet they earned only 18 times as much as their average worker.[65] When Steve Ross, the CEO of Time-Warner, pays himself seventy-eight million dollars and then lays off six hundred people because of declining advertising revenue, he is just practicing what Americans preach. Income-maximizing generals pay themselves the highest incomes they can get away with; empire-building generals don't.[66]

In American firms the chief financial officer (CFO) usually ranks second after the CEO.[67] The officer who watches after capital is number two. In contrast, the vice-president for human-resource development—the officer in charge of labor—is relatively unimportant. He or she will make 40 percent less than the CFO. In Japan the rankings are reversed. The officer in charge of the troops outranks the officer in charge of money.

As we have seen in Chapter 2, in the last two decades American managers have demanded, and gotten, real wage reductions from their work forces, even as sales and profits were rising. Partly to force American wages down and partly to get the even lower wages that exist abroad, American firms have also rapidly moved to offshore production bases. Lower-wage part-time workers have replaced higher-wage full-time workers. Japanese firms did not move production abroad or move to part-time employment to anywhere near the same extent. When a sample of Japanese companies was asked what they had done to reduce labor costs, only 2.6 percent listed discharging surplus workers or employing part-time workers.[68]

Studies of automation show that when automation goes up in America, wages go down. In contrast, when automation rises in Japan, wages rise.[69] In Japan these investments are used to enhance the productivity of labor rather than to replace skilled labor with unskilled labor, as happens in the United States. For American firms lower wages equal higher profits.

The United States is in a statistical class by itself when it comes to labor-force turnover.[70] A turnover rate of 4 percent per month is about equally divided between quits and firings. From an income-maximization perspective, this is a sign of efficiency. Workers are dismissed when they aren't needed, and workers accept new job offers whenever wages, and hence productivity, are higher. In Japan lifetime employment is offered to core workers in Japanese firms. Japan's turnover rate is just 3.5 percent per year—fewer job switches in a year than the United States has in a month.[71]

Successful armies know the value of a central cadre of experienced troops. Armies continually need new blood and new recruits, but they need a core of committed, trained troops. The employment guarantees made to a core group of workers by Japanese firms goes far beyond those given to the temporary workers on the fringe of the firm and is in accordance with military practice.[72] Turnover is limited to maximize training and experience, to promote bonding, and to increase the willingness to sacrifice oneself for the good of the group.

The U.S. Army decided that excessive individual turnover was one of its major mistakes in Vietnam. Rather than rotating groups (platoons and companies) in and out as their enlistments were up, individual soldiers were rotated in and out, and the bonding necessary to make soldiers willing to sacrifice for each other never developed. Without this bonding, the U.S. Army failed on the field of battle. Economic armies worry about similar problems; consumption maximizers do not.

In armies teamwork is always stressed as more important than individual brilliance. Medals are given for individual heroism after the battle is over, but prior to battle, teamwork is stressed. After the Persian Gulf War, some American generals argued that individual medals for bravery should not have been given. It detracted from the team nature of the victory.

In Japan the ceremony that new employees participate in when joining their lifetime company is in fact very similar to that of baptism (joining the Empire of God) or giving allegiance to medieval lords. Leaving the Kingdom of God or a Japanese company is viewed as "treason."[73] Loyalty is to be given by the employee in exchange for the security to be given by the firm. As stated by a Japanese business publication, "the majority of new recruits would appear to subscribe to the old proverb, 'Search out a big tree when you seek shelter.'"[74] One becomes part of a group that has a bigger purpose than simply raising one's own individual income. The Japanese unionization rate is far above that of the United States (26 percent versus 17 percent of workers in 1989). Its unions are real. Substantially more days are lost in labor disputes in Japan than in either Germany or France. But Japanese unions are organized on a company basis where they are part of the team rather than an external adversary.[75]

Following army practice, in the first year of employment in Japan, the company indoctrination process occupies a substantial amount of time. Management believes that the firm that best succeeds in bonding its employees to the company will simply have more reserves of goodwill, which in turn will create a work force more willing to make short-term sacrifices than those who cannot bond their employees to them. In contrast, U.S. firms make very little effort to indoctrinate their employees.

When it comes to training, a very different pattern of expenditures emerge in Japanese firms.[76] Americans invest less per worker and concentrate their investments more heavily on management education. If one looks at training investments, Americans invest less in general background skills and focus their investments more on the narrow job skills required for the next job. Army generals, in contrast, want an over-trained labor force, and the American armed forces do much more training than most American firms. In the Persian Gulf, that training paid off. In producer economics the goal is the most productive (best-educated, highest-skilled) work force that can be had. High wages are a good thing as long as productivity is even higher.

Bonus systems are also different. The American bonus system is keyed to rewarding individual performance, while the Japanese system is keyed to stimulating teamwork. Narrow profit centers are a much more widely used form of corporate organization in the United States than they are in either Japan or Europe. Quarterly profits in narrowly defined profit centers are the American way. In Japan bonuses are not normally keyed to profitability but to the growth, productivity, and market share of the entire company. The American system fits into a model of the world where individuals are motivated solely by their income and where group efforts are not important. It doesn't, however, fit into a world where the group's output, and not the individual's output, is believed to be the dominant factor in total production.

In the American system narrow profit centers often lead to noncooperation between different parts of the same firm, since no one wants to sacrifice one's own output (and, hence, bonus) to help some other part of the firm raise its output, even if that sacrifice would lead to higher output by the firm as a whole. In testimony to the Productivity Commission at MIT, the former head of research at one of the major American steel companies stated that he could not do the research projects that he thought he needed to do because plant managers did not want him using their facilities since it might lower their annual throughput and, hence, their annual bonuses.

In one system success is believed to flow from a skilled team; in the other system success is believed to flow from individual brilliance.

Cycles in Investment, Research and Development, and Training Expenditures

In the United States private research and development (R&D) spending falls in recessions and rises in booms.[77] In

Europe and Japan it does not. To an American firm, cutting R&D is a technique for maintaining profits during a period of declining sales. In Europe and Japan, R&D is not cut, since it is seen as the source of long-run competitive strength. The same spending patterns can be seen in investment and training expenditures. Cycles are sharper. American firms simply cut back on long-term investments much more sharply during recessions than the Japanese.

Accounting systems both change behavior and reflect attitudes about what is important. In American accounting conventions, since R&D is expensed, cutting R&D spending leads to higher bottom-line profits immediately. In Japan, where R&D is capitalized, it does not. The Japanese accounting system is set up to discourage short-term behavior. The American counterpart is set up to encourage it.

One hears differences in motivation in the very language of conversation. The average Japanese employee loves to tell you how he works for a company with the biggest market share in its industry. He or she will even take pride in having the third-largest market share—in being a soldier under the third most powerful warlord in the industry. No one from the head of a company to the lowest worker ever refers to a high rate of return on investment as an aspect of success in which one should take pride. Expanding market share is the objective.

The Takeover Wars

In Japan and Germany business groups essentially prevent the takeover wars so common in the Anglo-Saxon world. In 1991 Continental Tire was rescued from the clutches of the Italians when the big German banks bought enough shares to stop Pirelli from completing its takeover bid.[78] German businesses are for sale only when the Germans want them to be for sale.

In individualistic capitalism no one worries about preserving institutions. Since the group is not important, preserving any particular firm is not important. The book *Barbarians at the Gates* is an interesting story of complete individual income maximization, even if it means destroying the industrial empire (as it did in the case of RJR Nabisco) to which the individuals belong.[79] The profit maximizer simply doesn't care about destroying his company. The name of the game is raising his own income. Institutions and corporate loyalties are irrelevant. From what we know about the demise of the investment-banking firm Drexel Burnham Lambert, some of the same individuals who played a central role in the takeover of RJR Nabisco were also willing to destroy their own firm just to get their annual bonuses. Today's income is more important to profit maximizers than the firm's existence tomorrow.

To the income maximizer, destroying a company does not matter. Institutions take care of themselves, and if old institutions are destroyed, new ones will emerge to replace them without effort, cost, or lost opportunities. To the Japanese, such behavior spoils the sense of community necessary for success.[80]

Size and Profitability

On average, societies espousing market-share maximization should show up with firms larger than those that are found in societies based on profit maximization, while profit maximizers should make more profits. And so they do! If the world's 50 largest companies are listed by sales, 17 are American, 10 are Japanese, 6 are German and 5 are British. If one corrects for the size of the home market and a shorter history as a wealthy country, there are many more large Japanese firms than large American firms. If one lists the world's 50 largest companies by profits, 18 are American, just three are Japanese, only four are German and 11 are British. If one looks at the rate of return on stockholder equity, American firms in the top 50 earn 13.3 percent, or 50 percent more than the 9.1 percent earned by the Japanese firms in the top 50. Objectively, American firms are more profit-oriented than the Japanese.[81]

Similarly, if one lists the world's banks by asset size, nine of the ten largest banks in the world are Japanese; none is

American. If banks are listed by return on equity, however, six of the ten most profitable banks in the world are American; none is Japanese.

The largest nine diversified service companies are all Japanese. The tenth firm—AT&T—is American.[82] Of the top 50 service firms, 18 are Japanese (15 of these are in the top 25) and 14 are American (only five of the top 25 are American). But if one looks at profits per dollar of assets, the American rate of return (3 percent) is more than four times that of the Japanese firms (0.7 percent), despite the fact that two of the American firms were reporting huge losses because of debt burdens assumed in the takeover wars.

Ranking by sales and ranking by profits leads to very different conclusions about who is most successful. The differences between the two sets of rankings are not accidental. They are exactly what one would expect given the theories underlying the two sets of companies.[83]

National Strategies

Consider the comments of Ichiro Fujiwara, former vice-minister of the Japanese Ministry of International Trade and Industry (MITI), on national strategies:

> Let's take the case of the mainframe computer as an example. After the war, Japanese business firms had to start from scratch. To survive, they had to struggle with outmoded technology and meager capital to fend off foreign competitors armed with computerized manufacturing systems and management. No responsible government leaders, faced with such a situation, would have sat on their hands and watched domestic industries crushed under the juggernaut of foreign competition. We had to help the domestic computer industry to get on its feet. Government leaders of other countries had done, and are still doing, the same thing.[84]

A wide variety of techniques were used to develop the Japanese mainframe computer industry. To set up a wholly owned subsidiary in 1960, IBM had to make its basic patents available to Japanese manufacturers.[85] A government-financed computer-leasing company made it cheaper and less risky to buy Japanese computers. Directly and indirectly, large government investments were made in establishing a successful computer industry in Japan.

The Japanese government has never picked winners and losers. Their strategies have always been bottom-up, industry-led strategies, where government was a participant but never a dictator. Companies could, and do, reject government initiatives. The auto manufacturers rejection of a consolidation plan in the 1960s is only the most dramatic of many such examples.

In developing national strategies, the Japanese goal is to focus on those industries with high income elasticities of demand, high rates of growth in productivity, and high value added per employee. High value added means that high wages can be paid. When productivity has a high rate of growth, wages can go up rapidly even as product prices are going down. With falling prices and a high income elasticity of demand, markets will be expanding rapidly as consumer incomes grow, and labor won't need to be fired. Those trained and added to the work force can remain as permanent employees. In the 1990s there are believed to be seven industries that meet these criteria—microelectronics, the new materials-science industries, biotechnology, telecommunications, civilian aircraft manufacturing, robots plus machine tools, computers plus software.

Business firms are believed to be too risk-averse when it comes to projects that require large investments. Rationally, private firms see a riskless project with a payout of $1 billion as much better than a project with a $2.4 billion expected payoff but a 50 percent risk of failure. What is rational for business firms is, however, irrational for nations. Nations can average out their risks across many such projects. Government support encourages private industries to make the *right* market choices—like getting into aircraft manufacturing in the 1990s.

Similarly, private time horizons are believed to be too short. Private hurdle rates used in business-investment calculations are always far above the economy's long-term rate of return on assets. In the United States the private hurdle rate is 15 to 20 percent, while the historical rate of return on business assets is 7 percent. Banks such as the Japanese Development Bank or the Long-Term Credit Bank are designed to finance the long-term investments that normal banks and firms avoid.

Private firms invest too little in research and development (R&D) and don't want to diffuse the fruits of such activities fast enough. All empirical studies show that the social rate of return on R&D is far above the private rate of return. This occurs because new technologies often prove to be of most use to a company other than the one that paid to develop them. As a result, firms invest too little in R&D.

Those who invest in private R&D also want a monopoly on their ideas, so that they can earn the largest possible rate of return on their investments. To encourage R&D investment, monopolistic patent rights are given. Yet any society is much better off if the ideas developed within its jurisdictions are diffused to every producer as fast as possible. What is needed to stimulate R&D investments (patents) reduces their payoff (diffusion). Joint, partly government financed, cooperative R&D projects such as those found in the Japanese Key Technologies Center are one way to simultaneously get more investment and more diffusion. The former head of R&D at Nippon Electric Corporation notes that "R&D resources in the world are scarce; even big companies scream for these resources. If we don't collaborate, we can't advance. It's too expensive even for NEC. MITI is the third party needed to coordinate industry."[86]

Certain industries are seen as key industries with linkages (externalities) affecting other industries. Strengthen them, and other industries get stronger. Machine tools and key component suppliers, such as semiconductor chip manufacturers, are seen as linkage industries. A stronger machine-tool industry and a stronger semiconductor industry allows Japan to be more competitive in automobiles and consumer electronics. As a result, the total return to these investments is higher than the returns that show up in machine tools or semiconductor manufacturing alone.

Above all, government has an important role to play in accelerating economic growth. This means raising investments in plant and equipment, skills, infrastructure, and R&D above the levels that would occur in unfettered markets. Market participants are believed to have too much interest in the present. Government essentially represents the interest of the future in the present. It works to speed up markets and to encourage firms to go down their learning curves faster than they would if they were on their own.

As an illustration, the Japanese Development Bank provided funds for the Japanese semiconductor firms to continue building production facilities during recessions when their American competitors would stop construction. This gave the Japanese the capacity to service demands that could not be met by the Americans during the next cyclical boom. A government-financed short-term robot-leasing company persuaded firms to use robots faster than they otherwise would have. As a result, the market for robots grew far faster and became far larger in Japan than elsewhere in the industrial world. With larger and faster-growing markets, Japan's robotic firms could go down their learning curves faster and get a cost advantage over the rest of the world.

If Japanese firms are not yet prepared to compete, foreign firms are held at bay. Satellite television is such an industry at the moment. To give the domestic industry time to get organized, the Ministry of Post and Telecommunications prohibits Japanese citizens from having the dishes necessary to receive satellite signals from foreign broadcasters.[87]

Over time the instruments used to implement national strategies have changed. The foreign-exchange controls of the 1950s were replaced with capital allocation in the income-doubling decade of the 1960s. Today the focus is on research support, as in the case of the Japanese Key Technologies Center, where government and private funds are commingled to lower private risk.[88]

MITI's vision for the 1990s calls for securing the foundations for long-term economic growth. A flexible industrial infrastructure is to be combined with a better public infrastructure and improved capital and human resources. Despite the shift to services, manufacturing continues to be seen as crucial to technological innovation and growth. Basic science is to be strengthened, and the country is to make whatever efforts are necessary to stay at the forefront of the information revolution.[89]

These strategies create a problem for nations that do not believe in national strategies. How are countries without national strategies to compete? Japan recently announced a national strategy for capturing 10 percent of civilian aircraft manufacturing by the year 2000. A 10 percent market share must be dislodged from one of three competitors—Airbus Industries in Europe, Boeing in the United States, or McDonnell Douglas in the United States. Since McDonnell Douglas is the weakest of the three, its market share will probably go to the Japanese.

Historically, Americans have never had comprehensive civilian economic strategies. Only in wartime have such efforts occurred. Until recently, Anglo-Saxon economics denied the validity of national strategies. Economies of scale were exhausted, and diseconomies of scale set in long before any one supplier could capture an industry. If economies of scale were not exhausted, monopolies emerged, and these had to be broken up with antitrust laws to maintain a competitive market. No industries were believed to have externalities that were important to the existence of other industries. One could always buy one's supplies on the same basis as any other buyer—even if the seller were foreign. Profit-maximizing sellers do not discriminate, since to do so is to fail to maximize profits. Yet according to the U.S. General Accounting Office, American firms seem to find that when supplies are scarce, they don't get their equipment as fast from Japanese suppliers as the Japanese firms who belong to the same business group.[90]

In Anglo-Saxon economics there are no intrinsically high value-added industries. High-wage industries only look like high-wage industries because they use more skills. Higher wages are merely compensation for the costs of creating those skills. Once returns on human capital investments are subtracted, wages—the bribe for sacrificing leisure—are the same in every industry.

Even if national strategies could be made to work theoretically, many Americans argue that they cannot work practically. Sometimes this argument is narrowed still further to state that even if national strategies are shown to work abroad, they could not work in the United States because of its brand of special-interest-group politics.

Others argue that Americans should just accept the below-cost (subsidized) goods that they are getting as a result of these foreign strategies and withdraw from the businesses that are being targeted by others. If foreigners raise their prices when there are no American producers left, Americans will simply get back into those businesses. This argument ignores what happens when an American industry is driven out of business. The Japanese business firm is not in the business of making permanent gifts to Americans. When competition is gone, prices rise. American competitors do not come back into business because of the high transition costs of going in and out of business and because they know that if they were willing to come back into business, those fat Japanese profit margins would promptly disappear.

WHO WINS?

Abstractly, firms based upon the motivation of value added or market-share maximization and those based upon the motivation of profit maximization would each seem to have advantages. The strategic-conquest firm is willing to work for a lower rate of return and can use this ability to force profit-maximizing firms to drop out of an industry. It simply accepts a rate of return below the minimum thresholds of the profit-maximizing firm.

From the perspective of Anglo-Saxon economics, however, the profit-maximizing firms should win. They should be better cost minimizers. They are both more concerned about lowering costs and more willing to do it (i.e., fire workers), and this advantage should be large enough to allow them to meet their rate of return on investment targets and still sell products at prices equal to, or lower than, that of empire-building firms. Empire-building firms may not have a high demanded rate of return on investment, but they do have a profit constraint. They cannot grow unless their profits are positive. If profit-maximizing firms costs are low enough, they can defeat empire-building firms by forcing consistent losses upon them.

Recent empirical evidence would also seem to favor the long-run success of the empire-building firms. Firms based on the principle of producer economics are clearly on the offensive in international markets, while those based upon profit maximizing are on the defensive. But perhaps this is just the ebb and flow of economic battle. In the 1950s and 1960s the profit-maximizing firms of the United States put their competitors on the defensive.

Which of the two is to triumph will depend in the long run upon the extent to which the problems of growth (economic dynamics) are different from those of competition in a static environment (comparative statics). The theoretical advantages of profit maximization were in fact mathematically derived under the assumptions of what economists call "comparative statics." In comparative statics, a stable no-growth environment, firms prove their effectiveness by becoming efficient (moving from inside the production-possibilities curve to a place on the maximum production-possibilities curve). The cost minimizer wins. In getting onto that maximum production-possibility curve, Japanese lifetime employment and seniority wages should, for example, be a handicap. Labor is not paid in accordance with its individual marginal productivity. It is not laid off when it should be laid off. It is not paid the wages it should be paid.

In economic dynamics the central problem is rapid growth (getting the production-possibility curve to move to the right as rapidly as possible and to make productivity grow as rapidly as possible). Being on the curve, being the most efficient at any moment in time, is unimportant.

In reaching this growth goal, many of the cost-cutting advantages of comparative statics may be liabilities. Reducing wages and firing people may allow the firm to cut costs, but it lowers the willingness of the work force to accept new technologies, leads to a less well trained labor force, and eliminates loyalty—the willingness to make short-run self-sacrifices for the good of the firm. Similarly, the Anglo-Saxon willingness to reduce R&D spending, investment, and training in recessions may similarly be a short-run static advantage that turns out to be a long-run dynamic handicap.

By reducing the individual's risks with lifetime employment and seniority wage systems, the Japanese firm handicaps itself in the world of comparative statics. It cannot efficiently cut costs. But if the name of the game is dynamic growth, lifetime employment means that no one will become unemployed if new technologies reduce the demand for labor. Workers will be retrained if new technologies come along and make one's skills obsolete. With seniority wages, whatever happens, one's wages will not be reduced. Producer economics forces investments in skills and creates motivation that may offset its static inefficiencies. It has what Ronald Dore, an MIT Japanologist, calls "flexible rigidities."[91]

The economic risks of change are the same in the two systems, but in one system the risks of economic change are carried by the individual, and in the other, by the group. When the risks are carried by the group, individuals lose their rational incentive to fight technical change. What is good for the group is automatically good for the individual. In contrast, in the American system, what is good for the group—higher productivity from new technologies—is often bad for particular individuals.

In the long run history will tell us which theory is right. An empirical experiment is now under way. The profit-maximizing firms of the United States have faced off against the empire-building firms of Japan. Individualistic capitalism meets communitarian capitalism. Eventually, the winners will be known. In the end the winner will force the losers to change and play by the winner's rules.

Chapter 5

THE UNITED STATES OF AMERICA: THE GREAT WALL IS DOWN

Suppose that someone had told a keen fifteenth-century observer that some part of the globe was about to conquer the rest of the world and then asked that observer to guess whom the conqueror might be. The right answer would, of course, be Europe, but basing his reply upon his knowledge of the world at that time, our observer would probably have answered China. China was the first to invent gunpowder, printing, and the compass. China had an efficient unified national government while Europe was still a group of quarreling principalities. A Chinese armada with more than one hundred thousand soldiers had already set foot on the east coast of Africa. In comparison, Europe's explorations were very small-scale. No nation could match the power of China. If there was a country about to conquer the world, it had to be China.

Of course, our observer would have been wrong, because China was about to retreat behind its Great Wall and slowly

153

sink into poverty and powerlessness. Despite having a much larger population than Europe, by the nineteenth century it was itself under European domination, with different countries claiming their specific spheres of influence.

Economically, in the years after World War II, the United States, like China five hundred years earlier, was effectively living behind its own great wall. It was the "middle kingdom." Instead of being built of stone, however, its great wall was built of five overwhelming economic advantages.

First, in 1950 the American market was more than nine times as large as the next largest market, the United Kingdom.[1] As a result, American industry enjoyed economies of scale and scope that no other national economy could hope to achieve.[2] Mass manufacturing was effectively an American monopoly, where unit costs in industries such as autos or steel were beyond the dreams of the largest foreign producers. Serving such a large internal market, specialty firms could thrive.

Second, when it came to technology, Americans were superior. World War II had destroyed the scientific establishments in much of the rest of the world, and Europe had given America some of its finest brains—Albert Einstein and Enrico Fermi, to name two. American firms did not compete with foreign firms; they built products foreigners could not build. The Boeing 707 flew. The British Comet suffered from metal fatigue, and all too often did not fly. Industries where the technological leader was not headquartered in America were few and far between.

Third, American workers were more skilled than those found abroad. Americans had invented mass compulsory public elementary and secondary education. When the GI Bill was added to the Land Grant college system, America was also the first nation with mass higher education. Far larger proportions of its population were highly educated and, because of this education, capable of acquiring skills that were simply beyond the abilities of much of the rest of the world. Higher skills led to the use of technologies that would simply have outstripped human talent in any other country. As a result, costs were lower. No other industrial democracy could have even thought of putting a man on the moon in the 1960s, and the one country that tried—the Soviet Union—did not succeed.

Fourth, America was rich, while others were poor. In 1950 its per capita GNP was 50 percent higher than that of Canada, three times that of Great Britain, four times that of West Germany, and fifteen times that of Japan.[3] Americans could simply afford to do things that others could not.[4] Because Americans had more discretionary income than anyone else, the first mass market for almost everything began in the United States. This gave American firms an opportunity to go down the learning curve before anyone else could even get on it. America was not a high-saving/high-investment nation after World War II, but it was so rich that the modest proportion of GNP it devoted to investment still gave it much more capital per worker than other nations, even though they were saving and investing a much higher proportion of their total income. If America's per capita income was fifteen times that of Japan, a Japanese family could save three times as much of its income as an American family, and total investment per worker could still be five times higher in the United States.

Finally, American managers were the best in the world. America had a skilled cadre of middle- and upper-level managers because the most talented Americans prior to World War II had gone into management. Management was the route to the top. Prior to World War II the military was the route to the top for talent in Germany and Japan. England and France had their colonial empires. Talented individuals went into the colonial service, where one might dream of eventually ruling a whole country (India) rather than being the manager of a mere company. After the war the best and the brightest of the older generations were without business management experience and did not want to acquire it. For a while the young reflected the attitudes of those older generations. As late as the early 1960s, students at Oxford looked down on those who dreamed of managerial careers.

Put a huge market together with superior technology, more capital, a better-educated labor force, and superior managers, destroy most of the rest of the world in a major war, and the result is an economic middle kingdom protected by superior

technology and enjoying effortless economic superiority. Both
outside and inside the great wall, changes were occurring. But
Americans living in the middle kingdom did not notice and
did not change their behavior. As the rest of the world began
to catch up with income levels in the United States, the relative size of the American market got smaller and smaller. In
1990 the American market was only 40 percent larger than the
Japanese internal market.[5]

Partly because of worries about their inability to generate
economies of scale commensurate with those in America, the
Europeans created the Common Market in the 1950s. At the
time they promised that they would fully integrate their markets in 1992. As a result, on January 1, 1993, the United States
will become for the first time in more than one hundred years
the world's second-largest integrated market. The economic
major leagues will be in Europe—a unified market of 337 million people with a per capita income somewhat below that of
the United States but with an aggregate GNP substantially
bigger than that of the United States. If the rest of Western
Europe were to be attached, that market might easily grow to
four hundred million people. Add all of Middle and Eastern
Europe, and a market might be created with 850 million people. Starting in 1993, the Europeans believe that it is they who
will have the advantage when it comes to economies of scale
and scope.

In addition, modern telecommunication, computer, and
transportation technologies have created a world where the
size of one's internal market is less important than it used to
be. The Japanese can produce and sell six times as many video
recorders as they themselves buy. Global market economies
of scale and scope are open to everyone—even if they live in
relatively small countries.

There is also some evidence that the economies associated
with mass production may be less important than they once
were. With greater wealth, people are willing to pay a pre-
mium for variety. A higher-cost product tailored precisely to
their needs is better than a cheaper product designed for the
average consumer. Smaller production runs and shorter product life cycles are the wave of both the present and the future.

One can find industries where Americans still maintain a

technological lead (aircraft), but one can also find industries (consumer electronics) where Americans clearly lag.[6] Japanese companies understand that if Japan is to win, they must be technological leaders in generating man-made comparative advantage. In 1990, 32 percent of all Japanese firms believed that they were technologically more advanced than their American rivals, 63 percent claimed parity, and only 5 percent admitted inferiority.[7] America is technologically average if one includes both product technologies (where it is, on average, still a leader) and process technologies (where it is, on average, now a laggard). Whereas there used to be only products that foreigners could not technologically produce, there are now products where Americans cannot technologically build a product that is competitive in both quality and price. (Apple Computer could not build a laptop that was light enough to be competitive and had to announce a joint-production agreement with Sony.[8])

American research and development (R&D) spending used to lead the world, but that is no longer true. Today American nondefense R&D spending is lower than it was twenty years ago, while the Germans and the Japanese have upped the intensity of their effort. Total R&D spending (defense plus nondefense) matches that of Germany and Japan but nondefense spending has been flat at 1.8 percent of the GNP, for most of a decade, while German and Japanese spending is rising and now stands at 2.6 and 2.8 percent of the GNP respectively.[9] Looking at total R&D spending as a fraction of the GNP, America holds the fifth position, Japan the third, Germany the fourth. First place is held by Sweden. If military spending is subtracted and only civilian spending is evaluated, America slips to tenth in R&D spending. If all government spending is subtracted and only private R&D spending remains, America was almost at the bottom, ranking twentieth out of twenty-three industrial countries.[10] Unless one believes that Americans are smarter than the Germans or the Japanese, today's spending levels will eventually lead to a secondary position for American science and engineering and lower rates of growth in productivity.[11]

Patents confirm that judgment. In 1980 seven of the top ten patent winners in the United States were American firms, and only one of the top six was foreign. Ten years later only three of the top ten firms were American, and the best American firm could do no better than a fifth-place finish.[12] In a recent survey of high-quality, frequently cited patents, Fuji had surged ahead of Kodak and Hitachi was ahead of IBM.[13] At the end of the 1980s the gap in high-quality patents between Japan and the United States was half that at the beginning of the decade, and on a per capita basis Japan was ahead. When examining the U.S. technological position, the American Council on Competitiveness gave America a B minus grade. Strong performances in some areas were offset by weak performances in others (see Table 5.1). Americans are not smarter. When the rest of the world puts in more effort, it gets better results.[14]

TABLE 5.1
America's Technology Report Card*

A	Data-based systems, biotechnology, jet propulsion, magnetic-information storage, pollution reduction, software, voice recognition and vision in computers, computers
B+	Design and engineering tools, portable telecommunications equipment
B	Automotive power train, gallium arsenide, information networks, joining technologies, superconductors
B−	Electronic controls, materials processing, microelectronics
C+	Advanced materials, manufacturing processes
C	Precision machining, printing and copying equipment, optoelectronic components
D	Chip-making equipment and robotics, electronic ceramic materials, electronic packaging, flat-panel displays, optical storage

SOURCE: Thomas A. Stewart, "Where We Stand," in *The New American Century*, *Fortune*, Special Issue, 1991, p. 17

The rest of the world noticed the payoff from America's system of mass education, copied it, and upped the intensity level. Comparative international examinations reveal that Americans at all age levels know less than citizens abroad in other advanced industrial countries. The math test scores of the top 1 percent of America's high-school seniors would place them in the fiftieth percentile in Japan.[15] The older the student, the larger the educational achievement gap. In science subjects Americans place eighth in a ranking of ten-year-olds from fifteen countries. By age 13 their position has slipped to thirteen.[16] Not surprising, given that America has one of the shortest school years and school days to be found in the industrial world—180 days in the United States, versus 220–240 days in Germany, 240 days in Japan, and 250 days in Korea.[17] Combine a shorter school day and year with many fewer hours of homework, and less is learned.[18] Top this off with a much lower high-school graduation rate (71 percent in the United States versus 94 percent in Japan and 91 percent in Germany), and the United States has a grossly undereducated work force.[19]

Those who graduate from college catch up with their foreign counterparts, since most of the rest of the industrial world has not made the human and physical investments necessary to shift from elite education to mass education, and America's graduate schools have no equal, but successful economies are not built upon college-educated labor forces alone.

American higher education has a weakness when it comes to science education. Relative to the rest of the world, too few engineers and scientists are being produced. America now produces fewer than half the Ph.D. engineers and scientists per capita that it did in the early 1970s. Much of this can be traced back to bad science and math education in high school. By age eighteen many Americans have already shut the door on a scientific career. But that is not an excuse for failing to insist that every college graduate be numerate, that is, mathematically literate. The new technologies that are coming into the office and factory are going to require everyone to have levels of math competence that are far above those needed in the past. By refusing to insist that every college graduate take enough math to be numerate, universities are failing to give their graduates the skills Americans will need in the twenty-first century.

For those that do not go on to college, a poor educational starting position is compounded by less on-the-job investment in skills. Whatever the reason (be it higher labor-force turnover rates or a cultural inability to see the work force as a strategic asset), American firms systematically invest less in the skills of their work force than their foreign competitors. And what they do invest is targeted heavily on professional employees. Ordinary workers receive little beyond the detailed training necessary to do the next job. Almost never do they receive the general background training necessary to absorb complicated new technologies when they emerge.

At the same time technology has moved in directions that require a much better educated and more skilled work force. To make today's complex semiconductor chips, a company must use statistical quality control. To use statistical quality control, every production worker must master it. To do so requires learning some simple operations research, but to learn what must be taught, workers must know algebra. Americans are not used to a world where ordinary production workers have to have mathematical skills.

Technically, America has not been the richest country in the world for some time (one of the oil sheikhdoms has held that distinction for several decades), but it is now in a world where there are other industrial countries that are its approximate peers if one looks at both external and internal purchasing power. In this context lower American savings rates now lead to higher real interest rates and lower investment rates—about half that found in Japan and two thirds that found in Europe. Of twenty-one industrial countries, no country had a savings rate lower than that of the United States in the late 1980s. While the American family was saving 4.6 percent of its disposable income in 1989, the Japanese family was saving 15.7 percent.[20] When all forms of savings were aggregated, the Germans saved 62 percent more than the Americans, and the Japanese saved 100 percent more. During the 1980s, savings rates fell in all major industrial countries, but at the end of decade savings rates were sharply rising everywhere except in the United States.[21]

Higher savings rates lead to more R&D and more plant and equipment, but they also lead to more and better public infrastructure.[22] The Japanese have their bullet train. The French have their even faster TGV (normal running speed 186 miles per hour; tested at more than 300 miles per hour).[23] The Germans claim to have something even better going into service.[24]

A channel tunnel is being built between Britain and France. The French telephone system links every household in a computer network. The infrastructure for electronic funds-transfer systems is being built.

In the United States infrastructure investments are running at less than half the rates of the 1960s.[25] Keeping its bridges from falling down is all that America can manage. None of the world's exciting new infrastructure projects are in America. Yet better infrastructure is closely linked with productivity growth. Historically, an increased investment equal to 1 percent of GNP in public infrastructure has been associated with a rise of a half percentage point in private productivity growth.[26] As much as 60 percent of the slowdown in productivity growth has been traced to falling levels of public capital per worker.[27] The faster, cheaper transportation permitted by America's interstate highway system was responsible for a substantial part of the high productivity gains recorded in the 1960s. The nation that leads in the construction of electronic highways, an effort that will require both public and private investment, may get a similar jump in productivity in the 1990s.[28]

With more discretionary income, new products are now increasingly introduced first abroad (digital tape recorders were for sale for a number of years in Japan before they reached America, and high-definition digital stereo TV will clearly appear in Japan and Europe before it appears in the United States). Because of cumbersome approval processes, new drugs are almost universally introduced first in Europe. Foreign firms are increasingly jumping on the learning curve first; Americans are increasingly having to play catch-up on the way down.

Managerially, the lure of alternative opportunities is now precisely the reverse of what it used to be. If one wants a route to the top, management is now the only avenue in Germany, Japan, the United Kingdom, and France. The armies and empires of these nations have vanished. Old and young are psychologically adjusted to this reality.

America is now the one with a large military-industrial complex, with all of its opportunities for advancement and high earnings—30 percent of its engineers work directly or indirectly for the military.[29] It offers the excitement of high-tech adventures that civilian products cannot begin to emulate. Outstanding people can dream of foreign-policy superpower jobs. The generals in the Persian Gulf War became cultural heros. America has also invented zero-sum activities, such as the legal ("let's-all-sue-each-other") profession, that have absorbed much of its talent. American management talent and experience are no longer clearly better than that in the rest of the world. If measured by outcome—by trade deficits or slow productivity growth—they are worse.

Every year the World Economic Forum, a Swiss-run organization, publishes a *World Competitiveness Report* wherein it attempts to rank the competitiveness of business firms in different countries on different dimensions. The Forum evaluated management in 23 industrial countries, and the managers who were best at some activity got a ranking of 1 and those who were worst got a ranking of 23.[30]

When it came to product quality, American firms were ranked number 12. Japan was number 1. Germany was number 3.

When it came to on-time delivery, American firms were number 10. Japan was again number 1. Germany was number 2.

The same results were found for after-sales service: Japan was number 1; Germany, number 2; America, number 10.

The quantity and quality of on-the-job training given by American firms received a ranking of 11. Japan was number 1. Germany was number 2.

When it came to future orientation (that is, do firms take the long view?), of the firms in 23 industrial countries, American firms had a ranking of 22—almost, but not quite, the bottom. Only Hungary was worse. Japan was number 1; Germany, number three.

These European evaluations are echoed in the Orient. In a survey of Korean businesses, after correcting for price, 80 percent preferred Japanese products, and only 6 percent thought that American products offered any nonprice advantages.[31] When the Japanese were asked to list the imported cars they wished to buy, no American cars appeared on the list.[32] They all come from Europe. Not long ago a Japanese acquaintance told me that "we will help you manage your decline."

To some extent Americans agree with these outside assessments. Japanese managers are rated as better than American managers by 48 percent of the American population. Only 11 percent believe the reverse.[33]

The implication of all of these changes is simply put. America no longer lives behind its great wall. The great wall is down! America has to adjust to the harsh reality of real competition. Its effortless technological and economic superiority are gone.[34] Economically, Genghis Khan has arrived.

MEANWHILE, WITHIN THE WALLS . . .

As America's great wall was being dismantled by the success of the rest of the world, something was happening within America's great walls, something very similar to what China experienced behind its physical walls. Within the walls the American economy was also becoming less and less dynamic.

Biting critics of America such as Shintaro Ishihara of Japan see decline. The "predictions that Oswald Spengler made at the outset of this century in *The Decline of the West* have become a reality. The U.S., having converged the strains of European civilization, is now in decline."[35] While America is clearly not declining in any absolute sense, there are some real "falling behind" issues. In 1990 there were eleven countries whose wages exceeded those of the United States.[36] Manufacturing wages were higher in fourteen countries—nine dollars per hour higher in West Germany.[37] When fringe benefits are included, the wage gap is even larger.[38]

In the ten years from 1978 to 1988, the American economy generated 7.5 million new male jobs, but after correcting for inflation, 18.4 million males had 1988 earnings below 1978 levels.[39] On a net basis all of those millions of new jobs were below-average jobs, and another 10.9 million males were forced to accept real wage reductions. Over the decade median male earnings fell 9 percent in real terms, with the biggest losers being white male high-school graduates. They lost their traditional high-wage job opportunities in autos, steel, and machine tools.

Starting from much lower average earnings in 1978 (43 percent of annual male earnings, to be exact), and with time available to increase their average annual hours of work, female workers fared somewhat better. In the ten years from 1978 to 1988, 12.5 million new female jobs were created, and on a net basis only 2.7 million of these new jobs paid wages below 1978 levels. Real median earnings rose 17 percent, leading annual female earnings to rise from 43 percent to 54 percent of that of males.

With more women working in the 1970s and 1980s, real median family incomes rose slowly, despite falling male wages. In the 1990s, however, a greater work effort by women will not be available to offset falling male wage rates. Most women are already full-time workers, and the average family simply doesn't have a lot of unused female working hours left.[40] In the decade ahead American family incomes are apt to feel the effects of falling real wages.

If the real GNP is up and real wages are down for two thirds of the work force, as an algebraic necessity wages must be up substantially for the remaining one third. That one third is composed of Americans who still have an edge in skills on workers in the rest of the world—basically those with college educations. In the 1980s educational attainment and increases or decreases in earnings were highly correlated. American society is now divided into a skilled group with rising real wages and an unskilled group with falling real wages. The less education, the bigger the income reduction; the more education, the bigger the income gains.[41]

These wage trends have produced a sharp rise in inequality. In the decade of the 1980s, the real income of the most affluent five percent rose from $120,253 to $148,438, while the income of the bottom 20 percent dropped from $9,990 to $9,431.[42] While the top 20 percent was gaining, each of the bottom four quintiles lost income share; the lower the quintile, the bigger the decline. At the end of the decade, the top 20 percent of the American population had the largest share of total income, and the bottom 60 percent, the lowest share of total income ever recorded.

In the long run, productivity, or output per hour of work, is the central factor determining the ability of any society to generate a world-class standard of living. It is not possible to divide what isn't produced. In the short-run, other variables can be important. The economically active population, the labor force, can grow relative to the entire population. As unemployment comes down and capital capacity utilization rates go up, a society can produce more output without becoming more productive per unit of input. In the 1980s, American society did both; essentially, it increased its work effort and kept its GNP growing despite a poor productivity performance. But eventually, full employment for both men and machines is reached.

For substantial periods of time, nations can also import more than they export; that is, they essentially borrow resources from the rest of the world. The United States used this trick in the 1980s to keep its consumption growing faster than its productivity, borrowing about $1,000 billion from the rest of the world to finance higher consumption for Americans. But sooner or later any nation reaches the end of its borrowing capacity and has sold off the assets that foreigners wish to purchase. Its international borrowing exhausted, this source of consumption peters out. Higher productivity becomes the only path to higher incomes.

In the 150 years since the onset of the Industrial Revolution, American productivity growth averaged a little less than 3 percent per year. In the twenty years from 1947 to 1967, productivity growth was slightly better—3.3 percent per year.[43] With a 3.3 percent growth rate, living standards double every twenty-one years. From 1980 to 1990 American productivity grew at a 1.2 percent pace. With a 1.2 percent productivity growth rate, standards of living double every fifty-eight years. With productivity actually falling in 1989 and 1990, no turnaround, no light, is visible at the end of the productivity tunnel.[44] The mystery is simply compounded when comparisons with the rest of the world are made. Over the same decade productivity grew 3.1 percent per year in Japan, 1.9 percent in France, 1.4 percent in West Germany, and 2.8 percent in the United Kingdom.[45]

Manufacturing's productivity record is better than that of the rest of the economy. In the 1980s it averaged 4 percent per year. But this rate of growth was far below the 5.7 percent rate achieved by Japanese manufacturing.[46] This difference can no longer be attributed to the Japanese ability to play catch-up while the Americans were inventing new products and processes. Japanese manufacturing productivity levels were 30 percent above those in the United States in 1987.[47] If a country had the easy job of playing catch-up, it was America. While manufacturing is doing better than the rest of the economy, its performance is not world-class either.[48,49]

There are also reasons to believe that faulty measurements may exaggerate how well American manufacturing is doing. The Department of Commerce admits that it has been underestimating the extent to which American manufacturers use foreign components in their products and thus has been exaggerating the output and productivity of American manufacturing.[50]

Given this productivity performance, America would have had an economic problem even if no other country existed on the face of the globe. Americans would want to know why it was taking more than twice as long to double their standard of living. Issues of external competitiveness are merely visible symptoms of an internal productivity problem.

If productivity is growing more rapidly in other advanced industrial societies, then something is wrong with the way that America organizes itself. Studies show that Japan innovates both faster and more cheaply than America.[51] While Americans may not be superior to the rest of the world in native intelligence and drive, they are at the same time also not inferior. Any improvement possible in Japan is also possible in America.

Part of the decline in productivity growth is easy to understand. Americans simply weren't investing enough to get the new tools they needed to become more productive.[52] In the 1970s and 1980s investments in plant and equipment failed to keep pace with the rate of growth of the labor force. Capital per worker did not rise as it had in the 1950s and 1960s. In addition, the public sector was not contributing to productivity growth with new infrastructure investments as it had in the past. There was nothing new to speed the workings of the private economy such as the Interstate Highway System of the 1960s.

Educational skills quit growing or actually fell slightly if one believes the results of SAT scores. Increasingly, employers reported that their work forces could not learn new technologies unless they were given time away from work for remedial education. But longer training time shows up as less output and productivity.

As the military went into space, there seemed to be less and less spillover from military R&D to new civilian products. None of the new consumer products of the 1970s and 1980s could be traced to military research. Total R&D spending did not go down, but the dearth of civilian spending seemed to have a greater impact than in the past. Greater military efforts no longer seemed to compensate for lesser civilian efforts.

Much of the productivity problem is found in the service sector. Service employment boomed—twenty-one million new jobs were added from 1980 to 1990—but with lower average levels of productivity in services, rapid growth pulls down the national averages. Within the service sector, productivity is growing in some industries but falling in others.[53] By world standards the American service sector is simply inefficient. In West Germany service-sector productivity growth paralleled that of manufacturing. If American service-sector productivity had grown at the West German rate in the 1980s, only four million new employees would have been added to service-sector payrolls.

Much of the explanation for low productivity growth is to be found in wages. With falling real wage rates and very low minimum wages relative to average wages (which are, moreover, unenforced for all but large employers—almost 10 million people work at wages below the legal minimum wage), it just did not pay employers to invest in new labor-enhancing service-sector technologies in the United States. People were cheaper than machines. Abroad, minimum wages were much higher relative to average wages (and were also enforced), and real wages were continuing to rise. Machines were cheaper than people.[54]

Some of the service-sector drag on American productivity growth is apt to end in the 1990s. The end of the postindustrial era is probably already at hand.[55] In the 1990s services will not be growing faster than the rest of the economy. Over 90 percent of the growth of the service sector in the United

States can be traced to producer's services (principally, finance and the provision of office space), retail trade, and health care. In two of these three sectors, growth has already slowed. In the third, it is almost a national imperative to see it stopped.

The finance and office-building booms are over in the United States. Finance is laying off workers, and most cities now have enough empty office space to last them a decade.

In retail trade the shift to twenty-four-hours-a-day, seven-days-a-week shopping has been completed. New workers are no longer needed to lengthen shopping hours. Eating meals away from home is approaching saturation. New workers will not be needed to serve more meals away from home. In retailing, employment also grew as full-time workers who must legally be paid fringe benefits were replaced with part-time workers who were not guaranteed fringe benefits. With all of these transitions now essentially complete, retail-trade employment growth has simply reached a natural stopping point.

Health-care employment is still growing rapidly, but at some point in the next decade the United States will have to learn how to control its health-care costs. Health-care spending (now 12 percent of GNP) cannot continue to rise as a fraction of GNP. When costs are contained, health-care employment will quit growing.

White-Collar Productivity

Within each industry, much of the productivity problem can be traced to rapidly rising white-collar bureaucracies that were not tamed by investments in automating the office. While real output was growing 30 percent between 1980 and 1990, blue-collar employment grew by 2 percent, and white-collar employment grew by 33 percent. As a result, blue-collar productivity rose 28 percent, while white collar productivity was falling 3 percent.[56] When it comes to blue-collar productivity growth, America has a growth rate close to its long-run historic trend and not too far below that of the rest of the world. But since there are more than twice as many white-collar workers on American payrolls as there are blue-collar, the decline in white-collar productivity wiped out much of the gain in blue-collar productivity.

If the problem were a technological shift from blue-collar to white-collar workers (the white-collar robot programmer replaces the blue-collar welder), the same huge increases in white-collar employment would also be occurring in other advanced industrial nations. However, the same pattern is not found in Europe or Japan.

Studies of the relative cost of producing the Ford Escort in different countries show that 40 percent of the Japanese cost advantage is due to white-collar overheads that are lower in Japan than they are in the United States.[57] When Japanese managers take over existing American enterprises, they often find that they can dramatically reduce the number of white-collar workers.[58] If foreign managers find that they can manage American plants with far fewer white-collar workers than are needed by American managers, the problems cannot be traced to bureaucracy required by the American legal or governmental system.

This growth in white-collar employment is even more puzzling if one remembers that the United States is supposed to be in the midst of an office revolution, and that investments in office automation have accounted for a large fraction of total business investment in recent years. New technology, new hardware, new software, and new skills are all going into the American office, but negative productivity is coming out. In the 1980s American firms were investing more in computer technologies to automate the office than businesses in the rest of the world. This is the one place where the problem is not underinvestment.

Recently there has been a lot of talk in American industry about reducing white-collar overheads. Periodically, dramatic stories appear in the popular press about large numbers of white-collar workers being laid off. But in the aggregate white-collar employment continues to grow faster than output. Within American industry, there is widespread recognition of the white-collar problem, but very little action taken to address it.

If one asks seriously why office productivity is falling while investments in office equipment are rising, one must confront Anglo-Saxon management structures. Power (American bosses exist to boss), style (a good boss should know everything and in principle have the knowledge to make all decisions), institutions (most middle-level managers are paid according to the number of people who report to them), peer pressure (it is harder to fire those who work directly with you than those who work at a distance), and beliefs (if the system is based solely upon individual effort, there is no need to pay attention to group motivation, voluntary cooperation, or teamwork) have all contributed to an inability to take advantage of office automation.

Consider the conventional "do-no-harm" rule for deciding when medical treatment should be stopped. If every treatment is carried to the point where its negative side effects become worse than the original effects of the disease, doctors prescribe treatments far beyond the rational economic stopping rule (marginal costs should equal marginal benefits) and run up huge costs in situations where few benefits are to be expected—more than one third of all U.S. medical costs are incurred in the last year of life.

In the past employing every available procedure to the point where it actively began to harm the patient did not cost very much, since there weren't very many expensive technologies to be employed in most illnesses. But when such technologies arise and give doctors and their patients a lot of expensive technological options with submarginal payoffs, the old stopping rule can become a very expensive decision rule that can no longer be afforded. Yet thus far Americans have not been able to change their standard operating procedures in medicine.

What is true in medicine is also true in business. In business the equivalent of do no harm is the proposition that the boss should "Know Everything." In principle he should be knowledgeable enough to make every decision. As long as the technology did not exist to implement that decision rule, it wasn't very harmful. But when a technology (the computer) came along that makes it possible to attempt to know everything, that rule became a very expensive stopping rule.

Role models for what one "ought to do" are important in

determining behavior in every walk of life. Take the proposition that the best boss is the boss that has the most knowledge and can intelligently make the most decisions per day. In the late 1960s and early 1970s, the business press set up bosses such as Harold Geneen of ITT as role models for others to emulate. He was in the words of the business press of the day the "world's greatest business manager."[59] He had a "managerial system of tight control"[60] with "elements of a spy system."[61] He "worked extraordinarily long hours and absorbed thousands of details about ITT's business."[62] "Tales of Geneen's incredible stamina at these marathon affairs (affairs where he demonstrated that he knew more about their numbers than middle level bosses knew about their numbers) and of his brutality to any manager who dared to dissemble before him are retold today like epic poems."[63] "Everything the company does is totally number orientated."[64] "His unique form of management allows him finger tip control over his vast empire."[65] Was he "an ogre in a business suit? The greatest corporate manager of his time? An unimaginative numbers grubber? A great leader of Men?"[66]

Geneen, and managers like him, supposedly knew more about middle-level management's job than the middle-level managers themselves knew. He was famous for making thousands of rapid decisions. He was the prototypical boss who bossed. He was the macho manager whom lesser managers attempted to emulate. In lists of America's toughest bosses, he was regularly at the head of the list. He knew the numbers. Management by the numbers became the American way—it was how management was supposed to manage.

Such beliefs about the ideal boss may have long existed, but most managers could not implement them without the technological office revolution of the 1970s and the 1980s. Previously, firms had to decentralize and bosses had to delegate decisions to those on the scene since there was no feasible way for them to know what they had to know to make good decisions. But with the onset of the new information technologies, ordinary bosses could implement what extraordinary bosses had always preached. Bosses could do a lot more bossing, just as doctors could do a lot more doctoring.

To do so, however, one had to build up enormous information bureaucracies. Information could be gotten, but only at the cost of adding a lot of white-collar workers to the system. The problem is graphically seen in accounting. During the period when accounting was being computerized, from 1978 to 1985, the number of accountants on American payrolls rose 30 percent from 1 million to 1.3 million, while output was rising only 16 percent.[67] Accounting productivity fell 14 percent, despite the computerization of accounting.

Computers made accounting faster, but that speed was used not to reduce the employment of accountants but to increase the frequency and types of accounting. Old accounts that in the past had been calculated every three months were now ordered up every day. Whole systems of new accounts (management-information systems, cost accounting, inventory control, financial accounting, etc.) that had been previously impossible to calculate were put on-line. Yet there was no evidence that all of these new accounts improved decision making enough to justify their cost. In fact, given the huge increases in white-collar employment required to generate all of this new information, there was evidence to the contrary. But power and style called for ordering up all of those new accounts, and so it was done.

To the boss, more information seems like a free good. He orders it from subordinates, and the cost of acquiring it appears on the budgets of his subordinates. Subordinates in turn can neither refuse to provide the requested information nor know if the information is valuable enough to justify the costs of its acquisition. To the subordinate, costs are irrelevant. They are not even calculated. One does what one's boss orders. Essentially, both bosses and subordinates are imprisoned in standard operating procedures that create an institutional set of blinders. While efficient firms that do not operate in this way will eventually drive inefficient firms out of business, nothing guarantees that the efficient firms won't all be Japanese, while the inefficient ones will all be American.

Beliefs about the *right* management styles change very slowly and only under great duress. To do away with those white-collar workers and the information system they support is to delegate one's decision-making power to those on the spot who have the necessary information without the benefits of an information system. To do so is to become a boss who does less bossing. But this is contrary to one's conception of one's own role. No American becomes a boss to do less bossing.

Participatory management is a case in point. It may be an efficient way to cut white-collar overheads and raise productivity, but it requires a reduction in the boss's power. In experiment after experiment in participatory management, the problems have not been found among workers but among middle-level managers who feel threatened.[68] They block experiments with new, more efficient forms of production because they fear the loss of their job or their authority. The personal dangers in the American system are not imaginary. They are real. Personal rationality intervenes to prevent system rationality from being achieved.

As stated in a *Fortune* magazine article on "The Revolt Against Working Smarter," ". . . the participative process doesn't always fit easily with traditional management methods and measurements. . . . Fearing a loss of power, many middle managers torpedoed early participative programs. . . . It is tempting for some of our managers to say, 'it's our turn; we've got the club.' . . . The higher up the corporate ladder, the tougher seems the shift to participative mode. . . . Information is power and it remains a clear badge of rank with managers. . . . The skills required for would-be participative managers—communicating, motivating, championing ideas— are sandy intrusions in the gearbox of many traditional executives."[69]

Consider shop-floor just-in-time inventory-control systems. Letting assembly-line workers do inventory control may increase the variety in the tasks performed by blue-collar assembly-line workers and may as a result increase their motivation to do a good job, but the major efficiency gains are not to be found in enhanced motivation among blue-collar workers. They are found in eliminating white-collar inventory-control workers and the information systems necessary to support them. But to do so is to become a hostage to those assembly-line workers. They can, if they wish, now sabotage the system.

Allowing shop-floor employees to directly purchase the ordinary equipment they use rather than using purchasing agents or industrial engineers has a similar payoff. Motivation may increase when workers want to prove that their purchasing decisions have been good ones, but the real efficiency gains are to be found in reducing the number of purchasing agents or industrial engineers (and their supporting staffs) who used to be responsible for such investment decisions.

Traditionally American plants have had "locked" numerically controlled machine tools, while the Europeans and Japanese have had "unlocked" numerically controlled machine tools. Those terms refer to whether blue-collar workers are allowed to change the programming (unlocked) or whether only white-collar programmers are allowed to alter the programming (locked). In the latter case the machines are locked to prevent blue-collar workers from altering the system. Efficiency seems to be all on the side of the unlocked machines; a large staff of white-collar programmers does not have to be maintained, an information system does not have to be developed so that blue collar operators can tell white-collar programmers that something has gone wrong, and downtime is reduced, since the program corrections can be made instantly without waiting for the white-collar programmers to show up. But American firms have mostly opted for locked machines.

The issue is one of power and control. With a locked machine, management has more control and can set the pace of work. Numerically controlled locked machine tools were in fact sold in America as devices for recapturing the initiative in the pace of work from blue-collar assembly-line workers. In the words of *Iron Age*, a machine-tool journal, "Workers and their unions have too much say in manufacturers' destiny. Many metal working executives feel that large, sophisticated Flexible Manufacturing Systems can help wrest some of that control away from labor and put it back in the hands of management where it belongs."[70] If control is the issue, locked machines dominate unlocked machines. If enhanced productivity is the issue, unlocked machines dominate locked ones.

American managers also face a direct reduction in their own salaries if they become efficient in reducing white-collar overheads. Traditionally, they get paid based on the number of workers that report to them. To take actions to make the firm more efficient is to reduce their own salary and employment opportunities, since a reduction in white-collar employees will reduce the number of people that report to them and the need for bosses. When faced with a current and future reduction in their own prospects, few executives are going to enthusiastically support any reduction in white-collar overheads.

Consider word processors and the failure of office automation to yield the predicted gains in productivity. The source of the failure is to be found in the interaction of a number of institutional realities. To use office automation efficiently requires major changes in office sociology. The efficient way to use word processors is to eliminate secretaries or clerks and to require managers to type their own memos and call up their own files. But a personal secretary is an office badge of prestige and power. No one wants to give up that badge. To shift to new technology also requires those managers without good keyboard skills to go through a transition period where they will look clumsy and where they will get work done more slowly as they learn how to type. Few American bosses can maintain their prestige, power, and self-respect while publicly looking clumsy in front of their subordinates. As a result, they will order the assembly-line worker to shift from welding by hand to robot welding, but they will not order themselves to shift from manual typing and filing to computer typing and filing. Those who might consider doing their own typing and filing face peer pressure not to upset standard office procedures and are reluctant to adopt a new technology that will require them to fire those who are physically close to them. If those below you can be fired, then those above you can fire you.

No one likes to be reminded of that fact, and as a result American industry is much more ruthless when it comes to eliminating blue-collar workers than it is in the case of white-collar workers. Almost every American firm has a vice-president for factory productivity; almost no American firm has a vice-president for office productivity. In the 1981–1982 recession, 90 percent of the firms that laid off blue-collar workers did not lay off a single white-collar worker.[71] In 1991 New York City announced plans to lay off twelve thousand employees—only forty-nine were managers.

In Europe and Japan, where management salaries are more dependent on seniority (that is, less dependent upon merit or the number of people reporting to them), keeping white-collar overhead low is not seen as a personal threat to one's own wages or prospects as it is in the United States. With lifetime employment in Japan and severe legal restrictions on firing workers in Europe, it is also very difficult to fire blue-collar workers while hiring white-collar workers. To know *everything* and to give a lot of orders are not European or Japanese management styles. Paradoxically, the real threat of firing managers if efficiency rises, even if it is seldom done, ends up producing an American system with more managers than the European or Japanese systems, where there is little real danger of a manager being fired because of improvements in management efficiency.

Standard operating procedures have a strong hold on the human mind. An executive of an American electronics firm recently told me about an incident where management investigated a Taiwanese facility to determine why it had much lower production costs than an identical American facility, even after correcting for wage differences. The cost differences were to be found in a lot of small standard operating procedures such as the provision of telephones for every white-collar worker. Most white-collar workers make very few business phone calls, and when they do, they could easily use a central phone bank. No one phone is terribly expensive, but when one adds up the costs of phones for thousands of white-collar workers, it becomes an important cost. Blue-collar workers aren't given private phones, but taking phones away from white-collar workers would be traumatic for them, a symbol that they weren't important. Replicate such factors a few times, however, and one is talking about significant cost savings. The savings aren't made, however, because to do so would require changes in standard operating procedures.

What one believes makes a difference. Ideological blinders can imprison anyone in low-productivity modes of behavior.

ANALYSIS OF THE GAME

A smart coach, knowing that he has a group of American football players who must be transformed into world football players, watches a lot of game films to see how the pros in the rest of the world play soccer. He seeks to understand his opponents. What they do cannot always be copied, but it must always be understood.

The following eight industry "game films" (semiconductors and computers, commercial aircraft, consumer electronics, materials, chemicals, textiles, motor vehicles, and machine tools) are derived from my participation in MIT's *Made in America* study. More details on these eight industries are available in that three-volume work.[72] In the United States, of the eight game films, one describes a winner (commercial aircraft); one describes a failure (consumer electronics). Two are key support industries (machine tools and materials), while two others are key determinants of our national income (motor vehicles, textiles). One is a process industry (chemicals) and the final grouping represents product industries (semiconductors, computers, and copiers).

While it should be said that somewhere in America one can find firms and individuals who are cognizant of all of the weaknesses about to be seen in these game films (many successful turnaround stories are chronicled in the MIT study), these individual efforts have not yet translated themselves into a national effort similar to the one that followed the post-Sputnik shock of the 1950s and the man-on-the-moon effort of the 1960s. Collectively, these eight industries are a story about Americans having to play defense for the first time in half a century and finding it difficult to do so.

Information Industries: Brilliant but Unstable

Microelectronics began as an American industry. All of the great scientific advances necessary to permit the development of this industry—big and little computers, the transistor, the semiconductor chip—were American advances. Huge fortunes have been made in new start-ups in this industry, and it has given the word *entrepreneur* a new vitality and validity. Its firms—IBM, Digital, Intel, Apple, Xerox—are some of the leading lights of American industry.

Yet the world of microelectronics is a world where America's market share is falling rapidly.[73] Semiconductor production has fallen from 60 to 40 percent of the world market in less than a decade. The three leading merchant semiconductor companies (by *merchant* is meant a company that sells to others) are now all Japanese—NEC, Toshiba, and Hitachi. The National Advisory Committee on Semiconductors report to the president and Congress was entitled *A Strategic Industry At Risk*.[74]

The behavior pattern that leads to this industry-wide weakness begins with a high-tech start-up firm exploding into prominence with some brilliant initial products. The firm, however, cannot repeat its successes; it does not grow into the IBM of tomorrow. Earlier products become obsolete. As old markets become more competitive and sales decline, the internal funds to finance new growth dry up, fully vested employees begin to defect to other newer firms to make their own entrepreneurial start-up fortunes, proprietary knowledge is sold (often to foreign firms) to raise funds, and foreign competitors use this knowledge to push prices and profits down. Unable to make the necessary rates of return on investment, the American firm exits.

If one looks either abroad at those who have come to dominate the semiconductor business or at those that remain successful in the United States (IBM and AT&T, which produce semiconductor chips for their own internal consumption), one sees the same vertically integrated firms. The only difference is that the Japanese firms produce more semiconductor chips than they can use internally and sell their excess production on the open market. The American firms typically produce less than they need and use outside sources as buffer producers to smooth the inevitable upswings and downswings in the market.

The pattern of decline is clear. Licensing agreements in exchange for market access and government-financed cooperative R&D projects brought the Japanese firms up to speed technologically. World market demand fell, excess production capacity rose, and American firms quit investing to maintain their profit margins. The Japanese firms continued to build capacity, and on the next cyclical recovery, they had the capacity to insure prompt delivery. The Japanese market share went up in the early stages of a cyclical recovery and stayed up, since their new customers remained loyal to insure prompt delivery on the next cyclical rebound. American producers began building new capacity during the upswing, but when it came on-line a year or two later, it was often too late. The new plants failed to earn the required profits that would allow the next generation of plants to be financed.

Because the main users of semiconductors were also their main producers in Japan (especially when one widens the definition of a firm to include the large industrial groups, such as Mitsui or Sumitomo), much of the Japanese market was effectively closed to American competition. Because of this secure domestic market, Japanese firms could weather cyclical downturns and continue to invest in both R&D and new production facilities. Within a few iterations of the business cycle, American producers found themselves having slipped from being the dominant producers to being marginal producers.

As the American industry shrank, the domestic manufacturers of semiconductor materials and equipment vanished. Here again, the equipment makers in Japan were not stand-alone firms. Sometimes they were direct subsidiaries of the large firms that also made semiconductors, but they were always firms with close associations with those semiconductor makers and their industrial groups. Given these relationships, American firms were not going to be given preference on the first shipments of any new equipment or new materials that were in short supply. Not surprisingly, companies supply their own needs before they supply outsider needs. If American firms had to rely on Japanese equipment makers (and they increasingly did), they were not going to be on the leading edge when it came to new products.

The result was an uneven contest between small, single-product, inexperienced, underfinanced start-ups and the heavyweights of Japanese industry. In this case David did not defeat Goliath. The moral of the story: A solid industrial structure beats individual brilliance.

America is not used to having to design national strategies in order to help its industries catch up with dominant producers in the rest of the world, but in this case it had to do something. A cooperative R&D program, Sematech, was organized, but it had to be hidden as an effort necessary for national defense (half the funds come from DARPA—Defense Advanced Research Products Agency) rather than admitting its true purpose. This handicapped the effort. What the military wants in a semiconductor chip (unsurpassed performance) is not what civilian industry needed (reliability and cheapness). In 1990 a cooperative civilian production consortium, U.S. Memories, could not get off the ground and Motorola announced that it was making its next round of major investments in chip production in Sendai, Japan.[75]

In contrast to semiconductors, the computer market has remained much more of an American preserve. In 1990 America still had a 65 percent overall market share, although its worldwide market share had fallen 17 percentage points in the previous four years.[76] Only in laptops do the Japanese dominate, and even here an American design (Zenith—now part of a French company, Bull) has the largest market share. Outside of Japan, the market shares of American computer companies are not eroding, although America's export-import balance in computers has declined sharply.

In this industry, to be there first is to have a powerful built-in defense mechanism. Enormous investments have been made in computer software. No one wants to buy computers that are quickly obsolete or require a disruptive changeover from one software system to another. But the same will be true if the Japanese come to dominate the first widespread civilian applications of supercomputers.

Knowing this, the Japanese are trying to develop computer-software factories that they think will allow them to dominate the computer-software industry in the twenty-first century. Instead of letting every programmer write his or her programs as an individual artist might, their strategy is to attempt to force everyone to write programs with the same reusable modules. If successful, this allows the use of less skilled programmers and makes it much easier and faster to modify existing programs. While program quality might be slightly inferior, Japanese computer-software costs would be much lower. The aim, as in other industries conquered by the Japanese, is to dominate in process technologies.[77]

Commercial Aircraft: New Competition

America's commercial-aircraft industry grew up in a symbiotic relationship with government. The production of military aircraft financed research and development on products and processes that could often be carried over into commercial products (the Boeing 707 was a modified military-transport plane). Regulated airlines were guaranteed the fares necessary to pay for high-tech engineering staffs and to finance rapid shifts to more sophisticated aircraft. Most of the markets for commercial aircraft were in the United States, and suppliers and users worked together much as if they were in the same business groups. Technologically sophisticated users pushed technologically sophisticated suppliers. After initially defeating the efforts of the British Comet to become a major supplier, the American commercial-aircraft industry came to be dominated by three firms (McDonnell Douglas, Lockheed, and Boeing).

Given the enormous amounts of up-front development money (between two billion and four billion dollars), long periods of negative cash flow (five to six years), and even longer time lags until costs are covered (ten to fourteen years), no private company was ever going to break into this market against the entrenched American position. But the Europeans were determined to break in, especially the West Germans, who had been prohibited by treaty from building aircraft for a number of years after World War II. The Europeans' first attempt to break into the industry, the supersonic Concorde, was a technical success but an economic failure. The second attempt, Airbus Industries, was organized by the British, French, West German, and Spanish governments. Years have passed and twenty-six billion dollars has been put into the effort, but Airbus has become a serious competitor that is now planning to double its production capacity by 1995.[78, 79] Without government help, Airbus could not have gotten started and could not have survived. The Europeans claim, however, that they are only doing overtly what the American government had done covertly twenty-five years earlier through military procurement.

Meanwhile, the government-industry partnership in the

United States has frayed. Deregulation and lower fares led American airlines to cut back on their engineering staffs. Increasingly, planes were sold to leasing companies and not directly to airlines. Airline financiers replaced airline engineers as purchasing decision makers. Attractive financial packages came to be more important than technological sophistication. With route instability, the business became riskier, and it was harder to predict what the demand would be for aircraft of different sizes. Boeing delayed the introduction of new aircraft, leaving holes in its family of aircraft that Airbus could fill.

As the rest of the world became wealthier, less and less of the market for aircraft was located in the United States. In Europe, Airbus Industries effectively had a captive home market, since their owners, the governments, also owned their national airlines. As a result it was easier for Airbus Industries to pick off an American airline customer than it was for an American manufacturer to pick off a European airline customer.

While the U.S. civilian-aircraft industry had military roots, its principal producer (Boeing) for many years had no orders for military aircraft. Even if it had had orders, the characteristics of military aircraft were becoming so different from those of commercial aircraft that the easy transfer of research and production processes was probably a thing of the past. What had been a close relationship with government became a distant one.

Americans claim that Airbus is not making, and will never make, a profit. Europeans counterclaim that Airbus Industries climbed into the black in 1990.[80] The truth depends upon how the cost accounting is done. If interest is paid on the government funds that have been advanced, Airbus Industries is losing money and will probably never be able to repay its initial start-up costs. If government funds are treated not as loans but as equity investments, and governments are paid a fee based on the number of planes produced (as they are), then Airbus Industries is profitable and will be profitable. Profitable or unprofitable, there is no doubt that Airbus is a serious threat to the American producers.

Meanwhile, Japan sits in the wings, wanting to put together a successful government-industry partnership to make it a player in the market for commercial aircraft. How does one play against foreign "industrial policies"? The current American strategy is to force the European governments to quit subsidizing Airbus Industries with a GATT ruling that what they are doing is illegal. Make them play by American rules!

Can a commercial-aircraft manufacturer survive without an interested government partner? No one knows for sure. America might run an experiment to see if Boeing can survive alone, but if the experiment turns out to be a failure and Boeing does not survive, what happens then? Aircraft are America's largest single export. The Airbus experience suggests that getting back into commercial-aircraft manufacturing is very expensive and will be very lengthy if the United States is pushed into a marginal position.

Consumer Electronics: Sequential Retreat into Oblivion

The history of consumer electronics is a history of sequential retreat into oblivion from which an American industry may never again emerge. Radios and other audio products were the first to go. Ninety-six percent were produced in the United States in 1955, 30 percent in 1965, and nearly zero in 1975.

Then television went. Here the retreat was helped by the unrestricted licensing policies of the technical leaders, RCA and Philips, of the Netherlands. By the late 1980s the U.S. television industry had dwindled down to one survivor, Zenith, which had a 15 percent market share. In 1991 it reached a broad agreement to share its technologies with a Korean firm, Goldstar. The Korean firm wanted to use Zenith's flat-screen technologies on high-end televisions, since it was worried that its supply of Japanese technology was being choked off by Japanese manufacturers that saw it as a future threat in the market place.[81] Yet televisions represent a huge market—six billion dollars, or 22 percent of all consumer-electronics products sold.

Home video recorders never got going. Ampex held the

original patents and was active in the professional market, but it lacked the resources in engineering and manufacturing to successfully bring costs down to a level where home systems could be sold. Today, foreign producers are successfully moving upscale and threatening its professional market.

A wide variety of new products are on the way. Digital audio tape (DAT) was introduced into Japan and Europe in 1987, but not into the United States until 1990. High-definition television (HDTV) for production, broadcasting, and video recording is coming, but it is coming faster in Japan and Europe than in the United States. Interactive video disks will be used to store sound and computer data. None of these products are apt to be American success stories.

American firms run research operations where R&D spending is roughly proportional to sales. As sales decline, research declines along with it, and it becomes harder and harder for firms to bounce back on the next generation of new products. Lacking the manufacturing experience in building the last generation of products, firms become less and less competent to build the next generation of products.

Autos and consumer electronics are the only places where one learns mass manufacturing. The consumer-electronics industry buys half of all of the semiconductors sold in Japan. Without consumer electronics, it is difficult for either the robotics or semiconductor industry to get the volume to lower unit costs to the point where they can compete. Since the Japanese semiconductor firms are members of the same business groups as the consumer-electronic firms, American sales to Japanese consumer-electronics firms are minimal.

Once mastered in consumer electronics, mass-manufacturing techniques can often be transferred to other areas, among them, industrial electronics. Having conquered consumer electronics, foreign competitors are now focusing their attention on industrial electronics—a profitable and still American industry. Military electronics, the next step, is just coming into view on the horizon.

The consumer-electronics industry is dominated by the Japanese, but it need not be so. Philips, a European company, had sales of eight billion dollars in consumer electronics in 1986, second only to Matsushita. It is successful in the American market. What is the difference between the European firm that succeeded and the American firms that failed?

To some extent, the American government thought that consumer electronics was not a market worth keeping. During their initial incursion into the American market, Japanese TV manufacturers were selling sets in the United States well below the prices at which they were selling in Japan—a practice known as "dumping." The American government was basically indifferent and did nothing. But the real difference was commitment. Philips was not going to be pushed out of the industry. It committed itself to the necessary product and process R&D. It committed itself to achieving competitive manufacturing costs. The American firms were not committed to consumer electronics. Their commitment was to their historic rate of return on investment.

The sequence of the American retreat was as stylized as a Kabuki play. American firms would set high return-on-investment (ROI) goals. Foreign firms would force ROIs below these hurdle rates with aggressive pricing in some market segment. Within a short period of time, the American firms would retreat from that market segment, since they were not making the necessary ROI. Once that market segment was conquered, the foreign firms would move on to price aggressively in some other market segment. The American firms would once again retreat. The most recent example of this behavior was the sale of GE/RCA's remaining consumer-electronics business to Thomson, a French firm. Those running the GE/RCA consumer-electronics divisions were told by headquarters that they had to earn a 15 percent rate of return on investment or be sold. They couldn't, and they were sold.

Publically announced, high-ROI requirements allow foreign producers to play their American counterparts like violins. The Americans announce that they must make a 15 percent rate of return, or they will leave the industry. The foreigners price aggressively to guarantee that no one, including themselves, can make a 15 percent rate of return. Within a relatively short period of time, foreigners know that this pricing behavior will cause the Americans to exit. Once the Americans have been driven out of the market, foreign firms take over the American market share and raise prices to earn good rates of return. The only uncertainty is which of the foreign producers will inherit the biggest market share when the Americans exit.

For a time American firms can retreat to high-ROI market segments, but eventually they reach the point where there are no high-profit areas left. Further retreat becomes impossible. This point has been reached in consumer electronics, and American firms have retreated into industrial electronics where the ROI is better. But this is merely a temporary resting place. When the attack comes in industrial electronics, those higher rates of return will also vanish. Where then will pro- ducers retreat—to military electronics?

Insisting on a 15 percent rate of return when the rest of the world does not insist on a 15 percent rate of return is in the long run a strategy for going out of business. Going out of business is not a business in which Americans should want to excel, but in consumer electronics they became very good at it.

Steel: Missing or Catching a Technological Revolution

The American steel industry is a simple story. Demand per unit of GNP fell as alternative materials replaced steel and as steel become more efficient (stronger and lighter), with the result that, for example, fewer tons were needed per bridge built. Use per unit of GNP was essentially cut in half in the thirty years between 1950 and 1980. High-cost, integrated American producers watched as their markets shrank, and ever-larger shares of it were lost to imports and minimills.

One part of the industry, the larger integrated steel produc- ers, were laggards when it came to three technological revolu- tions—oxygen furnaces, continuous casting, and computer controls. Contrary to popular opinion, in the 1960s and 1970s the United States spent amounts equal to Japan on research and on new equipment. The problem was not inadequate spending but spending on the wrong research and the wrong equipment.

Another part of the industry, the ministeel mills such as those operated by Chaparral, were technologically advanced.

Their managers aggressively built new mills that used electric furnaces and continuous casting, pioneered new management techniques, built cooperative labor-management relations that cut labor costs (wages were high—$17 to $22.50 per hour—but restrictive work rules were absent), aggressively scoured the world for new technologies that they could buy, and sought close connections with their customers. In 1987 the hours of labor necessary for these plants to produce a ton of steel (1.8 hours) were less than one third those of the integrated producers. In contrast, the integrated producers never participated in joint R&D projects with the auto makers (their major customers) to improve steel stamping—projects that led to significant gains in Japan, where 50 percent of new product ideas were thought to originate with customers.

Not surprisingly, the laggards, companies years behind in technology, shrank, and the leaders, those firms ahead in technology, grew. Recently, the laggards have closed the gap separating them from their foreign competitors (hours of work per ton of steel are only slightly higher than those of Japan—6.4 versus 6). While the productivity of basic operations is now approaching the Japanese level (although the five most productive mills in the world still lie outside of the United States), the quality of the output does not yet match the best in Japan, Korea, or Germany in products such as high-grade arctic pipe, high-performance light and heavy plates, and sheet products. The quality of flat-rolled sheet can, for example, be improved by continuous casting, continuous annealing, vacuum degassing, and computer controls. In the late 1980s no U.S. firm had incorporated all of these techniques—though most Japanese firms had.

The real question, however, is not the past but whether the integrated American firms will be able to catch the next technological wave. Have the factors that led them to miss past technological waves been corrected?

Bureaucratic pressures seem to explain many past mistakes. Upper management had a large financial and technical stake in the open-hearth process, and builders of open hearths applied pressure on steel firms not to adopt the basic oxygen furnace (BOF). American engineering firms opposed the BOF, since they did not have the expertise to design the new plants. Makers of refractory brick were unable or unwilling to produce the new types of bricks that were necessary to line the inside of a BOF. Once BOFs were being built, the shorter tap-to-tap times required immediate results from metallurgical quality tests. The most obvious answer was computer controls. U.S. management backed off from this solution, citing the difficulty of developing sensing devices that could withstand the extreme conditions in the BOF vessel and the problems of developing software. Even as late as 1980 there were no genuine control-feedback systems used on American BOF plants.

Where Americans were technological leaders, such as in the development of the argon-oxygen-decarburization process (used to make stainless steel), the American industry retained its economic leadership. In 1986 Inland was the world's low-cost producer for cold-rolled steel coils, and Armco's new vacuum-degassing system produces a superior product at a cost lower than any other steel supplier.

Technological leaders remain economic leaders; technological laggards become losers.

The history of the steel industry is less interesting for what it says about the future of steel than for what it says about the revolution that is coming in made-to-order new materials such as ceramics, composites, and superconductors. There is a new technological wave clearly visible on the horizon. But these new materials won't be produced in America unless Americans are better at being technological leaders in the materials of the future than they were at being technological leaders in the materials of the past.

Chemicals: German Skills

Prior to World War II, chemicals were at the center of German economic strength. After the war, for a period of time American firms were large investors in Europe, but in the last two decades those investment flows have reversed. Many of the earlier American investments have been sold to the Europeans, and the Europeans now own 25 percent of what used to be American output. While Dow Chemical, America's second largest producer, divested $1.8 billion in assets and pulled out of Japan, Saudi Arabia, South Korea, and Yugoslavia, in 1986 alone European firms acquired eight U.S. chemical companies or major chemical units of diversified companies at a total cost of nearly $6 billion.

The three largest firms (Bayer, BASF, and Hoechst) are each more than 50 percent larger than the largest U.S. firm (Du Pont). Imperial Chemical, a British company, is also almost 30 percent larger than Du Pont. After Du Pont, size drops off very rapidly in the United States. The fifth largest producer (Atlantic Richfield) produces less than half the chemical sales of Du Pont and would lie far down on the world's tables of the largest producers. American firms are essentially successful as niche players—only Du Pont plays in the big leagues.

Germany has long dominated the chemical business. Chemicals were the first of the science-based industries, and in the first half of the nineteenth-century, Germany was the leader in science. Other major industries, such as steel or autos, were based on brilliant tinkerers rather than deep scientific understanding. It was not until many years after Henry Bessemer, for example, that anyone knew exactly what, scientifically, was going on inside his blast furnace. Henry Ford's assembly line was a brilliant innovation but not one based on high science. Individuals like him, as brilliant as they were, could not have been successful in chemicals, since from the very beginning scientific knowledge was necessary to construct new compounds or synthesize those found in nature.

The reemergence of Germany as the dominant player is not surprising when one thinks of the two basic ingredients of a successful chemical business—enormous amounts of capital and a strong scientific and engineering establishment. Germany, with its much higher savings and investment rates (and, hence, lower real rates of interest), and with a higher education system that is tuned to educating more than twice as large a proportion of its university students in engineering and science when compared to that of the United States, relied on exactly the same factors to recapture the chemical industry after World War II that it used to create the industry almost one hundred years earlier.

In the pharmaceutical area the American industry is handicapped by a slower approval process for its new products. If one looks at the twenty new drugs approved in the United States in 1986, 10.5 years elapsed from laboratory development to FDA approval. Abroad, only 6.2 years were required. Not surprisingly, fifteen of these twenty new drugs had already been approved abroad when they were approved in the United States. In the countries that approved these drugs first, the average legal approval time was ten months—or less than a third of the time necessary to get the formal approval of the FDA in the United States. Because of faster approval, even U.S. firms choose to introduce their new products abroad.[82]

No one can run a successful industry with such handicaps. If American players are to be niche players, they must be quick on their feet. A big part of being quick on one's feet is a government civil service that is equally quick on its feet.

Textiles: Beating Wages Down Is Not the Name of the Game

The history of the American textile industry is essentially a search for low wages. Established in New England, it moved first to the Southeast, and then to offshore production bases. But today's offshore production bases are only a temporary solution. Americans have no long-run competitive advantage when it comes to managing in the Third World. Third Worlders can sooner or later do it better. If the only issue is low wages, there are always others who are or will be better at playing the game. The trends are clear: Apparel imports rose from 2 percent in 1963 to 50 percent in 1988, and foreign manufacturers doubled their market share in the past decade.

If lower wages were the solution, American firms should be more successful than those in other developed countries. The American firms have more fully developed offshore production bases, and onshore American textile wages are well below those found in the rest of the industrial world. Yet the industry has not achieved the success found in other high-wage countries.

The route to success is not low wages. All one has to do is to look at the successful textile industries in other high-wage countries to see that something other than wages is at issue. Germany, for example, is the world's largest exporter of textiles, despite wages that are four dollars per hour higher than those in the United States. Successful textile-machinery industries—an industry in an advanced state of collapse in the United States—exist in Switzerland, Germany, Italy, Japan, and France. These firms simply offered products (no water- or air-jet looms are manufactured in America), quality, reliability, and, ultimately, service that wasn't offered by American machinery producers. If anything, the European producers have been successful despite facing more handicaps than the Americans. Unions are much stronger in Europe, and restrictive labor legislation is much more constraining. Layoffs and plant closings are highly regulated.

Instead of disinvesting in the domestic industry or switching to offshore production, the Germans invested heavily in new technologies, labor-saving machinery, and new plants to turn out higher-quality goods. Investments per employee more than doubled between 1970 and 1986, and the capital-labor ratio in German textiles is now more than 40 percent higher than it is in autos, and almost double that in machine tools—ratios not to be found in the United States.

Foreign success is not to be found in better government protection. Germany is the largest per capita importer of textiles and apparel, importing four times as much as the United States. Yet at the same time, Germany has successfully modernized and transformed its own textile sector. Productivity jumped 24 percent from 1980 to 1986. Exports have risen from 11 percent of total output in 1960 to 48 percent of production by 1984.

Both Italy (the world's second largest textile exporter and another country with textile wages above those found in the United States) and Germany operate in market niches in which they experience relatively little competition from low-wage producers. These are niches where design, quality, responsiveness to fashion, and rapid adjustments are important. The Italians developed close collaborations with well-known designers who produced signature collections for ready-made production. The introduction of this system was facilitated with substantial governmental aid.

In contrast, U.S. producers have traditionally focused on long production runs of standard goods for mass markets. As incomes rise, however, individuals want to differentiate themselves with their clothes, and the mass market becomes increasingly a series of niche markets. Only now are the American producers starting to organize themselves to serve these markets. Milliken, for example, has reduced its average lot size from 20,000 yards a few years ago to 4,000 yards today, and jet dyeing permits it to dye lots of 1,000 to 2,000 yards.

Flexibility is key in a niche strategy. To get it, the cooperation of the work force is central, but that cannot be won if the goal is to beat down wages. The comments of a manager of a successful high-fashion denim mill in Bergamo, Italy, illustrate the way in which workers are wooed by his firm, while his memories of a visit to a denim manufacturer in Texas, where the workers' faces were so blue from denim dust that they could not even be identified, reflect American management indifference: "I have no blue workers! The union wouldn't let me get away with it. I have had to invest in air cleaning systems that remove all that dust. And it's far better for us that we've done this. We operate better in a cleaner plant. Most important, you can't hope to get real cooperation from 'blue men.' We're at a point now with the unions that when we decided we needed to move to seven-day-a-week operations and the bishop attacked us publicly for Sunday shifts, it was the unions that came to our defense."

Similar efforts are starting in United States textiles. Milliken now channels about 2 percent of sales into R&D. It builds many of its own machines to protect its proprietary ownership. New products, such as a soil-release process that is embedded in a polyester fiber, have been invented. Most of its cash flow is reinvested, and its time horizons are much longer than most of the rest of the industry. Today it is attempting to do what the Germans did fifteen to twenty years ago.

If the American textile industry is to survive, it will have to eliminate the obstacles that now exist to the diffusion of the successful strategies found in other high-wage countries. The survival of the mass-production model is a monument to the tyranny of old ideas. Mass production built the American textile industry in New England, but it is not the wave of the future. Small, high-quality production runs are the name of the new game. Many American textile-mill managers have had few, if any, contacts with the apparel firms that purchase their fabrics. Close customer contacts are necessary in the German or Italian model. One needs to know what the customer will need tomorrow.

A different human-resource strategy is central. A good firm is not one that pays low wages. A good firm is one that has the productivity to pay high wages so that it can hire high-skilled individuals who can operate sophisticated new technologies. Many of the processes found abroad could not be used in the United States because of the unskilled nature of the American work force. Yet American plant managers do not seem to recognize this. They still have the American tinkerer in the back of their minds. They don't see a high-technology textile industry.

Firms in different parts of the industry have to be willing to work together to help each other solve common problems. Apparel companies guard their predictions on annual demand, but this prevents suppliers from stabilizing their operations. Unexpected demands are intrinsically low-wage, offshore demands. No one builds capital-intensive plants without assured markets. In America six-month time horizons are common. These time horizons fit the old labor-intensive American industry (rent a loft and lay them off when you don't need them), but they do not fit the high-tech, capital-intensive industries that have been the source of success in other wealthy countries.

The Formula for Success: High Skills + Flexible Specialization

Autos: The Difficulty of Changing When Successful

The auto industry is America's largest and the major customer for many other industries, purchasing 21 percent of our steel alloy, 16 percent of our aluminum, and 53 percent of our rubber. Without an auto industry, it is difficult for a machine-tool industry to survive. Without an auto industry and a consumer-electronics industry, it is impossible for machine tools to survive.

For all practical purposes, the mass auto industry was invented in America, yet combined imports (Japanese and European) and transplant production (Japanese) have risen from less than 1 percent of sales in 1955 to more than one third of sales in 1991.[83] In twenty years America has gone from an auto-export surplus to an auto-import deficit of sixty billion dollars—the largest single element in its poor trade performance. Imports continued to rise after 1985, even though the dollar fell sharply in value and imported car prices rose sharply. The rest of the world was offering something Americans wanted.

Imports are squeezing the American producers at both ends. Korean and Japanese imports dominate the low end of the market, and European imports dominate the high end of the market, although the Japanese are rapidly moving upscale. Only 17 percent of the cars imported into the United States come from Western Europe, but they account for one third of imports on a value basis. Since per unit profits are much higher on expensive cars, European firms probably earn more profits on auto sales in the United States than do their Japanese counterparts.

However, U.S. car makers must accept some of the responsibility for this dual squeeze. They did not foresee the oil shocks and the shift in demand to small cars and were not interested in producing small cars since profit margins were low. But the American producers also ceded the most profitable high end of their market—a segment that was growing rapidly with rising per capita incomes.

In an industry where American production used to dwarf that of the rest of the world, Americans now stand third. Japan builds more cars; Europe both buys and builds more cars. To the extent that the auto industry is built on scale economies, those economies increasingly belong to foreign producers.

Unions and managements can both be blamed. Managers were inward-looking and shortsighted; union work rules stifled productivity and led to wage claims that productivity could not support. But the problems go much deeper. The last major innovation that was first installed in an American car was the automatic transmission in the 1940s. Four-wheel steering and drive, turbocharging, and antilock braking systems were all first adopted on imported models. In 1985 the three leading Japanese producers recorded more than twice as many new patents as the three American producers—Ford, General Motors, and Chrysler.

Past American success was built on a few simple axioms. The American consumer wanted variety only as long as it did not cost very much. Skills were narrowly tailored in accordance with the dictates of Taylorism named for the father of scientific management. (There were, for example, door-lock engineers.) Beyond this, human investments were not needed. Labor was a commodity to be hired and fired as demand rose and fell. Designs were to last for years. As a result, tooling was locked into particular models for years at a time with dedicated machines.

Suppliers were treated in much the same fashion as the work force—marginal elements in the production system that were utilized in boom periods but jettisoned during the troughs. Reducing suppliers' profits and workers' wages were equivalent ways to raise company profits. Neither workers or suppliers were expected to show any initiative to improve the way the job was done. "Don't think—do what you are told!" might have been the organizing axiom.

The system was to be robust so that no strike or supplier bottleneck could bring it to a halt—hence, large inventories. The quality levels necessary for salability were to be achieved with checking and rework. For forty years it was a system that worked brilliantly. But the system of production organization and the accompanying market strategy perfected by the American auto industry in the 1920s was eventually surpassed by foreign competitors that developed better production systems and coupled them with market strategies better attuned to a rapidly changing motor-vehicle market.[84] What had worked before, ceased to work. The American industry could not return to the most central of its ancient virtues—cosmetically differentiated mass production. New modes of operation were required.

The Europeans and the Japanese had been forced to change earlier. Their internal markets were small and segmented. And in export markets, a car suitable for Italy was not suitable for Sweden. Consequently, they had to be efficient at a much lower level of production and had to produce cars that were really different—not cars that were only cosmetically differentiated with a few pieces of external sheet metal. As a result, the Europeans pioneered real product differentiation. Assemblers were aided in this effort by technologically oriented suppliers such as Robert Bosch.

The Japanese pioneered flexible manufacturing, in which within minutes, the same plant is shifted from the production of one model to another. Die changes that took eight to twenty-four hours in American plants could be done in five minutes in Japanese plants. They could not afford to build the separate plants that the Americans built. Perfect first-time quality—not acceptable rework quality—was the goal. Waste, including inventories, defects, excess plant space, and all unnecessary human effort was to be totally eliminated. Continuous incremental improvements were every worker's major job. Because workers could not be laid off, the human-resource base had to be made into a strategic asset. Above all, management organized a team—assemblers, workers, and suppliers—it did not enter into adversarial relationships. Using these techniques, the Japanese planner could work on a seven-and-half-year cycle (from the initial conception to the last vehicle to roll off the assembly line), while the American product planner was stuck with a thirteen-to-fifteen-year cycle. Since people want new and different cars, the speed of the Japanese becomes an overwhelming advantage.

By copying foreign practices, American firms have improved in "time to market," productivity, and product quality. But they have not yet achieved parity. The best American plants are not quite as good as the best Japanese plants, and the worst American plants are far worse than the worst Japanese plants. Japanese plants in the United States cannot yet duplicate the results of the best plants in Japan, but they demonstrate that real improvements can be made using American workers, and that American culture is more attuned to Japanese practices than many thought. The most famous instance of an American manufacturer adopting Japanese methods is the NUMMI GM-Toyota plant in California, which has demonstrated an ability to sharply raise productivity and quality using an existing plant and work force.

Change has been hard in the auto industry, and even though the American auto companies know that they need to change and have already made many changes, they do not yet have it made in the sense that one can with high probability predict that their market share has bottomed out. The difficulty of the problem can be seen in the J. D. Power survey of the ten cars sold in the United States that produced the greatest consumer satisfaction. At the beginning of the 1980s, the American auto companies knew that they had a job to do. Only two of the top ten cars were made by the Big Three American producers. In the 1980s they worked hard and made many improvements. But at the beginning of the 1990s, only one of the top ten cars were made by the Big Three.[85] The Big Three had gotten better, but the rest of the world had also gotten better and at an even faster rate. American car makers had reduced a 300 percent difference between themselves and foreign competitors in defects per car to 50 percent, but there still was a difference.[86] The quality gap had not closed.

If current trends are also an indication of the future, eventually, the gap in defects per car will close. But Japanese producers are now widening the gap in time to market and in their ability to produce niche-market cars where one has to be profitable on smaller volumes.

World-Class Manufacturing Without World-Class Tools

If you buy the very best from Japan, it has already been in Toyota Motors for two years, and if you buy from West Germany, it has already been with BMW for a year-and-a-half.
—director of GM machine-tool study

In good times we were too busy getting product out to develop new ones; and in bad times, we didn't have the money or the people.
—machine-tool-industry veteran

If you tried to get a license, the auto companies tried to break it. They didn't want one source, so they refused to pay the royalties, and the small guys couldn't fight it. That destroyed incentives to innovate because you would only get one-third of the order at most.

—machine-tool builder

U.S. companies hesitate to go to high-tech systems because they don't have the people.

Americans think that their people are too dumb to buy sophisticated equipment.

—two machine-tool builders

We saw 50 or more FMS (flexible manufacturing systems) vendors, each of whom had shipped at least 10 systems that year. We, on the other hand, can do maybe two a year, and have 100 customers waiting. What's the difference?

The users. In Germany users install the systems because they are more technically sophisticated than Americans. They have the manufacturing engineers, the shop floor people, the skills to take responsibility for their systems. We can't do as many systems as their builders—first because ours are more sophisticated than many of theirs, and second, because our manufacturers don't have the skills. We must rebuild our manufacturing engineering base in this country.

—American builder at Hanover trade show

Is it possible to have world-class manufacturing without world-class machine tools? No! Is it possible to have world-class tools if one has to depend upon imports? No! Countries with superior machine-tool industries exhibit superior industrial growth, yet by the end of 1990 the United States had dropped out of the top five in machine-tool production.[87] The decision of IBM, the world's largest and most self-sufficient computer company, to enter into cooperative arrangements with American semiconductor machine toolmakers dramatizes the problem. IBM found it could not count on getting the first shipments of new machine tools from foreign manufacturers. What IBM can't do, no American manufacturer can do.

Yet the American machine-tool industry is dissolving. In 1964 America was a net exporter. In 1986, 50 percent of its machine tools were imported, with most of this increase having occurred since 1977. Production is now only half of what it was at its peak. As in the case of autos, the Japanese are pushing up from the low end, and the Germans are pushing down from the high end.

The Japanese success was based upon a MITI industrial policy. The industry standardized its products, firms were pushed to specialize in one or two products, electronic controls all came from one firm (hence, insuring compatibility), and major R&D support was provided for cooperative development of generic flexible manufacturing systems (FMS), advanced FMS, and ultrahigh performance laser systems.

In Germany machine-tool builders usually have a parent manufacturing group that supports a machine-tool arm. Cooperative specialization on high-end niches is the basic strategy. Customers are very sophisticated and work with suppliers. Both users' and builders' work forces are technologically sophisticated. There is an infrastructure of apprenticeship, polytechnical schools, universities, and technical institutes that produces multileveled manufacturing expertise. This educational system provides skilled shop-floor people—practical engineers who can make things work. More research-minded engineers push the limits of process understanding but do so in close association with industry rather than in an ivory tower. Twenty university institutions are dedicated to research in machine tools. These institutions are supported by cooperative linkages with industry, trade unions, state and federal governments, and trade associations.

The sources of the failures in the American machine-tool industry are clear. The industry is highly fragmented into small firms that do not have an infrastructure of support from sophisticated users or government. As the industry moved from being a tinkerer's industry to being an industry based on high science, it fell behind. Users were slow to adopt new technologies, but machine-tool builders were also laggards when it came to using their own products in their own firms to build their own products.

To smooth production, firms backlogged orders when times were good, but this led to long time delays (sometimes years) before customers could get the products they wanted. These long order books could be cherry-picked by foreign firms that could offer quicker delivery. Military production often sent firms off in high-tech directions so complex that no civilian firm could afford to use them. Most important, neither universities nor industry accorded high status to manufacturing engineers and process technologies (something MIT is trying to remedy with its Leaders in Manufacturing and Management of Technology programs). The best students were not drawn into manufacturing, let alone into what was perceived as the mature, conservative, grubby world of machine building. Yet more glamorous activities cannot survive without sharp improvements in this grubby world. In the fall of 1990, Cincinnati Milicron, the last remaining American maker of heavy robots, sold out to a Swiss company. *The New York Times* headline for the article describing the sale read, "America's Last Robot."[88]

WHO IS US?

One can argue, as the Harvard analyst Robert B. Reich does, that as long as the rest of the world is building some of their products in America, "they are us."[89] "The cosmopolitan corporation, eager to avoid the appearance of national favoritism and desirous of a familiar and reliable image wherever it does business around the world, hires and promotes citizens of many nations to its executive ranks." This is a statement with an element of truth and a lot of half truths.

Japanese companies are good citizens in their host American communities.[90] There is no issue about that. He is certainly right when he points out that aid (an R&D subsidy, for example) to American corporations won't necessarily help Americans if the corporation immediately takes whatever is discovered and uses it abroad. American firms are very good—perhaps too good—when it comes to running offshore production facilities. (Foreign sales from such facilities are five times their exports from America.[91]) To insure that government aid ends up helping Americans, it should be focused on increasing the skills of American workers or improving American infrastructure, and not upon financial subsidies for American corporations.

But the last part of the Reich statement quoted above is, as has been shown earlier, wrong. The Japanese corporation does not "promote citizens of many nations to its executive ranks."[92] They are us only if Americans have an equal shot at the good jobs. If the top management jobs are back in Japan and the highest-wage jobs are back in Japan, they are not us. If the best technology is kept back in Japan, they are not us. In fact, Japanese transplant factories in the United States almost never make the most sophisticated, highest value-added products that the company makes. Transplants are also much less likely to make purchases from local American suppliers. On average, foreign firms in America import twice as much per worker as American firms in the same industry. Japanese firms are even worse, importing four times as much per worker as American firms.[93]

In the summer of 1991 Bridgestone Tire announced that it was laying off 5 percent of its work force. All of the workers fired were foreign; none were Japanese.[94] In this case there was no doubt about who was us.

The nature of the problem can be seen in the case of Canada, where the majority of manufacturers are owned by foreigners. Canadians have a good standard of living, but they can never have the best. The best jobs (CEO, CFO, head of research, etc.) are back at headquarters, and that is somewhere else. Even if Canadians were to get those jobs, and they don't, they would have to live abroad. There is something at stake!

AMERICA'S ROLE IN THE TWENTY-FIRST CENTURY

In the second half of the twentieth century, America was the instigator, Japan and Europe, the reactors. In the first half of the twenty-first century, the roles will be reversed. America starts the twenty-first century with a position second to none, but it has lost the big lead that it had in the last half of the twentieth century, and it will succeed or fail in the century that lies ahead to the extent that it learns to play the new economic games being defined by the Europeans and the Japanese.

Chapter 6

GETTING RICH

History teaches a very clear lesson: it is very difficult to become rich. Note the twenty richest countries in the world in 1870 and again in 1988 (center and right) in Table 1. These two lists, dated 128 years apart, are dominated by the same European and North American players.

If the 1870 list is compared with the 1988 internal-purchasing-power list (center column), two very lightly populated, natural-resource-rich oil exporters whose natural resources were unknown in 1870 (the United Arab Emirates and Kuwait) made the list, and three natural-resource-rich countries whose particular natural resources have become less valuable (New Zealand, Argentina, and Chile) fell off the list. In Europe, in a game of musical chairs, Portugal, Spain, and Ireland were replaced by Finland (the twenty-first country in 1870), Luxembourg, and Iceland. None of the three additions

TABLE 6.1
The Richest Countries Per Capita in 1870 and 1988

1870	1988*	1988†
1. Australia	1. United Arab Emirates	1. Switzerland
2. United Kingdom	2. United States	2. Iceland
3. Belgium	3. Canada	3. Japan
4. Switzerland	4. Switzerland	4. Norway
5. Netherlands	5. Norway	5. Finland
6. United States	6. Luxembourg	6. Sweden
7. New Zealand	7. Australia	7. Denmark
8. Denmark	8. Iceland	8. United States
9. Canada	9. Kuwait	9. West Germany
10. France	10. Sweden	10. Canada
11. Argentina	11. West Germany	11. Luxembourg
12. Austria	12. Finland	12. France
13. Italy	13. Japan	13. Austria
14. Germany	14. France	14. United Arab Emirates
15. Spain	15. Denmark	15. Netherlands
16. Norway	16. United Kingdom	16. Belgium
17. Ireland	17. Italy	17. United Kingdom
18. Portugal	18. Belgium	18. Italy
19. Sweden	19. Netherlands	19. Australia
20. Chile	20. Austria	20. New Zealand

SOURCES: J. Bradford De Long, "Productivity Growth, Convergence, and Welfare: Comment," *The American Economic Review* 78, no. 5 (December 1988): 1140–1141. Robert Summers and Alan Heston, "The Penn World Table (Mark 5): An Expanded Set of International Comparisons, 1950–1988," *The Quarterly Journal of Economics* 106 (May 1991): 351–354. *Vital World Statistics* (London: The Economist Books, 1990), p. 40.
*Based on internal purchasing power.
†Based on external purchasing power.

were far off the list in 1870; none of the drop-offs, with the exception of Portugal, are far off the list in 1988.

In 128 years there is really only one success story—Japan! It is the only industrial country to make it onto the list in 1988 that wasn't even close to making the list in 1870. But even

Japan did not start from ground zero in 1870. Its population was as literate as that of the United Kingdom early in the nineteenth century. Technologically capable, it could fight and win a war with a European power—Russia—at the beginning of the century. Its Zero fighter aircraft was perhaps the most sophisticated in the world at the outset of World War II. Japan was poor in 1870, but in a sociological sense it was in many ways not an underdeveloped society.

Many other countries, Brazil among them, have had a decade or two of economic progress but have been unable to sustain their success and fallen back. In the mid-1960s it was not absurd to believe that Puerto Rico could catch up with the income levels in the rest of the United States before the end of the century. It was then being touted as a miracle of economic development. Today it is no closer than it was thirty years ago. Korea, one of the success stories of the 1980s, was seen at the beginning of the decade as a candidate for bankruptcy along with Brazil and Argentina. In the early 1990s its social unrest would give anyone pause before they bet on Korea's ability to make it into the select circle of the world's twenty wealthiest countries a hundred years from now.

The economic race does not go to the short-term sprinters. It requires a marathoner's ability to put together a century of 3 percent or better annual growth rates. The task is very hard. The likelihood of any particular nation making it onto the list of the richest nations at the end of the twenty-first century is low—regardless of how successful they look at the beginning of the twenty-first century.

But there is a further requirement that guarantees that most of today's Third World countries will be poor one hundred years from now. It is simply impossible for any country to become rich in the context of a rapidly rising population. The reasons are simple. To make new human beings into modern productive workers takes a lot of investment. If there are going to be very many of these new human beings, existing human beings have to be willing to severely restrict their own personal consumption in order to make the investments needed by those new human beings.

A few American numbers illustrate the problem. If a new American is to have the average amount of space, a $20,000 investment has to be made in his or her housing. Until that new American is old enough to begin work, he or she will require feeding—another $20,000. To get to the average American educational level, he or she will require $100,000 in public and private expenditures. For that individual to attain the average American productivity at work, another $80,000 investment will have to be made in plant and equipment. Yet another $20,000 will be necessary to build the public infrastructure (roads, sewers, water mains, airports) needed to support that individual. Basically, each new American will require an investment of $240,000 before he or she is capable of fitting into the American economy as a self-sufficient, average citizen-worker-consumer.

Simple multiplication reveals that if the United States were to have a 4 percent population growth rate, more than 40 percent of its entire GNP would have to be devoted to providing for these new Americans. Existing Americans would have to take a sharp cut in their present standard of living if new Americans were to have a chance to become average Americans. It does not take a deep understanding of human nature to know that existing Americans would not be willing to make the necessary sacrifices. They say so every day by having small families.

The absolute investments necessary to give new citizens the existing standard of living differ from country to country, but the fractions of the GNP that must be devoted to this effort do not. In the Third World the funds to support such an effort simply aren't there, regardless of willingness. A 40 percent reduction in current consumption leaves both new and old citizens near starvation, with no resources left over to devote to improving their collective future.

What was to be done can be seen in Japan, the United States, and Germany.[1] Over the past one hundred years, Japan averaged a 4 percent per year real growth rate while its population was growing 1.1 percent per year. This produced a 2.9 percent yearly rise in per capita income. Over the same one hundred years, the American growth rate averaged 3.3 percent per year while its population was growing 1.5 percent per year. (The growth rate of its native population was much lower.) The result was 1.8 percent per year growth in per capita incomes. Even though per capita growth in the United States has been substantially lower than that in Japan over the past one hundred years, Japan has still not caught up (where performance is measured by internal purchasing power) with the United States. Japan was simply very far behind one hundred years ago. In Germany growth averaged 3 percent per year over the last one hundred years, and the population grew 1 percent per year, leading to a 2 percent per year rise in standard of living.

The histories of the world's richest countries illustrate an iron law of economic development. No country can become rich without a century of good economic performance and a century of very slow population growth. Many of today's poor countries have population growth rates between 3 and 4 percent. If Japan, Germany, and the United States had had such rates of population increase, their standards of living today would be no higher than they were one hundred years ago.

Getting rich is also probably going to get harder in the century ahead. In both of the last two centuries, there were countries that became rich through natural resources, most recently those with oil. Given long-term trends in natural-resource prices and usage, there are unlikely to be additions to the list of the twenty wealthiest countries in the century ahead simply as a result of abundant natural resources. With higher incomes, the developed world's markets for tropical fruits will expand, and there will be increasing demands for the Southern Hemisphere's fresh fruits and vegetables during the Northern Hemisphere's winter. But traditional agriculture (cereals, meat, dairy products) is not a growth area that can support economic development. Developing countries need efficient agricultural sectors to feed themselves (the first element in any increase in the standard of living in countries that start out with most of their populations in rural areas) and to reduce the need to use their scarce foreign-currency reserves to import food, but agriculture will not generate the resources necessary to pay for development.

WHO PLAYS?

In the late nineteenth and early twentieth century, world trade was seen as a back and forth flow between underdeveloped countries (colonies) that exported raw materials to developed nations (the mother countries) and developed countries that exported manufactured products back to those underdeveloped countries to pay for raw materials. But in the last half of the century, the growth in trade has been almost completely between developed countries. Less and less of world trade is accounted for by the trade between developing and developed nations. And without foreign aid from the developed world, the trade between developed and underdeveloped nations would have been even smaller.

As man-made comparative advantage becomes more important, many countries are becoming economically marginalized. What these countries do simply isn't important to the standards of living of those that live in the rest of the world. As a result, not every country that exists on the face of the globe is, or will be, a player in the world economy. To determine who is, and who is not, a player is to perform what the Germans call a *Gedanken* experiment. Imagine countries that could suddenly disappear off the face of the globe with no news reports of their demise. Would average citizens in the developed world be able to tell that something had happened from what they observed in their daily economic life? If they can, the country plays in the world economy. If they cannot, the country does not play in the world economy.

Saudi Arabia, for example, is a player. Without it, a shortage of oil would rapidly show up in much higher energy prices for the average consumer. Bangladesh does not play. If it were to disappear, economic life would not be noticeably different in the rest of the world.

Broad technological forces are making it harder for countries to play in the world economy, but this harsh reality is also being reinforced by the changes in the world's trading regime. As the world breaks up into quasi trading blocks, all of the developing world is going to face a common problem of market access. In the 1950s market access was not seen as an important ingredient of economic success. "Import substitution" was the route to development. Poor countries would look at what they were importing from the developed world, stop those imports from entering their countries, help local businesses get started producing those goods, and substitute local production for foreign production. Import substitution did not work anywhere it was tried. Living in protected markets, local producers never became efficient. Korea, Taiwan, and Singapore taught the world that the way to efficiency was *export-led* growth. Home companies were given protected local markets where they could not be run out of business by foreign competition—but only if they were able to export.[2] To export to the developed world, they had to become efficient, and once efficient in their foreign operations, they could bring this expertise home.

Market access is central in export-led growth. To become a little economic dragon, such as Singapore or Taiwan, two requirements must be met. A country must get itself organized to compete; but it must also have a place where market access is relatively easy—a "market of first resort." In the past half century the market of first resort has been the United States. But generating just 23 percent of the world GNP, America cannot continue to buy almost half of the Third World's manufactured exports. During the 1990s the United States will probably be forced to cure its balance of payments deficit. When it does, imports will have to go down and exports will have to go up. As this happens, the American market for a time will effectively be closed to the developing world. As a consequence, if Europe and Japan aren't willing to become markets of first resort, there may well be no new little economic dragons in the years ahead.

The development of quasi trading blocks is going to make market access difficult in general, but if some developing nations, such as Mexico or North Africa, are given special privileges in one of the three wealthy areas, their access will create enormous problems for other poor nations without such preferences. If a firm can export freely from Mexico to the United States but not from the rest of Latin America to the United States, the rest of Latin America has a major problem. No investor will want to locate where, relative to those who invest in Mexico, he has to work with a handicap.

What nations not now on the list will be on it in 2100? In all probability the number of successes in the next century are apt to be no higher than they were in the last century.

China

China is, of course, the world's largest country in terms of population. As a maker of textiles and running shoes, it is a player in the world economy. Its disappearance would be noticed.

During the 1980s, as it liberalized and introduced market incentives, it was one of the world's most successful economies—growing at almost 10 percent per year.[3] Rural incomes doubled in just six years. With the political events in the summer of 1989 (the Tiananmen Square student uprising) that progress slowed to a 2 percent annual rate but then reaccelerated into the 4–5 percent range in 1990. Gross investment is high (40 percent of GDP), and the state sector is shrinking.

Whether China will or will not move to real capitalism depends upon the directions taken by the next generation of Chinese leaders—those too young to have been on the Long March. The leaders of a revolution never lead a counterrevolution; the builders of socialism will not be the builders of capitalism. To expect this is to expect too much. No one knows, however, what these new, as yet unknown leaders will do. Until the next generation of leaders is known, the prospects for China have to remain shrouded in the oriental mists that cover its mountains.

If the movement toward a market economy resumes, China will have all of the problems now seen in Middle and Eastern Europe. China's 1989 retreat from the market occurred precisely because China could not solve some of those problems—in particular, corruption and inflation.

While China will always be important politically and militarily, it will not have a big impact on the world economy in the first half of the twenty-first century, even if it successfully resumes its progress toward becoming a market economy. The reasons flow from the numbers. China has a per capita annual income of $300.[4] Suppose it were to grow 10 percent per year—a rate equal to the very highest rates achieved in Japan or Korea. That would amount to $30 per person. Multiply 1.2 billion Chinese by $30 per person and China would have $36 billion in annual extra output—most of which would neither be imported nor exported but used to feed and house its people. But even if all of it were to be used to buy goods from the rest of the world, $36 billion is just 0.7 percent of the American GNP. Until China gets to much higher income levels, its economic impact on the rest of the world is going to be small.

Korea, Taiwan, Hong Kong, and Singapore

Among those in the Third World, the little dragons on the Pacific Rim have been the most successful. While specific details differed, each followed the Japanese model, where government offered a sheltered home market to firms that vigorously competed in foreign markets. Protection and competition existed simultaneously in a symbiotic relationship with aggressive national strategies that pushed key industries.[5] While very successful in the 1980s, each, for different reasons, will find it difficult to repeat their successes in the 1990s.

Hong Kong's fate depends upon what happens in China.[6] The treaty between Great Britain and China governing the transfer of Hong Kong to China in 1997 promises something—one country, two economic systems—that cannot be delivered. No country can allow the citizens in one of its cities to live by rules that allow them to become rich while forcing citizens in other cities to live by very different rules that leave them poor. The rules will have to be the same everywhere.

Those who argue that China cannot destroy the goose that lays the golden egg simply haven't looked at the arithmetic. Divide Hong Kong's GNP among 1.2 billion Chinese, and it comes to less than forty dollars per person if those in Hong Kong get to keep nothing. Hong Kong's golden egg is too small to matter to China. China will make its decisions on other grounds. Hong Kong's economic survival depends upon a China that has decided to move toward the market in a major way. If it does, Hong Kong and the area around it could easily be the most dynamic in the world.

The other three little dragons face a common problem.[7, 8] With per capita incomes between four thousand dollars and ten thousand dollars, they are no longer low-wage economies.

How do they go upscale in technology to the higher-productivity activities that can support world-class wages—per capita GNPs above twenty thousand dollars? This requires massive investments in plant and equipment, infrastructure, technology, and skills plus an aggressive effort to raise productivity. Singapore calls its plan for doing so "The Next Lap."[9]

Getting the technology necessary to move upscale is going to be difficult. Easy access to American technology is a thing of the past. Recognizing that they can no longer afford to give their technology away, American firms are now guarding their technology much more carefully and demanding much bigger fees when they do license it. Getting advanced technology from the Japanese has proven to be very difficult. Goldstar, a Korean electronics firm, had to buy into Zenith, the one remaining U.S. electronics firm, to get flat-screen TV technologies that it could not purchase from the Japanese.

There is also a major clash between the interests of business firms in Singapore and Taiwan and the interests of their governments. Governments want their firms to go upscale in technology so that their citizens can get world-class wages, but for individual firms there is a much easier road to higher profits. They can simply move today's low-wage activities abroad (to mainland China if the firm is Taiwanese; to Indonesia if the firm is Singaporean) and continue to do what the firm has successfully learned how to do. Few firms are going to do all of the difficult things that are necessary to move to the higher-productivity levels that support world-class wages if they can easily make a lot of money by simply moving abroad and continuing to use the technologies that they already have mastered.

In both Singapore and Taiwan, activities are now moving off shore at a much earlier stage in economic development than they did in Japan, America, and Europe. Japanese firms did not move offshore to low-wage countries in a major way until they had already achieved a world-class per capita GNP. Taiwanese and Singaporean firms are now moving offshore in major ways, even though the GNPs of Taiwan and Singapore are each only 40 percent that of the world's leaders.

Korea has the lowest annual per capita income of this group (four thousand dollars), but in terms of expenditures on R&D,

the buildup of brand names, and resisting the temptation to go offshore and simply repeat one's low-wage successes, it may be the best positioned of the three. Politically, however, it is the most unstable. Growth has slowed substantially in the early 1990s.

All four little dragons face a major market-access problem in the 1990s. Europe is going to keep them out of its markets since Europe will want to reserve its markets for middle-wage products from the countries of Eastern Europe, at least some of which will be offered associate memberships in the Common Market. As America cures its balance of payments problems, it will be importing less and exporting more. Since America already runs a trade surplus with Europe, most of the improvement in its trading position will have to come at the expense of the Pacific Rim countries.[10] Moving from a $120 billion deficit to a surplus of $80 billion (the sum necessary to make interest payments on America's international debt) would cost the Pacific Rim a minimum of 10 million jobs (see Chapter 7).

In theory, Japan could become a net importer and be the center of a Pacific Rim quasi trading block, pulling the little dragons along with it—a theory sometimes called the "flying-goose formation."[11] If this is to happen, however, Japan must become the prime market to which members of its trading block sell their products. In recent years imports into Japan from the little dragons have increased, but most of the increase has been in low-wage components destined to be installed in Japanese products exported to the rest of the world. Such exports to Japan are merely indirect exports to the United States or Europe.

The little dragons have found it no easier to sell directly to the Japanese consumer than any other nation. Yet they would have to be able to do so if a Pacific Rim quasi trading block were to help them close the gap with the world's richest nations. What is sold has to be sold through Japanese business firms, with the little dragons playing the role of low-wage manufacturers. As stated in a Japanese newspaper, "Asian dragons have discovered that Japan is still king of the jungle and that Japanese offshore production is squeezing their firms out of the low end of the market."[12] Where the little dragons' exporters have been successful and have been able to threaten Japanese industries, they have often found their efforts curtailed by the Japanese government. Despite a large trade deficit with Japan, Korean knitwear exports to Japan are "voluntarily" controlled.[13]

Instead of having a trade surplus with Japan, these countries, like all others, find themselves with bilateral trade deficits that only grow larger. Yet if a block is to be formed, Japan must become a large net importer. Only it has the wealth and the international assets that allow it to earn the income necessary to support a persistent trade deficit.

While geographically closer to Japan than to the United States (although Singapore is still very far from Japan), these countries are economically much more integrated with the United States than they are with Japan. They sell much more to it, and they have independent access. They do not have to work through American firms to reach the American consumer. Their best strategy might be to seek to join the American trading block. For them, America is a better trading partner than Japan; for America, they are a better trading partner than Latin America. With modern technology, quasi trading blocks need not be based on geographic propinquity.

Latin America and Africa

Some of the countries of Latin America should be rich; some of them (Argentina and Chile) once were rich.[14] Some of them have from time to time looked very promising (Brazil in the 1960s and 1970s; Chile in the last five years), but what looked promising always turned out to be a mirage, and the promise sooner or later vanished. In Africa, little has ever even looked promising. In the 1980s real per capita incomes fell in both regions.

Four problems have to be solved. First, chaotic, cumbersome, bureaucratic internal administrations have to be replaced by governments that can govern efficiently and know when not to intervene in the economy. Internal distortions need to be eliminated[15] and replaced by the "centralized, disciplined, and long-term" policy-making of the little dragons of the Pacific Rim.[16] Second, technical progress has to replace raw materials as the source of comparative advantage.[17] Third, population growth rates (often in the 3 percent per year range) have to be brought under control. Fourth, something must be done about international debts.

The first three require local initiative; the fourth requires international action. Latin America and Africa cannot grow if they must service international debts as large as those that now exist. Too many resources have to be taken out to pay interest on those debts; too few are left for reinvestment. It is also true that no foreign company will invest in countries where it cannot get its money out if it wishes to do so. As long as there are massive overhanging debts in these parts of the world, no firm can count on getting its money out, no matter how successful the individual project. There are simply too many others already in line.

Latin America and Africa also cannot grow if they unilaterally repudiate their debts. Private creditors would simply get court orders to seize their assets abroad—essentially making exports impossible. With few exports, no funds would be available to pay for imports. Peru is an example. Not paying its debts didn't help.

In the developed world attention has shifted away from Third World debt problems. Because of much higher loan-loss reserves, Third World debts no longer threaten the solvency of the developed world's banks. Other problems, such as the savings and loan disaster in the United States, have become more important. But in the debtor countries, the problems still remain. Most are not growing; few have been able to reduce their debt obligations and reenter normal credit markets. At the end of the 1980s, five countries were growing in Latin America, eleven were stagnating, and five were declining.[18]

One can argue over which party is most to blame for these debt problems (the borrowers or the lenders), but that argument is now irrelevant. The debts exist and have to be dealt with regardless of fault. The solution to the debt problem lies in the developed world. It has to forgive the debts. Latin America and Africa have to get themselves organized to prevent a repetition of their debt problems, but they cannot solve the existing problem. Only the taxpayers in the wealthy industrial countries can forgive what must be forgiven.

Much of Africa and Latin America are going to be hurt by the special privileges that will be given to North African countries and to Mexico. These privileges will not be extended to the rest of Africa and Latin America. They can't be. The more widely given, the less impact special access can have on any one area, and if too widely given, special access won't help slow America's Mexican migration problem or Europe's North African migration problem. To keep Mexicans and North Africans at home, it makes sense for America and Europe to insure that their low-wage imports come from those regions, so that people who live there have jobs and will stay at home, but this will mean that other low-wage areas elsewhere in Africa and Latin America will not have equal access.

Africa south of the Sahara, with the exception of South Africa (a country with its own peculiar political problems), is the world's economic basket case. If God gave it to you and made you its economic dictator, the only smart move would be to give it back to Him. Borders are in the wrong places to minimize ethnic animosities. The green revolution has not been made to work in the climates and soils of Africa. Effective, efficient governments do not exist. No economy has ever been able to cope with Africa's current population growth rates. Skill and education levels are the lowest in the world. Debts are large relative to earning power, although much smaller in absolute terms than those of Latin America and easier to solve, since they are mostly owed to governments and not to private banks. AIDS may be to Africa in the twenty-first century what the Black Death was to Europe in the fourteenth century. The falling per capita incomes of the 1980s are apt to be replicated in the 1990s. When it comes to southern Africa, the "dismal science" yields a dismal forecast.

The Middle East and South Asia

The Middle East is the one part of the world where it is possible for at least some to be rich because of oil. Exactly how rich depends upon how the oil wealth is shared among the residents of the Middle East. Those not producing oil in the region should be making goods and services for those who sell oil. Israel should bring technology, middle-wage industries, and organizational abilities to the table. But none of that can happen unless and until the political and military disputes between Israel and the Arab world are settled.

Whatever the appropriate number of countries or their precise geographic boundaries, there is only one healthy integrated economy in this region. Divided and not trading with each other, most nations are poor and will remain poor. General economic progress is held hostage to political and military solutions.

South Asia is highly diverse. Some countries, such as Vietnam and Cambodia, have the problems of Eastern Europe. How does a nation escape from the Second World into the First World? Other countries, Malaysia and Thailand among them, might become the next little dragons if they can get market access somewhere in the industrial world. But this is a big if. Burma and Bangladesh are two of the poorest countries in the world and nonplayers in the global economic game. That reality is unlikely to change.

Pakistan, India, and Indonesia are huge in population, have little control over their population growth rates, start from very low per capita incomes, and have massive skill and education problems. They also face the most severe market-access problems. Japan could give Malaysia open market access without disrupting its economy in a major way. Malaysia's population is small in comparison with that of Japan. But no one could give any one of these three countries, much less all three, open market access without being willing to undertake major structural readjustments at home. Industries such as textiles would simply have to go out of business. But no one in the developed world is now prepared to make the structural adjustments that would have to be made if these three countries were to grow rapidly.

WHO'S GOING TO MAKE IT?

Modern technology creates both advantages and disadvantages for Third World countries. Capital and technology flow to them more easily, but their raw materials are less valuable.

Modern medicine creates the population explosions that few of these nations have yet contained. The few that have done so are today's newly industrializing countries (NICs).

A hundred years from now, one or more of the NICs may have made it onto the list of the twenty richest countries in the world. The city-state of Singapore is probably the most likely candidate to succeed if its neighbors let it become the headquarters city for that part of the world and if these neighbors are moderately successful in their own economic growth. But Singapore is really a city and not a nation. Perhaps it should not be counted as a national success. To be considered a success, it would have to be among the twenty wealthiest cities in the world.

In the twentieth century the rich man's club let in only one new industrial member—Japan. It would not be a great surprise if no new members were to join during the twenty-first century.

Chapter 7

FESTERING PROBLEMS

In the 1980s much of the world faced slower growth, rising unemployment, and falling standards of living. This poor performance did not flow from a run of bad luck. It was produced by a number of festering problems that have a common denominator. They all arose from a world economy that had outgrown its post–World War II cooperative relationships; they all required the development of new forms of global cooperation if they were to be solved.[1]

GLOBAL ENVIRONMENTALISM

One of the major problems needing cooperative action is that of preserving and improving the global environment. When the post–World War II economy was designed, environmentalism was not an issue. But today institutions need to be built to deal with global environmental problems. These institutions have to be linked with those promoting economic growth, since pollution and species preservation are inexorably linked with economic development. They are linked because markets misprice the costs of pollution and place no value on the elimination of species.

To each economic actor, the environment is a place where wastes can be disposed of without cost. Pollution by any individual has no noticeable effect on his or her individual environment. As a result, all nations have an incentive to pollute rather than to incur the costs of producing their goods or services in a nonpolluting manner. But if the actions of all of the individual actors are aggregated, every act of pollution does count! The problem is to design a world economy where standards of living can grow rapidly, yet where pollution does not occur.

Species preservation, such as the attempt to save the spotted owl in America's Pacific Northwest despite protests from logging interests, does not show up in the economic calculus of timbering, since there is an incentive for everyone to be a free rider and let someone else worry about, and pay for, biological diversity. Those cutting down old-growth timber know that their jobs are at stake if the trees are preserved for the spotted owl. No one knows the future value of biological diversity, and there is no market where it can be purchased.

In principle, environmentalism is a place where the professional economist and the professional environmentalists should be working together, yet over the past twenty-five years no two fighting cocks have ever disliked each other more. Even when they start out sympathetic to each other's aims, they can barely sit in the same room. The dislike is not theoretical. Economists do not deny the validity of environmental concerns. A clean environment is seen as one of several desirable economic outputs. Economists talk about "internalizing externalities." By this they mean production should be arranged so that those who buy goods are forced to pay the full cost of producing those goods in a manner that does not pollute the environment. Given what looks like theoretical agreement, why then the dislike?

While a clean environment is a desirable economic output from the perspective of economic theory, it is just one among many desirable economic outputs, and it has no overarching claim to priority. Other economic outputs may be more valuable than a clean environment and worth having even if these mean a dirtier environment. This is common sense to economists but rank heresy to environmentalists.

Another part of the problem has to do with different beliefs about the efficiency of rules and regulations versus incentives. Economists believe that incentives work. If people are forced to pay what are called "effluent charges" when they pollute, they will pollute less, and if the charges are high enough, they won't pollute at all. States with bottle-deposit laws don't have discarded bottles littering their parks and highways. Conversely, economists don't believe that prohibitions against polluting will work any more than they did in stopping people from drinking during Prohibition. Alcohol taxes can be collected, but "Thou shalt not drink" doesn't work.

Environmentalists often believe that incentives don't work. Corporations and the rich will simply pay and go on polluting. More importantly, environmentalists are not just worried about the efficiency of current environmental rules and regulations. They want to persuade others to join them politically. For this purpose, thou-shalt-not laws play an important role in shaping beliefs and attracting supporters. Many environmentalists can be persuaded to fight for laws requiring no oceanic pollution; few environmentalists can be persuaded to fight for a 1 percent tax on ocean dumping.

Almost by the nature of their concerns, economists focus on goods and services as the primary focus of attention, with environmentalism as a secondary issue. Environmentalists see the world exactly in reverse. A clean environment is primary; more goods and services are secondary.

Economists, for example, see the generation of electricity as a highly desirable output and note that however it is generated, some environmental problems arise. If coal is used, the problem is acid rain and backfilling open-pit mines. Nuclear power leads to radiation dangers. Hydropower floods canyons and valleys. If oil or natural gas is used, a finite natural resource is being depleted. If solar energy is used, there are some very toxic wastes produced (arsenic, for example) in the process of making solar cells, and solar collectors are a resource-intensive technology that require enormous amounts of space and copper. Every conceivable technique for producing electricity produces waste and every conceivable technique kills people, but the benefits that flow from electricity are worth it.

In contrast, environmentalists focus on acid rain, natural-resource depletion, or radiation, and see more electricity as secondary. Conservation, they believe, could lead to the use of less electricity without any noticeable reduction in standards of living. But to the economist, that is impossible, unless people today are being inefficient and irrational in their behavior—a possibility that environmentalists believe and economists reject.

From the point of view of the environmentalists, those hurt by toxic wastes should always be compensated, even if those responsible did not know that it was toxic at the time. Economists tend to see environmental losses as just one of a large number of random elements that reduce personal incomes. There is nothing special about environmental losses.

Economics is essentially forward-looking. Prices should be set so as to make the economy run efficiently tomorrow. These prices should include charges to insure that today's pollution is under control, but they should not include charges to clean up the past (i.e., taxes should not be levied to support the Superfund to clean up old toxic-waste sites where those actually responsible are long dead and out of business). Those activities should be paid out of general tax revenue. To pay for the past's sins in today's prices is to distort the efficiency and beauty of the price mechanism.

Environmentalists don't worry about the beauty of a free market economy. A green environment is worth more than green money. When it comes to the famous bottom line (a term loved by economists and hated by environmentalists), economists and environmentalists are less likely to sign a peace treaty than Israel and its Arab neighbors.[2] But they should.

With potential and existing environmental disasters—ozone holes in the Antarctic and now perhaps in the Arctic, acid rain in New England and Sweden, global warming, the destruction of the tropical rain forests—seemingly all around, it is well to remind ourselves that these situations can be turned around if we have the will to do so. We do not live in some environmental Greek tragedy where the outcome is predetermined, regardless of the actions of the protagonists.

Recently, I was in Baltistan, a region in the far north of Pakistan, on the Chinese border. It is the home of some of the world's great mountains (including Godwin Austen—also known as K2—among others) and is often referred to as a vertical desert. No vegetation grows on the mountains, except where men irrigate, using water that comes from melting snow far above. I was first in Baltistan in 1972. Trees then were very few and very far between. By 1989 one sees a very different world. In regional capitals like Skardu there is a sea of green. Forests are growing where forests have never grown before. On the edge of town irrigation is being used to expand the forests. In villages far beyond the road's end, one will come across small nurseries where trees are being grown to be transplanted to other areas when they are strong enough to survive. These plots will often have a lock on the gate, even though one could easily step across the mud walls that surround them. The lock is more a symbol of the value of what is inside rather than an active deterrent to anyone who might want to steal a small tree.

This change did not occur spontaneously. It occurred because the Dutch used their foreign-aid money to expand the areas that could be irrigated so that farmers could plant forests without having to cut back on the area that they devoted to food production. Using their foreign-aid money, the Dutch made it profitable to plant trees. Illiterate peasants quickly learned that there was money to be made in planting trees. The Dutch can take pride on money well spent. Baltistan is clearly better off, and in a small way the Dutch are also better off. Every tree helps make our atmosphere better.

The Dutch activities indirectly cast shame on America. A number of years ago the United States led an effort to get all of the developed countries of the world to pledge to give 1 percent of their GNP to foreign economic assistance. The Dutch lived up to their pledge. America did not. Today it is giving about 0.2 percent of its GNP to foreign aid, but almost all of this money goes to Israel, Egypt, Turkey, and Pakistan, where it is effectively backdoor military aid. In a rather brief time America has gone from being the most generous of countries to being the least generous of countries. The way we Americans like to see ourselves (as generous) is a reflection of the past—not the present.

But if one wants to be hard-nosed, there is a hard-nosed problem to be solved. Tropical rain forests may generate the atmosphere that we all need for survival, but it is economically rational for the Brazils, Indonesias, and Chinas of the world to cut them down. No one pays for clean air, but people do pay for oranges or beef. They have every right to cut down their forests and turn them into orange groves and grazing land in order to get rich.

In the end the wealthy industrial world is going to have to do what the Dutch have done in Baltistan on a much bigger scale in the tropical rain-forest areas. The Dutch made it more profitable for the Baltis to grow trees than to do anything else. The rich part of the world is going to have to pay rent for rain forests so that the growing of rain forests becomes an activity more profitable than cutting them down.

Humans aren't used to having to pay to get breathable air and an atmosphere that will let them go outside without getting skin cancer, but they are going to have to learn to do so. They will pay the poor to grow trees, not because they are generous, but because they want to breathe good air.

The key problem is one of time lag. When something such as air goes from free to expensive, no one wants to face this reality. We would all like to find some way to go back to the good old days when we did not have to worry about clean air and did not have to pay for it. But nostalgia solves few problems. If we want good air thirty years from now, those trees have to be planted today.

A good environment is an important part of any human being's material standard of living.[3] Yet increasingly a good environment is not to be had by the actions of any one country by itself.[4] Global warming, excessive carbon dioxide in the environment, the ozone hole in the Antarctic, and too much fluorocarbon in the atmosphere are not problems that are controllable or remediable in any one country. Cooperative solutions are going to have to be designed.[5]

If I burn less fossil fuel and my neighbor doesn't conserve at all, I incur what may be a heavy cost with no corresponding benefit. If more trees are needed in the rain forests of the world to keep temperatures from going up, the trees will only exist if someone makes growing trees more profitable than cutting trees. It is neither fair, efficient, nor likely to happen that those who own rain forests can be persuaded to voluntarily (for free) keep the rest of the world supplied with enough carbon-dioxide removers. Those with high material standards of living will have to pay if they want a high environmental standard of living to go along with everything else they have.

As the Brazilians often point out when they cut down their rain forest, they are doing nothing that wasn't done in Ohio a hundred years earlier. The difference, of course, is that the Brazilian rain-forest trees work harder and are more efficient removers of carbon dioxide than trees in Ohio, since Brazilian trees have leaves on them twelve months a year. If the world needs trees, it is more efficient to use some of the income earned in Ohio to pay for more trees in Brazil than it is to reconvert Ohio to tree production.

This could easily be done by using satellites to measure acres of rain forest in Brazil and then paying Brazil an annual rent on its rain forest high enough to earn more by growing trees than it could by cutting its trees down and raising cattle. Systems such as renting Brazilian rain forests require cooperative governmental organizations. Because of "free-rider" problems, these institutions need the power to levy the taxes necessary to preserve the global environment.

Issues like global warming are not going to be easy to solve because of long-tail problems. (The CO_2 discharged today will be affecting the world's climate fifty years from now.) By the time it is absolutely clear that global warming is occurring, it will be too late to do anything about it. At the same time, it doesn't make sense to turn life-styles upside down and spend huge amounts of money on a nonexistent problem. There will be those who say wait,[6] just as there are those who say act.[7] The right answer is do those things that make sense, regardless of whether there is or is not a long-term problem of unbounded global warming. In the United States this means a high tax on gasoline—something that makes sense given bal-

ance-of-payments problems and insecurities in foreign oil supplies. On a world basis it makes sense to preserve the rain
forests.

Ultimately a good environment comes down to human carrying capacity. The use of almost everything and the disposal
of almost anything is directly proportional to the number of
people inhabiting the globe. How many people can the good
ship earth carry in comfort? The answer depends upon beliefs
about optimal life-styles.

If the world's population had the productivity of the Swiss,
the consumption habits of the Chinese, the egalitarian instincts of the Swedes, and the social discipline of the Japanese, then the planet could support many times its current
population without excessive pollution or deprivation for anyone. On the other hand, if the world's population had the
productivity of Chad, the consumption habits of the United
States, the egalitarian instincts of India, and the social discipline of Yugoslavia, the planet could not support anywhere
near its current numbers. Unfortunately, most humans seem
to fall in the America-India-Chad-Yugoslavia category.

The intimate interaction between the number of people that
a given area can support and expected life-styles can be seen
in what was known in the early 1960s as the "minimum diet"
problem. What was the minimum amount of money that an
adult American would need to purchase a balanced diet for
one year? Somewhat to their surprise, economists found it
was possible to buy a balanced diet for what was then $79 per
year and would today be $283. That diet, however, consisted
of meals depending heavily on soybeans and lard, with just
enough orange juice and liver to provide the minerals, vita-
mins, and proteins missing in soybeans and lard. And if one
was willing to eat nutritious, but not normally eaten, plants,
such as dandelions, a minimum diet could be had for even
less. Similar calculations were made for heat and space. Eski-
mos provide vivid evidence that not much of either is really
necessary. If people were willing to live in the cheapest style
consistent with a normal life expectancy, they would not need
very much in the way of goods and services and the carrying
capacity of the earth would be enormous.

The problem is not, however, what is economically feasible

but what is socially acceptable. Are most people willing to accept the assumptions that lie behind the minimum diet problem—that no one should have anything above and beyond what he or she needs to live a healthy existence? The answer is clearly no, and that unwillingness is the real limit on world's population. To improve upon their life-styles, those that "have" are willing to watch those that "have not" go without.

These attitudes, of course, might change. Beliefs about what is acceptable depend upon circumstances and change slowly over time, depending upon population densities. The Japanese, for example, live in crowded apartments that Americans would find oppressively small. Seeing how the rest of the rich world lives, discontent is rising in Japan, but at least until recently the Japanese had been socialized to accept cramped living quarters. But they did not jump to their crowded life-style quickly. It evolved slowly over centuries out of necessity in a country whose population grew to be almost five times that of California in an area about the same size. If California's population slowly increased by a factor of five, the acceptable California life-style would also change. Suburban yards and private swimming pools would disappear. Yet the Japanese have a high material standard of living. It is just very different from the American standards of living. With a high degree of social discipline and organization, the world could adjust to almost any population if that population grows slowly enough.

Realistically, a slowly growing world population is necessary for both economic development and environmentalism. Neither economic growth nor social discipline can keep up with rapid population growth. The question is how to get from here to there.

The richer the country, the slower the rate of growth of population. Most of Europe and Japan have growth rates below that necessary to maintain a constant population. Those that can afford children the most have them the least. What on the surface seems a paradox isn't. In rich countries parents understand that if they want to have a high-consumption standard of living and want to give their children a life-style at least as good as their own, they cannot afford to have very

many children. In poor countries children are less of a burden, since no one plans to make the investments necessary to
get rich. Not making these investments, however, means that
there is no chance that their children will live in a rich
country.

In poor rural countries during planting and harvesting
time, children are productive at a much earlier age than in
the industrial world. Most important, children are the old-age
pension system in poor countries. While I was working in Pakistan two decades ago, a peasant once told me why he had
to have 17 children. First, he really only had nine, since eight
would die before he did. Second, he really only had three,
since another six would be too poor to take care of him in his
old age. Third, he really only had one, since two of those rich
enough to take care of him in his old age would be mean and
selfish and refuse to do so. As a result, if he did not want to
starve in his old age, he needed at least seventeen children.

While populations are not growing rapidly in either the
First or Second World, rapid population growth in the Third
World creates a problem for the First World. The generation
of electricity in China by burning brown coal can turn Tokyo
into a sea of acid rain. With modern transportation, it is also
clear that much of the First World has lost control of its borders. Where there are enormous income differences between
contiguous regions (America/Mexico, southern Europe/North
Africa), human beings find a way to move. If a country wants
to continue as a member of the First World, it then has no
choice but to make the necessary investments in these new
immigrants and their children. But this lowers the standard of
living for those already living in the country just as much as
if they had had more children themselves.

Rich outsiders cannot force poor insiders to have smaller
families. But rich outsiders can focus their economic aid where
it will do the most good. Aiding countries with rapid population growth is a waste of time. They can never raise standards
of living, no matter how hard they try or how much they are
helped. Foreign economic aid should be focused on those
underdeveloped countries where population is growing the
slowest or where the best efforts are being made to reduce
population growth rates. To do otherwise is to waste limited

resources in a hopeless task. What Germany, Japan, and the United States cannot accomplish—become rich while populations grow rapidly—cannot be done by anyone else.

STRUCTURAL TRADE IMBALANCES

America's trade deficit and the surpluses of Japan and Germany (they are essentially mirror images of each other) are generating economic gravitational forces similar to those of a black hole in space. Black holes are thought to exist where nothing seems to exist—where everything that enters vanishes. Gravitational forces are so strong inside a black hole that not even light can get out—hence, the name. Since no one can devise a way to visit a black hole to report on what they find there, what happens in a black hole has to be deduced from what cannot be seen. Because of the intense gravitational forces, the very nature of matter is believed to be fundamentally altered.

So too with the current structural trade imbalances. While trade deficits and surpluses have existed before, they never have been this large or existed for this extended a period of time. The longer they endure, the greater their eventual impact. In the end, like a real black hole, these forces will become so strong that they twist and bend the very nature of the world economy.

Starting from a surplus of six billion dollars in 1981, the United States plunged into deficit as it played its traditional role of economic locomotive in the aftermath of the 1981–1982 recession. With the United States growing much faster than most of the rest of the world, its imports rose faster than its exports, but this normal state of affairs was magnified by the peculiar mix of fiscal and monetary policies adopted by the Reagan administration in its first two years in office. High interest rates were combined with large tax cuts and a big increase in defense spending. The tax cuts and the expenditure increases provided a Keynesian locomotive for the American and world economies, but the high interest rates attracted huge foreign-capital inflows, dramatically raising the value of the dollar and leading to a much bigger trade deficit than would have occurred if America had only been playing its traditional locomotive role of pulling the world out of its recession. Without those high interest rates, the dollar would have fallen much earlier.

In the mid-1980s it was hoped that a modest downward adjustment in the value of the dollar would cure the structural trade imbalances that had emerged in the first half of the 1980s. Everyone just had to be patient and give the lower-valued dollar time to work. Currency values changed, as they should have changed, and time passed, but the desired effects did not emerge. The value of the dollar fell 35 percent (trade weighted), and the value of the yen rose 35 percent, but the pattern of imbalances in 1991, although superficially better, was just as structurally intractable as it had been in 1985 when the value of the dollar was at its highest value.

The American current account deficit peaked in 1987 at $144 billion, but it was still $99 billion in 1990, even though the value of the U.S. dollar had been down for five years. Until 1991 the improvement in America's trading accounts was counterbalanced by a deterioration in the trading accounts of Great Britain. The United Kingdom went from a surplus of five billion dollars in 1985 to a deficit of thirty-four billion dollars in 1990, despite a 10 percent fall in the value of the pound. If one adds the deficits of the two big-deficit countries together, their combined deficits in 1990 were bigger than they had been in 1985.

In the spring of 1991, the U.S. deficit temporarily improved because of the American recession (with slower growth, America imported less) and the war in the Persian Gulf (what the rest of the world paid the United States for fighting the war—almost sixty billion dollars—showed up as the export of a service—waging war—and caused a temporary improvement in America's current account). When the American recovery starts, and all of the Persian Gulf War payments are in, the American deficit will rapidly deteriorate.

The West German trade surplus rose steadily from 1985 to 1989, despite a 20 percent increase in the value of the mark, peaking in 1989 at fifty-five billion dollars. The German surplus shrank in 1990 and disappeared entirely in the spring of 1991 as Germany diverted exports and increased imports to

TABLE 7.1

Current Account Surpluses and Deficits*

(in billions of U.S. dollars)

Country	1981	1982	1983	1984	1985	1986	1987	1988	1989	1990
U.S.	6	−7	−44	−104	−113	−133	−144	−127	−106	−92
West Germany	−3	5	5	10	17	40	46	50	55	44
United Kingdom	15	8	6	3	5	16	−7	−27	−34	−24
Japan	5	7	21	35	49	86	87	80	57	36
Newly Industrializing Countries†	—	—	—	—	—	—	28	26	19	28
Oil Exporters	47	−10	−20	−6	4	−23	−4	−13	6	—
Western Europe‡	−33	−32	—	27	3	8	−5	−7	−21	−13
Others	−107	−74	−38	−27	−34	−30	−5	−15	−53	—

SOURCE: International Monetary Fund.

*International Monetary Fund, *International Financial Statistics, Yearbook 1990* (Washington, D.C.: IMF, 1990), p. 142-143. "Ecoomic and Financial Indicators," *The Economist*, March 8, 1991, p. 102. "Economic and Financial Indicators," May 25, 1991, p. 104. "Economic and Financial Indicators," June 14, 1992. China External Trade Development Council, *Handy Economic and Trade Indicators* (Taiwan: The Council, 1991), P. 11. Monthly Statistics of the Republic of China, April 1991. International Monetary Fund, *International Financial Statistics, Yearbook 1991* (Washington, D.C.: IMF, 1991), pp. 246, 542, 550, 576.

†When not separately listed, included in Others.

‡Does not include West Germany and United Kingdom.

develop what had been East Germany. In the short run this shift gives the rest of the world a little economic breathing room, but what happens when eastern Germany has been re-equipped and integrated into a new, larger German exporting machine? Germany's structural trade surplus is apt to reappear larger than ever.

The Japanese surplus peaked in 1987 at eighty-seven billion dollars, fell to thirty-seven billion dollars in 1990 as a result of higher prices for middle-eastern oil, but then started to rise sharply once again in the spring of 1991. By the fall of 1991 it was running at an annual rate well in excess of one hundred billion dollars per year. Japan's bilateral surpluses with the United States were falling in 1991, but its surpluses with the rest of the world were rising by even larger amounts. Large increases in the value of the yen and six years worth of time have not eliminated the Japanese surplus.

Changes in exchange rates just did not do the job that they are supposed to do for either the deficit countries or the surplus countries. The fundamental disequilibrium that emerged in the world's trading accounts in the 1980s stubbornly remained at the beginning of the 1990s.

While structural trade deficits and surpluses can more easily be financed with a world capital market, this simply reduces their short-run braking power at the expense of increasing their long-run destructiveness. Large debtor-creditor positions can be built up before anything has to be done. No one can predict the exact timing, but no country can forever continue to run trade deficits.

The fundamental financial mathematics is clear. To run a trade deficit, a country must borrow from the rest of the world and accumulate international debt. Each year interest must be paid on this accumulated debt. Unless a country is running a trade surplus, it must borrow the funds necessary to make its interest payments. Thus the annual amount that must be borrowed gets larger and larger, even if the trade deficit itself does not expand. As debts grow, interest payments grow. As interest payments grow, debt grows. As time passes, the rate of debt accumulation speeds up, even if the basic trade deficit remains constant. Compound interest eventually insures that the required annual borrowings become so large that the rest of the world will be unable (unwillingness will undoubtedly come first) to lend the necessary sums. When that happens, dramatic changes occur.

Suppose that the United States starts with an annual $100 billion trade deficit (approximately the current figure). In the first year it must borrow $100 billion to finance its trade deficit. But as the process continues, debts pile up. With interest rates of 10 percent in the second year, it must borrow $110 billion ($100 billion to pay for its trade deficit and $10 billion to pay interest on $100 billion of outstanding debt). In year three, it must borrow $121 billion ($100 billion to cover its trade deficit and $21 billion to pay interest on an accumulated debt of $210 billion—$100 billion in year one and $110 billion in year two).

When the United States owes $1,000 billion, it must borrow $200 billion per year—$100 billion to finance its trade deficit and $100 billion to make its required interest payments. Running an annual trade deficit of $100 billion and paying a 10 percent interest rate, the first $1,000 billion in international debts is accumulated in 8.3 years, the second $1,000 billion is accumulated in 4.2 years, and the third $1,000 billion in just 3 years. Debts and interest payments pile up at an ever-faster rate.

Eventually, the rest of the world will be unwilling to lend the necessary sums. Nations will refuse to lend because the risks of not being repaid by the Americans in currencies of equal value to those that were lent is too high, or because the sums that must be lent require them to save more than they are willing to save—they wish to consume their income rather than lend it to Americans. When this happens, the structure of world trade must undergo a dramatic shift.

At American productivity levels, it requires about 2.5 million full-time workers to produce $100 billion worth of exportable goods and services. Since the rest of the world has been running a $100 billion trade surplus with the United States, at least 2.5 million workers in the rest of the world owe their jobs to that trade surplus—more if the export surpluses are in countries with productivity levels below those of the United States. When the lending stops, the trade surplus stops (Americans have no funds to buy foreign goods), and the jobs associated with those exports stop.

But that is just the beginning of the problems in the rest of the world. Without foreign lending, America must run a trade surplus to earn the funds necessary to pay interest on its accumulated debts. If the lending stops when these debts are $3,000 billion, then America must have a trade surplus of $300 billion to earn the funds necessary to meet its interest obligations, assuming a 10 percent interest rate. A $300 billion American trade surplus means a $300 billion trade deficit in the rest of the world. As $300 billion in American exports displace $300 billion of local production, the rest of the world loses another 7.5 million jobs—making a total of 10 million jobs. The required changes in the structure of world trade, and hence national production, are certain to be large, and may be sudden.

In the United States the restructuring is even more profound. When a country is borrowing money from the rest of the world, its consumption can exceed its income (production). With a trade deficit, Americans get to consume an extra $100 billion worth of goods that they didn't produce. When the lending stops, they lose that $100 billion addition to their consumption, but since they have to start paying interest rather than borrowing the funds to pay interest, there is a further necessary subtraction from their consumption. The $300 billion in interest payments owed to the rest of the world must now be taken away from it (in the past it was borrowed from foreigners and given to foreigners) and given to the foreigners that own those debts. Total American consumption tumbles by $400 billion.

Foreign borrowing is essentially a way to raise present incomes at the cost of lowering future incomes—the greater the addition today, the greater the subtraction tomorrow. Americans have gotten relaxed about this future subtraction because the borrowing has gone on for so long that it seems as if it can go on forever. But it cannot.

National net creditor or debtor positions are calculated by subtracting all American-owned assets in the rest of the world from all foreign-owned assets in the United States. In late 1982, at historical costs, Americans owned $152 billion more assets in the rest of the world than the rest of the world owned in the United States.[8] At the beginning of 1991, the rest of the world owns about $757 billion more assets in the United States than Americans own in the rest of the world.[9]

One can argue about the exact net-debtor position of the United States. It differs depending upon whether one is using historic costs or market values. The U.S. Department of Commerce estimates that at the end of 1990 America's debts were only $361 billion at market value.[10] American assets abroad had been acquired earlier than foreign assets in the United States and had therefore had more time to appreciate in value. But whatever the exact current-debtor status, the same limits apply. Lower debts simply mean that a country can run its trade deficit for a little longer than it could have if debts were higher.

While the language of foreign borrowing and lending is technically correct, it is misleading when applied to the United States. In recent years Americans have not so much been borrowing money from the rest of the world as they have been selling assets—Columbia Pictures and Rockefeller Center, for example. Functionally, in terms of their impact on future standards of living, the two are equivalent. Loans lead to future interest payments that must be sent abroad; the sale of assets leads to future profits or rents that must be sent abroad. Both are subtractions from future U.S. living standards. They are different, however, in that the United States does not quickly hit a sudden lending limit, such as that hit by Mexico on Friday, August 13, 1982. America has a lot of assets that could be sold and, as a result, can become a net-debtor nation to a much greater extent than Mexico.

To be precise, America has about $25,000 billion in private assets and could theoretically accumulate debts of this magnitude before the "lending" (selling of assets) would have to stop. At that time foreigners would own everything that could be owned in America. Americans often talk about foreigners buying America, but the reality is that Americans are selling America to support their consumption habits.[11] If they continue long enough, they will succeed in selling off their entire capitalistic inheritance. The lending will clearly stop before this happens (foreigners will rightly fear expropriation), but no one knows how far the process might go.

As time passes, the economic gravitational forces of the

trade deficit grow larger and larger. No one knows how long the deficit can be run, but it cannot be run forever. It is also stupid to test the limits of the system. Once in a black hole, it is impossible to get out.

Since it is the only way to avoid the black hole created by structural trade imbalances, cooperation becomes important. If the deficit countries must do all of the adjustment, they have only three choices: (1) They can cut their own economic growth rates and reduce imports; (2) They can let much lower valued currencies cut their imports and increase inflation; or (3) They can reduce imports directly with trade barriers. All lead to lower world growth. If the surplus countries adjust by growing faster, their imports rise and world growth accelerates—but they take a chance on inflation. There is no painless solution. The question is how to spread the adjustments or obligations around so as to cause the least amount of and fairest distribution of pain.

WHO'S THE COP ON THE BEAT?

Instead of having an international trading system with agreed-upon rules and some international system of dispute settlement, each country is now setting up its own rules, constituting itself as judge and handing out penalties to those who violate its interpretation of the rules. Instead of using the international definition of dumping—selling in foreign markets at prices lower than those in the home market—the United States, for example, passed a law defining dumping as selling products at less than full cost, plus 10 percent for otherwise undiscovered overheads, plus an 8 percent profit margin on sales. Using this definition, seventeen out of the twenty largest industrial firms in America could be found guilty of dumping, since very few firms make an 8 percent profit margin on sales. Armed with a law that makes almost everyone guilty of dumping, American firms then proceeded to keep foreign products out of the American market by bringing suit under America's new antidumping law.

Meanwhile, the Japanese use a variety of delaying techniques—known there as "administrative guidance"—to stop American firms with a technological edge from gaining positions so entrenched in the Japanese market that they cannot later be dislodged by the Japanese firms that wish to be in those markets. Corning Glass faced such delays with fiber optics; more recently, Motorola had the same problem with cellular telephones.

The rules that govern international trade are being unilaterally broken for two reasons. The world has outgrown the existing rules, and the flexible exchange rates that were supposed to guarantee a rough balance in trading accounts have failed to work. The pattern of surpluses and deficits is more uneven, more persistent, and greater in magnitude than has ever been seen in the past. The time lags are too long, and the misadjustments, too large to be tolerable. During the long period when they are in deficit, countries feel that they must respond with actions limiting their imports in defiance of the rules of international trade, since too many local producers are being hurt by imports and too few local producers are being helped by exports.

The developed world may be moving toward trading blocks, but it will still need trading rules and some mechanism for enforcing them. The rules for a world of quasi trading blocks will eventually need to be written. What techniques of managed trade are permissible? What rules will prevent trading blocks from succumbing to the temptation of self-sufficiency? At the meeting where the new rules are written, an institution will have to be added that was proposed, but ultimately omitted, when GATT was built—the International Trade Organization (ITO). The ITO was originally designed to be the judge and policeman of the world's trading system. America rejected the ITO because it did not want to be judged or policed. It wanted to be the judge and the policeman. But the United States is today no longer in a position to play that self-appointed role.

The world has to create an institution that will police a *fair* trading system, even if the system is a system of managed trade.

MACROECONOMIC COORDINATION

History teaches us that capitalism is inherently unstable and from time to time needs to be rescued from itself. Inflation, financial panics, recessions, or depressions—all are intrinsic parts of capitalism. Capitalism is a phenomenal generator of goods and services, but like a finely tuned racing car, it often breaks down and needs a lot of regular repairs, service, and tune-ups.

Just think of what would be happening at this moment in the United States if the American government had not come to the rescue of the bankrupt savings and loan banks when their deposit-insurance funds were exhausted. With depositors losing hundreds of billions of dollars, a cataclysm resembling the 1930s would already be under way.

With strong American Keynesian countercyclical aggregate-demand policies (in the form of a big tax cut, a big increase in defense spending) the sharp worldwide recession in 1981 and 1982 was converted into an OK performance for the rest of the decade. With conventional Keynesian countercyclical policies flooding the system with liquidity, the worldwide financial panic of October 1987 was converted into the best-growth performance of the decade in 1988.

But the real problem is probably not that of disaster. If a sharp worldwide economic downturn were to occur, the big three economies (Germany, Japan, and the United States) would coordinate to stop it. The real issue is a world growth rate so low that standards of living fall in much of the world, but not so low as to threaten the stability of the system—as happened for much of the 1980s. In such murky conditions, coordination does not occur. Without the creation of sufficient aggregate demand, the result is apt to be a world that in the 1990s grows even more slowly than it did in the 1980s.

One-country macroeconomic coordination is no longer possible. The American locomotive simply isn't big enough to continue pulling the world's economic train. With an already large trade deficit, with an already large federal government deficit, and starting from a position as the world's largest net debtor rather than its largest net creditor, the United States simply could not do in 1992 what it successfully did in

1982—pull the world out of a recession. America's strong macroeconomic stimulus in late 1982 was the last such solo effort the world will see. In the 1990s no one country starts with a position strong enough to be the world's economic locomotive.

Yet the world needs a locomotive. West Germany, one of the big lenders in the 1980s, is going to be a big borrower in the 1990s as it invests in eastern Germany to build the infrastructure of capitalism. The rest of Eastern Europe and Kuwait are also going to be big borrowers in the 1990s. National savings rates are down in all of the world's major countries. A world credit crunch looms.[12] If higher real interest rates occur, growth is apt to be slow in the developed world and negative in the underdeveloped world.

If this situation is not to occur, the big borrower of the 1980s, the United States, must become a big lender. But converting the United States from a borrower to a lender means cuts in public and private consumption. During the transition period Germany and Japan would also have to provide the markets—aggregate demand—the world needs to avoid a depression.

Together, America, Japan, and Germany are large enough to be the locomotive pulling the rest of the world into prosperity. If they act together, the rest of the world has little choice but to adopt similar policies. The problem is to get them to coordinate when what is good for the world economy is not narrowly good for their own home economies.

LENDER OF LAST RESORT

Nations have learned through brutal experience that they need managers for their financial systems. Usually, the necessary institutions were created after disasters such as the stock-market crash of 1929. With the development of a world financial system, the world needs a financial manager just as much.

Developed countries need lenders of last resort when financial panics, such as the crash of October 1987, strike. In that particular case close coordination between the world's major central banks essentially created a temporary world central bank until the crisis was over. But circumstances may well arise when ad hoc coordination does not work.

Developing countries need a real world central bank to clean up the mess in their financial systems, much as the American banking authorities are now cleaning up the mess in America's savings and loan industry. In both cases there is plenty of blame to be assessed as to who created the mess, but the real problem is not in assessing blame or in punishing the wicked but in restoring the financial system to health so that real growth can resume. If the Second World and Third World are to start growing (and it is in everyone's long-run self-interest that they do so as soon as possible), some system has to be devised for handling the outstanding international debts that they have incurred in the past but cannot be repaid in the future. As long as those debts exist, growth cannot resume.

Only a world lender of last resort can deal with the existing debt problems, since only it can assume the losses that will have to be assumed. To force the private banks that originally made the loans to assume the losses would simply be to create a commercial banking crisis that would rival the existing savings and loan crisis. In the end the taxpayer would have to pick up these costs, and they undoubtedly would be larger than any costs associated with a world central bank.

Second and Third World debt problems have been given to the World Bank and the International Monetary Fund to solve, but these institutions can only continue to put patches on a system that already has too many patches. Neither institution was designed to deal with debt problems; neither has the necessary instruments at its disposal. They can stave off collapse, but they cannot return Second and Third World financial systems to health.

FOREIGN-EXCHANGE STABILITY

Flexible exchange rates are an area where members of the economics profession, myself included, were simply wrong. Back in 1971, when the world went onto the current system of flexible exchange rates, economists were sure that it would be impossible to have large fluctuations in exchange rates between major countries over short periods of time, or to have currencies that were fundamentally over- or undervalued for any extended period of time. Yet in the past two decades, both have occurred.

If changes in productivity, inflation, and nominal exchange rates are added together, the real dollar-yen exchange rate rose an amazing 70 percent over a few months in the early 1980s. An American firm such as Caterpillar (a maker of heavy-duty earth-moving equipment), whose costs were equal to those of its Japanese competitor, Komatsu, suddenly found that through no fault of its own, it suddenly had costs that were 70 percent higher.

With such violent swings in exchange rates, it simply isn't possible to run efficient economies. Nobody knows where economic activity should be located; nobody knows the cheapest source of supplies. Wherever economic activities are located, they will be located in the wrong place much of the time. The result is a needless increase in risk and uncertainty, rising instability from protectionism, shortening time horizons as firms seek to limit risk and uncertainty by avoiding long-term commitments, reductions in major new long-term investments, large adjustment costs as production is moved back and forth to the cheapest locations, the expectation of future inflationary shocks when sudden shifts in currency values cause import prices to soar, and consequent instability in interest rates. Without clear signals to indicate where long-lived capital-intensive investments should be made, business firms have cut back on such investments. What company wants to make major investments in thirty-year facilities to find that unexpected currency swings have converted a profitable investment into an unprofitable investment?

Currency values have also often moved contrary to what would have been predicted by standard economic theory. In the first six months of 1990, the Japanese yen fell sharply in value, despite a Japanese trade surplus that was then the world's largest. Such currency movements can neither be predicted nor explained. Even after the yen fell in value in 1990, no one had a very good explanation for why it might have occurred.

The world has learned to live with currency volatility in the last two decades, but a large price has been paid. It is well to remember that the world's real growth rate in the 1980s was well below that of the 1970s, despite the food shocks, oil shocks, inflation, recessions, and hard times for which that earlier decade is now remembered.

To reduce currency volatility within Europe, the Europeans are reconstructing a system of fixed exchange rates for Europe. If currency stability is necessary for European success, it is probably equally necessary for success in the rest of the industrial world.

WANTED: A MANAGER FOR THE SYSTEM

If it is to work, a system of quasi trading blocks will need a manager just as much as the GATT–Bretton Woods system. Some nation has to take a leadership role and focus attention on the things that will need to be done to preserve and improve the system. Countries cannot watch out for their own narrow economic self-interest all of the time. If they do, no system can long sustain itself. Someone has to take a leadership role if the world is not to break into quarreling trading blocs where each seeks to exclude others from its domain.

America had this role in the last half of the twentieth century by virtue of the fact that it was by far the world's largest economy. As the only economic superpower, it did not manage by *diktat* in the second half of the twentieth century, but it was a dominant leader that could not be lightly defied. Everyone else needed access to the American economy if they were to prosper. America held the very real military threats of the Russian bear and the Chinese dragon in check. Military power could be used implicitly to purchase economic cooperation and acquiescence. That world is gone, but the world still needs a manager. In the twenty-first century the manager of the world economy will be a peer among equals—a leader in consensus building.

Neither Japan nor Germany can play this role. Germany's management talents will be focused on constructing the

House of Europe in the first half of the twenty-first century. It will have little time or talent to spare for wider problems. Japan's closed culture makes it virtually impossible for outsiders to participate in Japanese decision making. As a result, Japan's decisions could not possibly be sensitive enough to the needs and desires of the rest of the world for it to be willing to follow Japan's leadership. Both Germany and Japan also suffer from a military history whose lingering effects make it unlikely that many of their neighbors would be willing to follow their leadership.

Fortunately or unfortunately, international leadership is the one place where military power becomes important. As the United States will be the world's only military superpower in the twenty-first century, there is no other choice but to make it manager of the system. If it refuses to manage, something that may well happen, there will simply be no manager. Almost by definition, military superpowers are countries that cannot be managed by others. If some other nation attempted to manage the system, the United States could easily use its military power to frustrate their management.

Theoretically, Americans could smoothly and gracefully adjust to a situation where their per capita GNP was falling relative to that in the most developed nations and still be a benign manager for the world's trading system—a gentle military giant. But realistically, that is unlikely to happen. If Americans see themselves as persistent losers, they will sooner or later circle the wagons, keep others out, or strike out at those they blame, fairly or unfairly, for their failure. By refusing to cooperate, America has the power to blow up the world's twenty-first-century economic system.

Because of this reality, the rest of the world has a direct interest in the success of the American economy. The rest of the world can do little to help the United States solve its own internal economic problems, but the world needs a successful American economy. To fill this role, America does not have to have the world's most successful economy, but it does have to be in the race, running with the pack, if America is to play the role that only it can play.

A Reminder

In the intense competitive atmosphere that will exist in the twenty-first century, all of the participants should remind themselves daily that they play in a competitive-cooperative game, not just a competitive game. Everyone wants to win, but cooperation is also necessary if the game is to be played at all.

Chapter 8

WHO OWNS THE TWENTY-FIRST CENTURY?

In the twenty-first century the per capita incomes of the major industrial countries may converge, just as regional incomes have converged in the United States in the past sixty years.[1] As Japan catches up with America and Europe, its growth rate may decelerate and stop it from sprinting ahead of the pack.[2] But there are no automatic-feedback mechanisms in economics that lead to convergence. Precisely the reverse; the faster one grows today, the easier it is to grow faster tomorrow. The slower one grows today, the more certain it is that one will grow slowly tomorrow.

Current momentum, whether up or down, is hard to reverse. If incomes are rising rapidly with high growth, big investments can be made in the future without having to sacrifice a higher standard of living today. Both can be gotten from rapid growth. In contrast, transforming a slow-growth, low-investment society into a fast-growth, high-investment society requires sacrifices in today's consumption to secure the investment necessary for tomorrow's faster growth.

In the race ahead, one of the three great economic powers is apt to pull ahead of the other two. Whichever pulls ahead is apt to stay ahead. That country or region of the globe will own the twenty-first century in the sense that the United Kingdom owned the nineteenth century and the United States owned the twentieth century. It will have built the world's best twenty-first-century economic system.

While convergence is unlikely, the twenty-first century is unlikely to have an economic power as dominant as Great Britain was in the nineteenth century or as the United States was in the twentieth century. Britain's nineteenth-century dominance was based on having started the Industrial Revolution fifty years ahead of anyone else. In the first half of the nineteenth century, it had no competition. Once the Industrial Revolution had begun elsewhere, Britain was still the strongest power, but its position was very different from when it had had the economic playing field to itself. It was still first—but hard-pressed by others, especially Germany and the United States.

Similarly, the American dominance in the second half of the twentieth century was built upon a unique historical experience. In the first half of the century, America was the leading economic power. It had the world's largest GNP and highest per capita standard of living, but it also had challengers— West Germany and the United Kingdom. There were industries such as chemicals where America was definitely behind. High science—chemistry and physics—belonged to the West Germans.

But in the second half of the century, the destruction of World War II left the economic playing field empty except for the United States. Everyone else was far behind, struggling to rebuild. America's economic dominance after World War II (it had over half of the world's GNP and was the technological leader in essentially every industrial product) had not been seen since the Roman Empire and probably will not again be seen in the next two thousand years.

As a result, the twenty-first century is apt to be one where there is a definite economic leader but not a century where one country towers over all the rest.

EVALUATING THE TEAMS

Japan

While the three contenders have equal league records (roughly equal per capita GNPs if external and internal purchasing power are averaged) as they enter the twenty-first century, if one looks at the last twenty years, Japan would have to be considered the betting favorite to win the economic honors of owning the twenty-first century.

In just twenty years time, Japan has gone from having a per capita GNP just 50 percent that of the United States to having a per capita GNP technically 22 percent above that of the United States, if the two GNPs are evaluated using international currency values.[3] Where none of the fifteen largest banks in the world in 1970 were Japanese, ten of the fifteen largest banks in the world in 1990 were Japanese, and the top six were all Japanese.[4] Japan had 5 percent of the American auto market in 1970; in 1990 it had 28 percent.[5] In just twenty years' time, it completely wiped out the American consumer-electronics industry. Where it used to have a trade deficit and be a net-debtor nation (it just repaid its last debts to the World Bank in 1990), it is today the world's largest net creditor and has the world's largest trade surplus. In the last fifteen years, after correcting for inflation, its growth rate was 75 percent greater than that of the United States and twice that of the European community.[6] In head-to-head competition, its communitarian companies have been impossible to beat.

Japan's home market is the smallest of the three major contenders, but it has the advantage of a long unified history. Cohesion and homogeneity give Japan an ability to focus its economic might that few others can rival. No nation can organize better to march toward well thought out common goals. Japanese high-school students come near the top in any international assessment of achievement, and the nation's ability to educate the bottom half of the high-school class is simply unmatched anywhere in the world.

No nation is investing more in its future. Total fixed investment, including housing, is twice that of the United States.[7] Plant-and-equipment investment per employee is three times as high as that in the United States and twice that of Europe; civilian R&D spending as a fraction of GNP is 50 percent above that of the United States, slightly above that of Germany, but far above that of Europe as a whole. When it comes to investing for the future, firms organized on the principles of "producer economics" have some major advantages over those based on "consumer economics."

Japan's strength (its powerful cohesive internal culture) is also its weakness. Japanese firms have demonstrated a first-class ability to manage foreign workers (often they get more productivity out of foreign workers than foreign managers can), but to the extent that the economic game of the twenty-first century requires firms to integrate managers and professionals from different cultures and nationalities into a homogeneous team, Japan has a problem. Japanese history, traditions, culture, and language make it very difficult to integrate foreign managers and professionals as equals. If winning requires absolutely first-rate foreign managers, Japanese firms will have a problem. To hire the very best foreign managers, these foreigners must have a chance to get to the top, but such a chance cannot be provided in the closed Japanese corporate culture.

While every nation copies to catch up, those that have become leaders also eventually learn how to pioneer new breakthroughs. Japan has yet to demonstrate that it has this ability. Without such an ability, Japan can stay slightly ahead of the richest nations elsewhere in the world because of its demonstrated competence in process technologies, but it can never get very far ahead unless it also learns to invent new products. If products have to be copied from abroad, Japan's own economic advance will be limited by the pace of its competitors' inventions.

When trying to determine whether Japan will or will not become a leader in new product technologies, it is well to remember a little American history. In the nineteenth century the United States was known as a nation of copiers. The great inventions that started the Industrial Revolution (the steam engine, the spinning jenny, the Bessemer steel furnace) were British inventions. Americans were famous for taking these inventions and making them work 10 percent better than the

British—much as the Japanese are today famous for taking American inventions and making them work 10 percent better than the Americans. Historically, copying to catch up is the name of the game. After America caught up at the end of the nineteenth century, it eventually learned to be inventive in the twentieth century, but it took half a century to do so. It was not a scientific leader in the first half of the twentieth century, even though it had the world's highest per capita GNP. It did not sprint ahead of the rest of the world until it became a scientific leader at midcentury.

When Japan catches up, it will, I believe, also learn to invent. The ingenuity needed to improve processes is no less than that needed to shift to new product paradigms. The Japanese worry about their inability to make big breakthroughs, but an objective reader of history would not see cause for their concern. The only problem is the time lag. It may take Japan a half century, just as it took the United States a half century, to become inventive.

Japanese success has been based upon an export-led economy. Exports were the fastest growing part of the economy. Export industries were the productivity leaders. Exports pulled the domestic economy forward. Domestic industries were often very inefficient by world standards. But an export-led strategy will not be the route to Japan's success in the future.

To grow faster than the rest of the world, Japan's export industries had to capture larger and larger foreign market shares to insure that Japan could pay for the raw-material imports that it needed to keep its economy racing along. The rest of the world could tolerate this situation as long as Japan's exports were small. Japan is now so large economically, however, that the rest of the world cannot allow Japan's exports to rise and capture their markets at the rate that would be required if Japan were to continue to grow much faster than the rest of the world. The rest of the world is simply going to stop Japan from being an export-led economy in the twenty-first century, by instituting overt restrictions if necessary. If Japan is to grow faster than the rest of the world in the twenty-first century, it has to find a way to do so while exports are growing more slowly than its GNP. Essentially,

Japan must transform itself to become an economy pulled ahead by its domestic demands rather than an economy pushed ahead by exports.

The need to shift from an export-led to a domestically pulled economy will be accentuated by the development of quasi trading blocks in Europe and North America. A world of quasi trading blocks will require Japanese companies that are seen as insiders and not as outsiders in both Europe and America. This will mean more offshore production and fewer exports from Japan.

If Japan is successful in becoming a domestically led economy, housing and infrastructure investments will lead the way, since these are two areas where Japan is basically an underdeveloped country. Without housing, and without roads and parks, Japanese standards of living cannot rise to world levels, whatever the productivity its citizens achieve at work. Housing is the critical bottleneck that will require major changes in traditions, which have resulted in rice land in the middle of Tokyo as a result of low inheritance taxes on rice land but not on other assets, restrictive shade and earthquake laws that prevent high-rise residential buildings from being constructed in Tokyo, and an unwillingness to use eminent-domain laws to acquire the tracts of land necessary for large-scale housing and public infrastructure projects. Without breaking these traditions, there can be no major breakthrough in the construction of living space. Without a breakthrough in living space, the Japanese will remain a poor people in a rich country.

The producer-economics business firms of Japan may be the best in the twenty-first century's economic game, but for the Japanese to win, some consumer economics will have to be grafted on to their producer economics. The ultimate owner of the twenty-first century will have to balance these two sets of human drives. The discontent over the housing issue is so high among young Japanese professional workers, however, that it is difficult to believe that Japan will be able to resist change. Eventually, democracies, even one-party democracies, have to respond to the wants of their citizens.

Japan's history and culture may make it impossible for it to create a quasi trading block on the Pacific Rim to rival that of

Europe or the Americas. Korea and the Chinese-based economies (mainland China, Taiwan, Hong Kong, and Singapore) may prefer to have special arrangements with their best market—the United States—rather than their chief rival—Japan.

Trading blocks imply some level of labor mobility, but this means that the Japanese would have to be willing to digest guest workers. If Western Europe worries about labor migration from Middle and Eastern Europe, think what would happen if the border were opened between Japan and China. Millions of Chinese would move to Japan, yet the Japanese culture is such that it may be the country in the world that is least willing or able to absorb immigrants. The culture that is now the world's most difficult to join will have to become much easier for outsiders to join if Japan is to win. A few special trading arrangements may emerge, but Japan is not likely to be able to create a Pacific Rim common market to rival the European Community. There is simply no evidence that it is willing to make the necessary adjustments that it would have to make.

But any analysis of the strengths of the teams before the game begins would show that Japan comes into the competition with momentum on its side. It is simply growing faster and investing more in future growth than anyone else on the face of the globe. If the gambling casinos of Las Vegas had economic, as well as sports, betting, Japan would be the betting favorite to own the twenty-first century. One hundred years from now, historians looking back are most apt to say that the twenty-first century belonged to Japan.

Europe

While having been the slowest mover in the 1980s, Europe starts the 1990s with the strongest strategic position on the world economic chess board. Its position is very much like that shown in books on chess "endgames." The reader is shown a configuration of players on a chessboard and told that black can win in five moves, regardless of what white does. But the reader has the difficult task of finding and making those five moves. Economically, Europe holds just such a position. If it makes the right moves, it can become the dominant economic power in the twenty-first century, regardless of what Japan and the United States do. In this case the right moves are easy to see but very difficult to make.

If Europe can truly integrate the EEC (337 million people) into one economy and gradually move to absorb the rest of Europe (more than 500 million people) into the House of Europe, it can put together an economy that no one else can match. Europe's 850 million people are the only 850 million people on the face of the globe that are both well educated and start out not poor. Some of the countries that need to be added to the EEC, such as Sweden, Switzerland, Norway, and Austria, are in fact some of the richest in the world.

Europe's major advantage is that almost everyone starts out well educated. The communists may not have been able to run good economies, but they ran some of the best K–12 educational systems on the face of the globe. Europe is the only region where one of the countries, Germany, is a world leader in production and trade, and where one of the countries, the former Soviet Union, is a leader in high science. The former Soviet Union has many more space shots than the United States, and in many areas of theoretical science it leads the world. West Germany's 1990 trade surplus was the largest in the world; on a per capita basis, it was almost three times that of Japan. A decade from now, when eastern Germany is fully integrated and up to western German productivity standards, Germany is going to be even more formidable. Germany's traditional markets, Middle and Eastern Europe, are also apt to be the fastest growing in the world in the early twenty-first century.

If the high science of the former Soviet Union and the production technologies of the German-speaking world are added to the design flair of Italy and France and a world-class London capital market efficiently directing funds to Europe's most productive areas, something unmatchable will have been created. The House of Europe could become a relatively self-contained, rapidly growing region that could sprint away from the rest of the pack.

Since European countries represent both the communitarian and the individualistic strains in capitalism, the compromises necessary for the integration of Europe could lead to a mix and match of the best strains of both. The Europeans don't have to adopt foreign—American or Japanese—ideologies.

The Europeans also have the advantage of getting to write the trading rules for the twenty-first century. Those who write the rules will not surprisingly write rules that favor those who play the game the European way.

This does not mean, however, that Europe will win. It just means that it can win if it can make exactly the right moves—no matter how well either the United States or the Japanese play the economic game. The right moves involve two major problems. The economies of Western Europe really have to integrate, and that integration has to be quickly extended to Middle and Eastern Europe. The ex-communist economies of Middle and Eastern Europe have to become successful market economies. Neither is an easy task. Both will require European citizens willing to make sacrifices today to create an economic juggernaut tomorrow. Western Europe will have to be willing to give large amounts of economic aid to Middle and Eastern Europe in order to get capitalism started.

Ancient border and ethnic rivalries in both Eastern and Western Europe will have to be put aside. The English and the Germans will both have to become *Europeans*. Their different reactions to the Gulf War neatly illustrate the political problems that remain to be overcome. These obstacles notwithstanding, the House of Europe holds the strongest starting position on the world's economic chessboard.

The United States of America

The clash between capitalism and communism was an economic, ideological, and military clash. Capitalism, democracy, and a worldwide set of military alliances (such as NATO, for example) went up against communism, totalitarianism, and a worldwide set of military alliances (that of the Warsaw Pact, for example). In the end the economic weakness of communism led to the victory of capitalism, the spread of democracy, the abandonment of the Warsaw Pact in March 1991, and the final meltdown of the USSR itself.

The clash between individualistic and communitarian capitalism is strictly economic. All capitalists believe in democracy; all believe in private ownership of property. America will be the military superpower of the twenty-first century. But that, if anything, gives it a handicap in its attempts to remain an economic superpower in the twenty-first century. To be a double superpower, it will have to be willing to invest what others invest in being economic superpowers and, on top of that, make whatever investments are necessary to remain a military superpower.

Having been rich longer than anyone else, the United States starts the twenty-first century with more real economic assets that can be deployed in the twenty-first century's economic competition than anyone else. Technologically, it is seldom far behind and often still far ahead. Its per capita income and average productivity are second to none. Its college-educated work force is the best in the world; its domestic market is far larger than that of Japan and far more homogeneous than that of Europe.

But it squandered much of its starting advantage by allowing its educational system to atrophy, by allowing itself to run a high-consumption, low-investment society, and by incurring huge international debts. No one at the end of the twentieth century is less prepared for the competition that lies ahead in the twenty-first century.

American investment is simply not world-class. Plant-and-equipment investment per member of the labor force is half that of Germany, one third that of Japan.[8] Civilian R&D spending is 40 to 50 percent less than that of Germany and Japan. Physical-infrastructure investments are half those being made in the late 1960s. Europe embarks on an ambitious high-speed rail network to link its major cities while unspent funds pile up in highway and airport trust funds in the United States. And, America is not a leader in building the modern telecommunications highways of the future.

In the 1980s America's slow productivity growth was hidden by a rapidly growing labor force and an unused borrowing capacity that could be allocated to raising real family standards of living faster than was warranted by productivity growth. In the 1990s America's labor force will not be growing rapidly, and its borrowing capacity is already close to full utilization. As a result, the unseen and unsolved problem of the 1980s, slow productivity growth, will move front and center in the 1990s. America's chances of owning the twenty-first century depend upon the answer to a simple question. Can it get its productivity growth rate up to the standards of its chief rivals?

Paradoxically, if America wants to have a world-class consumption standard of living in the twenty-first century, it will have to shift from being a high-consumption, low-investment society in the 1980s to being a high-investment, lower-consumption society in the 1990s. From being present-oriented, it will have to become future-oriented. To raise investment, consumption (public and private) must grow more slowly than output for some extended period of time, so that investment (public and private) can rise as a fraction of GNP.

When it comes to the skills and education of the work force, the second understrength player on the American team, the picture is mixed. The college-educated part of the American work force is world-class. College is where the American work force catches up with the rest of the world. Americans simply work harder and spend more to insure quality at this level than anyone else. Luckily for Americans, most of the countries with good K–12 education systems have not built good mass university systems to go with them. Elite education systems have often become mass education systems with little investment in either human or physical facilities. Students who have worked very hard to pass tough high-school graduation examinations often make the first couple of years of university life into a sandbox. That part of the American work force that does not go to college, however, is not world-class, and that part of the American work force that does not graduate from high school (29 percent) is positively Third World when it comes to educational skills. Education has to improve if Americans want to win.

In chess the queen is the most powerful piece on the board.
Economically, it is the queen that Americans may have forgotten how to move. In economic terminology, to move the
queen is to play "catch-up; get back in." How does a country
catch up in a key industry where it is behind? How does a
country get back into a key industry where it has been pushed
out by aggressive foreign competitors. What strategy does a
country employ to insure that it gets its share, or more than
its share, of the new high-value-added, high-productivity,
high-income-elasticity-of-demand industries that flow from
man-made comparative advantage?

Americans may have forgotten how to play catch-up; get
back in, since they haven't had to do either for a half century.
In the past they could win without a game plan. But having
had to cope with American dominance for half a century, in
order to catch up, the rest of the world has become very good
at moving their economic chess queens.

America's natural geographic trading partner, Latin
America, is both poor and poorly educated. Latin America's
per capita GNP has been declining, and its debt problems
make rapid growth unlikely in the early parts of the twenty-
first century. Even if a North and South American common
market could be worked out, it would not help the United
States very much. But common markets between countries
with very different income levels are also very difficult to
establish, because the free labor mobility that is part of a
common market causes too many people to move from the
low-wage countries to the high-wage countries. America will
work out some special trade arrangement with Mexico in
order to increase job generation in Mexico to cut migration
into the United States, but it will not be able to build a
real common market with Mexico, much less with all of
Latin America. Such a common market would cause too
many people to move to the United States and cause too
much of a reduction in the wages of unskilled Americans.

At the same time, the United States has some real cultural
strengths. If Japan's culture makes it the country where foreigners find it hardest to participate as equals, America's culture makes it the country where it is the easiest for outsiders
to become insiders. Americans may not be great exporters,

but they are the world's best when it comes to running off-shore production facilities. If the sales of offshore American production facilities had been treated as exports, the 1986 American trade deficit of $144 billion would have become a trade surplus of $57 billion.[9] Americans quickly make the natives into successful American businessmen.

In crises (Pearl Harbor) or in situations which can be made to look like crises (Sputnik), Americans respond magnificently. Clear problems (Sputnik; Iraq's invasion of Kuwait) get clear, clean, well managed solutions. America is perfectly capable of claiming the twenty-first century for itself. The American problem is not winning—but forcing itself to notice that the game has changed—that it will have to play a new game by new rules with new strategies.

THE WINNER IS . . . ?

A case can be made for each of the three contenders. Momentum is on the side of the Japanese. It is difficult to bet against them. The Americans have flexibility and an unmatched ability to organize if directly challenged. They start out with more wealth and more power than anyone else. But strategic position is on the side of the Europeans. They are the most likely to have the honor of having the twenty-first century named for them.

In the end the Europeans will do what is necessary to complete the integration of the countries now in the Common Market, add the rest of Western Europe to it, and pay the taxes necessary to allow much of Middle and Eastern Europe to join the House of Europe, not because they are wise and farsighted, but because they have no choice. To prevent the Poles and other Eastern Europeans from all moving to Paris, London, Rome, and Frankfurt, the Western Europeans will do what strategic considerations dictate that they should do.

To win, Japan and America also have to seize the strategic opportunities in front of them, but they have to be able to see the positive benefits of change. They have no negative pressures, such as European migration, helping them to make the right decisions in spite of themselves. History and human nature tells us that it will be far easier for the Americans and the Japanese to avoid doing what they must do if they are to win.

Future historians will record that the twenty-first century belonged to the House of Europe!

Chapter 9

AN AMERICAN GAME PLAN

America's most comfortable hypothesis is to tell itself that it does not need an economic game plan. The old ways are the best ways. In the last twenty years, the rest of the industrial world has been catching up with America, but that was an inevitability. It took just fifty years for the rest of the world to overcome the handicaps that they imposed on themselves during World War II. When other countries catch up with U.S. productivity levels, their growth will slow down. They may catch up, but they won't pass. Books maintaining this hypothesis periodically top the list of best-sellers.[1]

Whatever Americans think, the wealthiest parts of the industrial world see themselves forging ahead of the United States. As stated by Jacques Attali, principal economic adviser to the president of France and head of the European Bank for Reconstruction and Development in a new book called *Millenium*, Americans refuse to believe that they are falling behind the most advanced parts of the industrial world and, because of this belief, will not make the changes necessary to remain competitive. No one can solve a problem they refuse to see.[2]

The rest of the world may be wrong. They may not forge ahead. But since the economic problems of playing catch-up are much harder than those of playing keep-up, it is very dangerous to wait until the verdict of history is clear. When the rest of the world seemed about to pass Great Britain in 1900, the British decided to wait to see if it would really happen. It did. Ever since then, the British have been rather unsuccessfully playing catch-up. A smart country, interested in insuring its future, assumes the worst and starts playing keep-up early.

INTERNATIONAL BENCHMARKING

A country that wants to win starts by closely studying the competition. The purpose is not emulation but what the business world calls "bench marking." Find those in the world that are the best at each aspect of economic performance. Measure your performance against theirs. Understand why they are better. Set yourself the target of first equaling, and then surpassing, their performance.

International bench marking reveals two decades of subpar American productivity growth. With productivity falling in 1989 and 1990, there is no light at the end of the tunnel. Technically, the solutions to the productivity problem are known—more investment, more skills, better strategies. The question is not "What should America do?" but "How does America force itself to do what it knows needs to be done?"

President Bush is fond of saying that the United States "has more will than wallet" when he discusses domestic issues. The truth, of course, is exactly the opposite. America's per capita real GNP is two and one half times as large as it was when it began to finance the rebuilding of the world with the Marshall Plan in 1948. America has a lot more wallet than will and could easily invest the sums that would be necessary to give it a competitive economy.

But the issue is also not just will. No society just summons up its will to change. National will flows from a widespread understanding that the world has changed and that external realities require internal changes. Americans are particularly resistant to changing their system, since they tend to believe that they got it right the first time. Given a chance, everyone in the world would like to be an American. The Japanese, in their secret souls, are really socially imprisoned, low-saving, high-consuming Americans.

Not long ago I was at a meeting in Tokyo, and during the question period a Japanese got up and asked, "Who's worrying about making the American system better?" The honest answer is, of course, no one. Why should one worry about making a perfect system better?

When the American system fails, as it does, of course, from time to time, Americans don't look for system failures. They look for human devils who have mucked up a perfect system. Thus, instead of reforming America's financial system when it essentially collapsed at the end of the 1980s, Americans found devils (Mike Milken, Charles Keating, Neil Bush) who needed to be punished (thrown in jail), but nothing was done to change the system to prevent a future repetition of these events.

The view that the American system is perfect and cannot be made better comes from America's peculiar history. America's Founding Fathers (Thomas Jefferson, George Washington, Benjamin Franklin) were gods, or if not gods, at least individuals more perfect than anyone now alive. They designed a unique system that could last forever without improvements. It was, and is, perfect. No other country has founding fathers in the sense that the United States has founding fathers. The only other country that did, the USSR with Marx and Lenin, has just officially rejected its founding fathers by returning Leningrad to its original name of St. Petersburg.

Consider the fifteen-thousand-plus independently elected local school boards that run America's schools—the ultimate in Jeffersonian local democracy. If an educational system that allows thousands of independent local school boards to run schools was a good one, one might reasonably expect that at least one of those fifteen thousand school systems could turn out high-school graduates whose achievement scores could match those of Europe or Japan. None can. When more than fifteen thousand experiments are run each year, and each of them results in failure year after year, the source of that failure is not apt to be found in local devils (such as the existence or nonexistence of schoolteachers' unions or merit pay). Something is wrong with the system itself.

International benchmarking reveals that no one turns out a high-quality product unless someone sets quality standards. The world's best school systems operate under a strong centralized ministry of education that sets tough standards that everyone must meet. No one passes without performing. In contrast, locally elected school boards have a direct incentive to cater to the lowest common denominator when it comes to setting standards. No substantial fraction of the students can be flunked, whatever their performance. If they were flunked, a different school board would be elected. Teachers would be fired. Yet no one in America can say that local school boards should be abolished. That would be un-American.

While the rebuilding of America's system will have to take American history, culture, and traditions into account, it will also have to go beyond those traditions, history, and culture to construct something new. Whatever their abilities, Americans will have to realize that the Founding Fathers did not get it right every time.

Consider the favorite phrase of President Reagan—Standing tall! To claim that America is standing tall is to claim that it has no problems and does not need to change. Unfortunately, good economics and good politics clash. Refusing to admit that there are problems is clearly good politics. The last two presidents have been elected three times on a there-are-no-problems-with-the-system platform. But without being willing to face reality, no economic restructuring can take place. Facing reality means preparing for the economic weather that actually exists. What used to be a tropical beach has become a howling blizzard. Appropriate dress has changed.[3]

STRENGTHENING AMERICA'S PLAYERS

Savings and Investment

While there are arguments over exactly what proportion of America's productivity problem can be traced to inadequate public and private investment in plant and equipment, R&D, infrastructure, and skills, it does not take a deep understanding of economics to know that America cannot have a competitive rate of growth in productivity when it invests half as much as the Japanese and two thirds as much as the Europeans. That would be possible only if Americans were substantially smarter than everyone else. We aren't!

From an economist's perspective, it is easy to restructure America to insure greater investments. But all routes to that objective require someone, somewhere, to consume less. How does a society force itself to go on a consumption diet? Dieting is technically easy. One just does not eat as much as one used to eat. Anyone can get thinner if they eat fewer calories than they burn up for an extended period of time. Similarly, more savings and investment is technically easy. One just does not consume as much as one used to consume. The trick in both cases is how to lock the refrigerator door in such a way that it will not be unlocked when the person who must hold the key to the door is the one who should be dieting. Designing a diet is not a major problem; putting one's self on a diet is an enormous problem.

Step one is for Americans to quit dissaving in their private lives (borrowing to finance consumption purchases). Step two is for Americans to quit dissaving in their public lives (running government deficits). Ideally, they would run surpluses in both their private and public lives. Step three is to adopt a tax system with powerful incentives to save and powerful disincentives for consumption. Step four is to establish strong incentives for private investment and larger government budgets for public investment. All of these steps point to the federal tax system as the place where America's consumption diet must be designed.

While America's private corporations are world-class savers, America's private citizens are not. Less is saved than is invested in housing (3.3 percent versus 4.1 percent of GNP in 1990), and as a result, individuals actually subtract from, rather than contribute to, the pool of savings available to finance output-enchancing forms of investment.[4] Voluntary personal savings (the savings made after Americans make compulsory contributions to their pension funds) are actually negative. In 1988 compulsory pension contributions exceeded net personal savings by 25 percent in the United States.[5] No economy can be competitive if the personal sector is a substantial net drain on its pool of investment funds.

In principle, societies do not need private savings. Governments could, if the system were so organized, run surpluses in their budgets large enough to finance private investment. Governments would simply lend, rather than borrow, in the nation's capital markets. In practice, however, the American system needs private savings. American governments are not going to run surpluses large enough to obviate the need for private savings.

But the public sector does need to be a net saver. If America's government deficits had been produced by increased public investment (infrastructure, education, research), one could be relaxed about the borrowing necessary to finance them—future standards of living need not fall if the return on public investment is higher than the interest rate that had to be paid on the borrowings. But America's budget deficit was not caused by higher public investment. It was caused by higher public consumption. As a result, the federal government's budget deficit led to less investment. Private savings was being borrowed to finance public consumption, and with fewer funds left for the private sector, investment had to go down unless additional funds could be borrowed abroad.

In 1981 President Reagan predicted that high-income Americans would save more if they were taxed less. Their income taxes were cut, but the American taxpayer spent his or her extra after-tax income on a consumption binge. Private-savings rates fell to all-time lows in the aftermath of the Reagan tax cuts (2.9 percent of disposable income in 1987).[6] On the expenditure side of the budget, defense spending (a form of social consumption) rose sharply, from $131 billion in 1980 to $314 billion in 1990.[7] At the same time, infrastructure and skill investments declined. The bottom line was a large government deficit used to finance consumption and a decade in which Americans made fewer provisions for their own future than they had in any decade in their history. There were those that warned of the dangers implicit in what was being done (the chairman of President Reagan's Council of Economic Advisers, Martin Feldstein, was one), but they were ignored.

Americans seemed to be able to run far larger federal budget deficits with far fewer adverse effects than anyone predicted. Neither the higher inflation rates nor the crowding out of private investment that had been so widely predicted occurred to the extent that had been predicted. Foreigners were simply willing to lend Americans more money than anyone dreamed possible. Investment did go down from 17.5 percent of GNP in the last four years of the 1970s to 15.3 percent of GNP in the last four years of the 1980s, but it would have fallen to 12.6 percent if foreign funds had not been available to augment American savings.[8] The inflow of foreign funds kept the value of the dollar high in the first half of the decade, and low-priced imports kept inflation in check. American firms simply could not raise prices without losing market share to their foreign competitors.

Because the timing of those predicting disaster was wrong, the public came to believe their predictions were also wrong. But to say that economic gravity has been defied for ten years is not to say that it can be defied forever. In 1991, for the first time in a century, the United States became a net payer rather than a net receiver of foreign-investment income.[9] Eventually, the lending will stop, and real interest rates will soar, reducing investment even further.

Like a trade deficit, a federal budget deficit has its own gravitational arithmetic. As budget deficits continue, total government indebtedness mounts and interest payments become a larger and larger fraction of total spending. In the 1980s interest payments rose from 9 to 15 percent of federal spending.[10] During the deficit period, tax rates can be set at levels below those necessary to cover normal government services. Money is borrowed both to make interest payments and to pay for some services. Conversely, when the budget returns to balance, tax rates have to rise to cover both the government services that were earlier being financed with borrowed money and the higher interest payments that are owed on a vastly expanded government debt. In 1990 the federal government collected 20 percent of the GNP in taxes.[11] If the federal government had run no deficits in the decade of the 1980s, 20 percent of the GNP would have been enough to balance the federal government's budget in 1990. With the deficits it did run, however, the federal government would have had to collect taxes equal to 23 percent of GNP if it was to balance its budget in 1990. The longer a deficit runs, the higher marginal tax rates must eventually become to finance any given level of public services.

If government deficits are financed by internal borrowing, average American take-home incomes are not affected. Taxes have to be collected from American taxpayers to make interest payments, but those interest payments are in turn made to American bondholders. If government deficits are financed by external borrowing, however, taxes have to be collected from Americans to make government interest payments to foreign bondholders. American incomes must fall.

In the decade ahead the American system will be tested to see whether it is run by an establishment or an oligarchy.[12] One often hears that Japan has an establishment, while Latin America has an oligarchy. In many ways both terms refer to the same group. Both are groups of well-connected rich people who go to the same schools, marry each other, and run their countries. But there is a key difference. The central goal of an establishment is to insure that the system works so that the country will in the long run be successful. An establishment is confident that if the system works and if the country does well, its members will personally do well. A confident establishment doesn't have to make its own immediate self-interest paramount when it makes, or influences, public decisions.

In contrast, an oligarchy is a group of insecure individuals who amass funds in secret Swiss bank accounts. Because they think that they must always look out for their own immediate self-interest, they aren't interested in investing either their time or their effort in improving their country's long-run prospects. Put bluntly, they aren't confident that if their country is successful, they too will be successful.

America's history is not as consistent as that of either Japan or Latin America. At some points in time, America has clearly had an establishment. The Founding Fathers—among them

George Washington, Benjamin Franklin, Thomas Jefferson—were an establishment. America also had an establishment after World War II. Rebuilding Japan and Germany, the Marshall Plan, and similar activities did not happen because of a spontaneous democratic outburst of altruism. Those programs had to be sold to a democratic electorate by the American establishment as good for the world—and as a result, in the long run, good for Americans. In the short run those programs cost Americans some of the resources that they might otherwise have spent on themselves—about 3 percent of GNP for ten years.

At other times America clearly has had an oligarchy. The 1920s were such a period. I suspect that future historians will also say that America had an oligarchy in the 1980s. The merger wars, junk bonds, business magazines whose biggest-selling issues were lists of the wealthiest Americans, the lifestyles of the rich and famous on TV, trade and budget deficits that remain uncured, financial scandals, tax cuts for the wealthy—all are manifestations of an oligarchy.

But what will America have in the 1990s—an establishment or an oligarchy? If one wants to know, watch the federal budget deficit. Does it get eliminated or does it remain a festering problem?

If an oligarchy is redesigning a tax system, it will rig the system so that it pays the least possible taxes. The recommended tax laws will be defended as good for the country, but the prime goal will be tax cuts for the oligarchs themselves.[13] When a public diet is required, the public services that go to the oligarchs will be the last to be cut.

In contrast, an establishment will lower its own taxes last, even if there is a good economic case that lower taxes would help the country. When it comes to public expenditures, it puts itself on a diet before it puts others on a diet. An establishment lowers its taxes last and cuts its expenditures first to be credible and to prove that it is an establishment when talking about the sacrifices others must make.[14]

It is completely rational for each individual to want to pay the least possible taxes and to shift the burden of paying for its public services onto others. Yet if each individual gets what is in his or her immediate self-interest, democracy itself breaks apart. It cannot do what has to be done. An establishment has to persuade the electorate to ignore its immediate self-interest and to focus on its collective health and long-run survival.

Americans believe that they pay the highest taxes in the world, when in fact they are at the bottom of the industrial league—ranking 24th among 24 major industrial nations in terms of tax collections as a fraction of GDP (see Table 9.1). Every American tax (income, payroll, property, and indirect) is far below those of most of the rest of the developed world.[15] Gasoline taxes of two dollars to four dollars per gallon are typical. A large gasoline tax would help both the federal budget deficit (every penny on the tax rate equals a billion dollars in federal revenue) and the trade deficit (America now imports half of its oil and cannot afford to price oil as if it were still an exporting nation). The rest of the industrial world uses value-added taxes to raise a lot of their revenue. Fifteen to 20 percent value-added tax rates are common in Europe.[16] The buyer of a car sends 20 percent to the government; a saver sends nothing. The result: a strong incentive to save. Simply raising taxes to eliminate the federal deficit would not be the end of the world. Americans would still be paying fewer taxes than their compatriots in most of the rest of the industrial world.

At the same time, there are real opportunities to cut spending. If fears of the Soviet bear more than doubled defense spending in the 1980s, the disappearance of the Soviet bear can more than halve defense spending in the 1990s. Even before the Soviet meltdown, Germany had committed itself to a 26 percent cutback in troops, from 500,000 to 370,000.[17] America does not need to spend more than 12 percent of its GNP on health care—one third more than the next-highest-spending country. The spending hasn't paid off. America is well down in the charts when it comes to every measure of health—life expectancy, morbidity, infant mortality.[18] Successful societies face up to such facts and find ways to cut their spending back to levels where there is some objective payoff. With the elderly on average now wealthier than the nonelderly, there is also a case for cutting back on the Social Security benefits that go to those with above-average incomes.

TABLE 9.1
Government Tax Collections as Fraction of GDP in 1990*

Country	Tax Rate (in percent)
United States	30.0
Australia	30.0
Turkey	30.0
Japan	30.0
Switzerland	31.0
Greece	32.0
Iceland	32.5
Spain	33.0
Portugal	33.2
Canada	34.0
Britain	35.0
Ireland	35.3
Germany	37.0
Finland	37.2
New Zealand	40.0
Italy	40.2
Austria	41.0
Luxembourg	41.5
France	43.0
Belgium	44.0
Netherlands	45.0
Norway	46.1
Denmark	47.5
Sweden	58.0

SOURCES: OECD.
*The Economist, September 21, 1991, p. 123.

While Americans love to fight about government spending, the real issue is not public versus private spending. The real issue is investment (public and private) versus consumption (public and private). America should set itself a goal to design a tax and expenditure system where consumption—public plus private—rises 1 percent per year less rapidly than GNP.[19] If this were done for a decade, America would have world-class savings and investment at the end of the decade, and no one's consumption would have to fall—it would just grow slightly more slowly. One does not need to devastate the present to protect the future. One just needs to be concerned about the future.

A system to raise investment by 1 percent of GNP per year could be designed from either a liberal or a conservative perspective. My optimal system would include value-added taxes to encourage exports and discourage consumption.[20] An offsetting income-tax credit would be established for the first ten thousand dollars in consumption for a family of four to make the value-added tax progressive. There would be tax-free savings accounts, but individuals would have to prove that they were adding to their savings accounts by reducing their consumption and not simply moving money from one account to another or borrowing the funds. America's Individual Retirement Accounts (IRAs) did not stimulate saving, since money was simply moved into IRA accounts from already existing accounts or borrowed and then deposited to get the tax deductions. If tax rates were then raised on that fraction of income not saved (consumption) so as to collect the same amount of government income-tax revenue, tax-free savings accounts would be a powerful vehicle for raising private savings. Savings would effectively be exempted from taxation, and this would turn America's progressive income tax into a progressive consumption tax.

The ideal system would also eliminate payroll taxes to encourage investment in human resources and eliminate the corporate income tax to stimulate physical investment.

As suggested by New York senator Patrick Moynihan, the federal government would take the very large Social Security surplus out of its budget calculations and balance what remains. The necessary revenue to balance what remains would be raised with value-added taxes and gasoline taxes.[21] Together with the existing state and local surpluses, such a strategy (balancing the federal budget, excluding Social Security) would double national savings.

Consumer and mortgage down payments would be raised to limit the dissavings of those that consume more than their income. Germany requires a 40 percent down payment to buy a house; Italy, a 50 percent down payment.[22] Americans could

do likewise. Sixty-month no-down-payment car loans are unknown in the rest of the world. If Americans can get everything they want without saving, why should they save? They
shouldn't and they don't. (Somewhat surprisingly, focus
groups indicate more support for credit restrictions than they
do for consumption taxes.[23])

These suggestions, however, reflect only my own personal
preferences. America would have to design a consensus system that could be supported by both liberals and conserva-
tives, so that as the political tides come and go, the tax system
could continue to provide stable long-run incentives for investment and growth.

Polls show Americans are worried about their economic futures but confused about why their incomes are falling relative
to those in the rest of the world.[25] For many, economic failure
is somehow linked with moral failure (crime in the streets,
drugs, family breakdowns). There is a jumbled stew of economic and moral problems that they cannot sort out. Others
wonder why, if there is a problem, the movers and shakers
of society don't articulate an overarching solution similar to
President Kennedy's man-on-the-moon response to the Soviet
Sputnik. Relentless presidential optimism leaves them confused. Perhaps there isn't a problem after all. But at the same
time they want to be led to a solution if the burdens of that
solution are to be shared fairly across the population.

Sorting out this stew of jumbled beliefs will require an
American establishment that can articulate the demands of the
future (today's investments) and that can suggest unselfish
self-interested programs for achieving this result. To do what
must be done, some president of the United States will have
to unlearn what every politician has been taught by President
Reagan. President Reagan taught every politician, Republican
and Democrat, one fact of political life and then redefined an
English word. His fact was simple: In American politics opti-
mists beat pessimists. Politically, the rhetoric of "standing
tall" is a winner. While Reagan raised standing tall to new
heights in the pantheon of political truths, being optimistic
has probably always been very important in getting elected in
America. The real damage was done by President Reagan's
redefinition of the word *optimism*. In the Reagan political dic-

tionary, an optimist is someone who denies that America has any problems. To admit that America has any fundamental problems or weaknesses is to be a pessimist and unfit for political office.

By this definition of optimism, President Kennedy was a pessimist when in 1960 he admitted that the Russians were ahead of America in space and had been growing faster economically in the 1950s. But at the time Americans thought of him as an optimist. He had solutions. He would get the country moving again by putting a man on the moon within a decade, and he would design new economic policies to stimulate economic growth. He succeeded. Americans got to the moon first; productivity grew at record rates in the first half of the 1960s. Today, President Kennedy would be labeled a pessimist; his advisers would warn against man-on-the-moon speeches.

Presidential elections have become contests to see who can most successfully deny that the United States has any problems. But once elected on a no-problems-exist platform, it becomes impossible to implement solutions to those nonexisting problems. The schizophrenia this produces was palpable in President Bush's 1990 State of the Union message. In the last half of that speech, he talked about improving K–12 education; in the first half of the speech, he talked about America having the most productive work force in the world. But if American workers were the most productive in the world, not much could be wrong with American education. The speech came and went—and not much has been done about education.

Compare Bush's 1990 State of the Union speech with Churchill's Dunkirk speeches. Those speeches are remembered for their fighting rhetoric: "We shall go on to the end. We shall fight in France, we shall fight on the seas and oceans, we shall fight with growing confidence and growing strength in the air, we shall defend our island, whatever the cost may be. We shall fight on the beaches, we shall fight on the landing grounds, we shall fight in the fields and in the streets, we shall fight in the hills; we shall never surrender."[25]

What is forgotten is how they began: "The news from France is very bad."

Americans cannot strengthen their economic team unless the president is first willing to tell them the news from the economic battlefields is very bad. If each new president insists that America has no economic problems, then there are no political solutions to America's economic problems. In America the existence of an establishment depends upon having a president who is willing to lead. America is not Japan, where an establishment among elite civil servants can keep the country on track, whatever the politicians do. In America each generation must rebuild anew an establishment that is forever in flux. Without domestic presidential leadership, America, by default, is led by an oligarchy.

The Skill Positions

If the "British disease" is adversarial labor-management relations, the "American disease" is the belief that low wages solve all problems. When under competitive pressure, American firms first go to the low-wage nonunion parts of America and then on to a succession of countries with ever-lower wages. But the strategy seldom works. For a brief time lower wages lead to higher profits, but eventually others with even lower wages enter the business (low wages are easy to copy), prices fall, and the higher profits generated by lower wages vanish.

The search for the holy grail of high profitability lies elsewhere—in a relentless upscale drive in technology to ever-higher levels of productivity—and wages. Since rapid productivity growth is a moving target and therefore hard to copy, high long-run profits can be sustained. But to get the necessary human talent to employ new technologies, large skill investments have to be made.[26] High wages have to be paid, but paradoxically high wages also leave firms with no choice but to go upscale in technology. High wages and high profits are not antithetical—they go together.[27]

To create the productivity that can justify high wages, American K–12 education will have to improve. Numerous studies have sharply defined the problem. The performance of American high-school graduates may have declined, it depends upon exactly how performance is measured, but the real problem is not deterioration. The rest of the world is simply reaching levels of performance far above those ever reached in the United States. This is especially true if one looks at performance standards for the bottom half of the distribution. Even in the good old days, America wasn't very good at the bottom. Blacks that are today left uneducated in America's central cities were yesterday left uneducated in its rural South.

While everyone sees the need for a better-skilled work force, each economic actor thinks that she cannot recoup her costs if she must bear the costs alone. The individual does not know where she will be employed and does not want to invest in skills that will become worthless if she is laid off. Someone else should make the necessary investments.

Because of high labor-force turnover rates, firms feel that they cannot educate their workers. If they did, their newly trained workers would simply go off to other employers who could pay higher wages because they did not have to incur training costs. Someone else should make the necessary investments.

Local governments don't want to pay for first-class schools. They know that less than half the population has children in school at any one time, that students will leave home and use their skills in different geographic regions of the country, and that the high taxes necessary to pay for good schools would drive industry away. Firms would locate next door and free ride on their well-educated work force. Someone else should make the necessary investments.

As state governments went through their budget-cutting exercise in the 1991 recession, no sector of public spending was cut more than education. Someone else should make the necessary investments.

In recent years the federal government has come to see education more and more as an individual or local responsibility. Student grants have been converted to student loans, and federal aid to education both at school and on the job is one of the few places where government spending was actually cut under the Reagan administration. Someone else should make the necessary investments.

When it comes to skill investments, individual rationality (let someone else do it) produces collective irrationality (it doesn't get done).

The United States is unique among industrial countries in that it does not have an organized postsecondary education system for the non–college bound.[28] Relative to their respective sizes, for every dollar in taxpayer's money invested in the education of the non–college bound, fifty-five dollars is spent subsidizing those going to college—a ratio that is neither fair nor efficient.[29] Other nations' governments invest heavily in the postsecondary skills of the non–college bound. Britain, France, and Spain spend more than twice as much as the United States; Germany, more than three times as much; and Sweden, almost six times as much.[30]

The rest of the world understands that a worker who moves to another firm may be lost to the company that paid for his training, but it knows he is not lost to the economy. There is a collective interest in insuring that private training occurs. Japanese firms talk about training workers to "add to effective battle strength."[31] The Europeans talk about "A Winning European Formula: Schools + Industry = Work Readiness."[32]

Consider the words of a German executive. "Germany is fighting to hold a quality edge over countries like Korea and Japan—not so much with the U.S. This is the reason for the great expansion of further education in Germany right now. The problem with the U.S. is that there are too many people in college and not enough qualified workers. The U.S. has outstanding universities, but it is missing its middle. Too much training takes place on the job, and therefore is too unsystematic."[33]

"Following Joe around," the American system of on-the-job training, simply isn't a system. The resulting skills are very narrow and do not lead to workers who can absorb new technologies.

The Germans have an apprentice system that is the envy of the rest of the world. With lifetime employment, Japanese firms know that they must either train or have an untrained labor force. The French have instituted a 1 percent sales tax to insure that firms train. If training is given, the 1 percent is refunded. If training is not given, the funds are kept to finance government-training programs. Singapore allows "bonding," where employees who receive training sign loan agreements that must be repaid if the employees leave the employment of those paying for their training before a specified period of time.

While the skill-deficiency problem has been well defined, the leverage point from which the system can be moved has not been found. Better working skills are a two-stage, public-private process. First, workers must come into the labor force with good educational skills when they leave the twelfth grade. In America this has historically been a government function. Second, firms must invest in the specific job skills that need to go along with these general-education attainments. In America this second step has been a private responsibility.

While the superior performance of European or Japanese high-school graduates is lost by the time they graduate from college, and while American graduate schools have no equal elsewhere in the world, there is still a problem in higher education. It produces too few scientists and engineers relative to the total college population—only 15–17 percent in the United States, as compared to about 40 percent in Germany or Japan. But this problem cannot be solved at the college level until high-school science and math education has been improved. Most Americans have effectively already closed the door on a science career by the time they graduate from high school.

Bench marking reveals that educational reforms should focus on math and science education for those that do go to college and on developing a first-class skill system for those in K–12 education who will not go on to graduate from college—about 75 percent of the population. Since most of the differences in educational achievement between America and the rest of the industrial world emerge between the seventh and twelfth grades, these grades should be the central area of concern![34]

America's high-school-dropout rate (29 percent) is positively Third World (Japan's rate is 6 percent; Germany's, 9 percent), but dropout prevention is not the most important problem.[35] Getting people through a system that does not provide them with usable skills isn't an achievement. The first goal is to make the American high school work for those that do attend—then worry about problems of the nonattenders.

The problem is not lack of information or studies.[36] The problem is generating action in a system with fifteen thousand independent local school boards whose incentives lie in other directions. To bring about the necessary reforms, a grand bargain needs to be struck.

In their part of the bargain, the taxpayers would agree to bring the wages of schoolteachers up to the levels found in Germany or Japan—$40,000–45,000 per year versus $30,000 in America.[37] When schools had a captive female labor supply, high-quality teachers could be hired without high wages. Today, quality and wages are directly linked. America cannot continue to run a system where one third of those teaching physics have never taken a formal college course in physics.[38] In a capitalistic society, if one wants skilled teachers in the classroom, one has to pay for them.

Wages should go up, but not without the rest of the grand bargain. The teachers, for their part, would have to agree to world-scale work effort and efficiency. The school day would be lengthened by a couple of hours per day in high school, and the school year would be at least 220 days long. A 35-year-old German teacher may make $51,000 annually, but he works a full day and year—220 to 240 days depending upon the Länder—not the 180 days common in America.[39]

In addition to working longer, teachers would commit themselves to bringing nonclassroom administrative costs down to the levels found in Germany or Japan. In most big-city school systems, less than half the employees are now classroom teachers. Over time, administrative jobs have grown to provide higher wage opportunities for low-wage classroom teachers. With higher wages in the classroom, most of those unneeded administrative jobs should be abolished, and teachers should return to teaching. Much of the increase in teacher's salaries would effectively be funded out of cuts in administrative costs.

Competitive wages would force Americans to spend more, but not a lot more. America now spends 4.1 percent of GNP on K–12 education. Germany spends 4.6 percent, and Japan, 4.8 percent.[40]

The fourth part of the bargain is to set a quality standard for the non–college bound. Here the high-wage business community in each state should write an achievement test that would cover what they think high-school graduates need to know to work at America's best firms. Local school boards could continue to graduate whomever they wished, but those that had passed this "business achievement test" would have their diploma so stamped. In accordance with a plan developed by John Bishop, a Cornell analyst of the American high school, leading high-wage business firms would commit themselves to hiring only those with stamped diplomas.[41] The state would pay to grade and administer the achievement test, but it would be written by employers to insure that Americans clearly understood that this is what their children must learn if they wished to have high-wage jobs. It wouldn't be a test written by ivory-tower professors or education bureaucrats.

If there were an objective quality standard for everyone, a lot of parental choice and school independence in determining the individual means to passing those achievement tests could be allowed. With everyone having to reach the same final goals, no one could spend too much time wandering off into irrelevancies. Completely free parental choice, unrestricted school vouchers, is not apt to work in the United States. Any system of free parental choice will quickly produce some schools devoted to black nationalism or white supremacy and little else. Just as quickly free parental choice will be abolished. The right answer is combining parental involvement with public education.

Parents will have to push harder. Fifty-one percent of the parents in Taiwan purchase an extra workbook to help their children in science—only 1 percent do in Minneapolis. Japanese students do five times as many hours of homework per week as their American peers. American students read only one third as much as those in Switzerland.[42]

In the same spirit, universities should admit students based upon achievement examinations and not high-school diplomas or intelligence tests.[43] Those who worked hard in high school should be rewarded with admission to universities, whether public or private. Those who did not work should not be admitted—no matter how smart they are.

Communities would agree to quit using schools as a dumping ground where they assign social problems that cannot be solved elsewhere. The school's prime responsibility is to insure that their students are educated. The front lines of the war on crime, drugs, teenage pregnancy, or housing desegregation should be established elsewhere. Better nutrition, drivers' training, and sports are secondary. The energy of our school systems should be focused on education—not dissipated on other goals, no matter how laudable.

Better schools are only the beginning. American firms do not invest as much in training their work forces as firms abroad, and what they do invest is much more heavily concentrated on professional and managerial workers.[44] The oft-cited reason is turnover. If turnover is the real reason, then firms need to take actions such as deferred compensation to reduce turnover. Without a much better trained work force, they will not be competitive.

A number of avenues exist for increasing the working skills of the average worker. One possibility is to pass the American equivalent of the French law that requires business firms to invest 1 percent of their sales in training. Firms must pay a tax of this amount but can deduct their own internal training costs from this tax. Since all firms have to pay for training, they might as well train.

Alternatively, the Social Security system could be expanded beyond health care and pensions for the elderly to include training for the young. Upon birth, every young person would have a training account set up in his name for use after graduation from high school in which a sum of money equal to the amount of public money that is now spent on the average college graduate (about $17,500) would be deposited.[45] Over their lifetime, individuals could draw upon this fund to pay for university training or to pay their employer for on-the-job skill training. Repayment would occur in the form of payroll tax deductions.[46]

Americans can, if they wish, have the most skilled work force in the world, but it does require being willing to build a new American system. No society likes to change, yet no society survives across the centuries unless it does.

Creating Business Groups

If productivity isn't rising at a rate commensurate with that of the best, and competitive bench marking reveals that it is not, American business firms are failing to do their primary job. The rest of the world thinks that America's failure lies in shortsightedness. Perhaps they are right. Seventy percent of the CEOs in America's largest one thousand firms think that they put too much emphasis on the short run, although they place the blame on the stock market.[47, 48] They are not completely wrong. Security analysts regularly object to firms spending too much money on research and development.[49]

Not too long ago I was consulting for a firm that had a problem. Its cost-cutting program had substantially exceeded expectations, and it had made 50 percent more money in one quarter than it had expected to make. This good news, learned near the end of the quarter and too late to be effectively hidden with creative accounting, was treated as a disaster. Management was sure that its stock would immediately rise on news of the record profits but then plunge in the next quarter when the firm could not duplicate the previous quarter's feat. Its fears were not unfounded. In other cases record profit results have been connected with tumbling stock prices.[50]

To compete in a world economy, products and services must be speedily designed and precisely tailored to the needs of the customer. To do this, corporations must work with their suppliers and customers, but in the American system of arm's-length business relationships, cooperation usually fails. A customer in one area is apt to be a competitor in another. How can any firm reveal its secrets to its competitor? A firm's supplier is also apt to be the supplier of its competitor. How can a firm be sure that anything cooperatively learned with a supplier won't be immediately passed on to a competitor? To work together, firms must trust each other, but in the American system, they cannot trust each other.

American firms play in a world economy where they face off against Japanese and German business groups. Business groups make it hard for American firms to penetrate foreign markets. Potential industrial customers are all locked into relationships with members of their group. Consumers are difficult to reach, since retailers give preferences to producers that are part of their group.

Shortsightedness, working with customers and suppliers, international competition—they all dictate a return to an era of business groups. Business groups insulate management from short-term stock-market pressures without creating incompetent managers. Sitting on each other's boards, members of the group know what is going on. Buying each other's products, they must insist on efficiency. They can cooperate with each other, since their place on the board means that they cannot in secret be double-crossed. Without such linkages, no one knows who is on who's side. With business groups, the American market becomes harder for foreigners to penetrate. No one should be forced to join a business group, but no one should be prohibited from doing so either.

American capitalism is rich in financial investors of every size and variety, from the man on the street to the giant pension funds to the get-rich-quick speculators and takeover artists. In the 1980s financial Vikings were everywhere raiding everyone. If the merger and takeover wars had tightened up efficiency, a case could have been made for the merger wars, but productivity was falling at the end of the decade. Like the real Vikings who laid waste to so many vegetable gardens that they were eventually forced to become farmers if they did not want to starve, the financial Vikings were temporarily driven out of business by their own excesses. But their temporary demise is not enough.

Put bluntly, American capitalism needs a heart transplant. The financial traders who have become the heart of American capitalism need to be taken out and replaced by real capitalists who can become the heart of an American industrial rebirth. What America lacks is genuine, old-style capitalists—those big investors of yesteryear who often invented the technologies they were managing and whose personal wealth was inextricably linked to the destiny of their giant companies. It misses them. Men like Henry Ford; Thomas J. Watson, of IBM; and J. P. Morgan were at the heart of the system that produced the greatest economic power and the highest standard of living in history.[51]

Old-fashioned corporations were run by individual capitalists—a shareholder with enough stock to dominate the board of directors and to dictate policy; a shareholder who usually was also the chief executive officer. Owning a majority or controlling interest, the old-fashioned capitalist did not have to concentrate his attention on reshuffling financial assets to fight off the raids of the financial Vikings. He was an industrialist who made his living by producing new products or by producing old products more cheaply. He was in control. But he was also locked into his corporation. He couldn't look to get rich by selling out for a quick profit—dumping his large stock holdings on the market would have simply depressed the price of his stock and cost him his job as one of the captains of American industry. His wealth, job, ego, and prestige were all locked up with the success or failure of his corporation. He had no choice but to work to improve the long-run efficiency and productivity of his company.

Today, with very few exceptions, old-fashioned capitalists are gone and cannot be brought back to life. In the aggregate, financial institutions such as pension funds, foundations, or mutual funds own 60 to 70 percent of most publicly listed companies. Collectively, they own the company, but individually, there are limits to how much of any one company they can own (usually no more than 10 percent), and how actively they can intervene in the decision making of the companies in which they do own stock (they cannot sit on the board of directors of any firm in which have substantial holdings, since this would give them inside information). Minority shareholders are, in the aggregate, majority shareholders. By law, the institutions are essentially forced to be traders and speculators. They cannot be active builders that seek to strengthen a company's long-run competitive position. They cannot act as real capitalists who control what they own.

Minority shareholders have agendas very different from those of the dominant capitalist. Since they do not have the clout to change business decisions, strategies, or incumbent managers with their voting power, they can only enhance their wealth by buying and selling shares in accordance with what they think is going to happen to short-term profits. As a result, earnings per share, judged on a quarterly basis, become the dominant factor in determining whether the institutional investors will buy, sell, or keep a stock. Hundreds of millions of shares change hands every day in a game that has nothing to do with beliefs about long-term success or failure, or with plans to convert failure into success.

As the financial institutions grew to their present size, they could make money by being better informed than the individual shareholders whose shares they were acquiring. But as they came to own a majority of the shares in the market, they were essentially buying and selling from each other. What one financial institution gained, another lost. Their only options were to buy stock-market averages (a dull option that does not yield high returns or take talented people to implement it) or to participate in the financial wars.

For these minority-majority institutional shareholders, the takeover game was simply the only money-making game in town. Opportunities existed to make a lot of money quickly. It was a game far better than the zero-sum game they were playing with each other on the stock market. America's laws could even be interpreted as saying that institutional investors that did not want to participate in the takeover game had to sell out to others who did. If a takeover artist offered a pension fund more for its shares than their current stock-market value and the fund did not sell out, perhaps it could be sued for not living up to its fiduciary responsibilities to maximize stock-market values for the benefit of future pension recipients. To ignore such short-run profit-making opportunities might actually be illegal. Recently, the financial institutions have organized to prevent management from adopting defense mechanisms such as poison pills to stop takeovers, since these devices undercut the value of the shares the institutions hold.[52]

In the absence of dominant shareholders, corporations are effectively run by their professional managers. Unlike founding fathers, the professional chief executive officers (CEOs) of large corporations usually reach that exalted position just a few years before they retire. Long-run careers at the top are very unusual. As a short-term CEO, they not surprisingly organize compensation packages for themselves that emphasize bonuses and salaries keyed to current profits or sales. These short-run compensation packages are unfortunately completely congruent with the short-run perspective of the institutional shareholders. Neither the manager nor the shareholder expects to be around very long.

For both managers and minority shareholders, mergers and acquisitions—the takeover game—represent an almost irresistible path to glory. The managers of acquiring companies can double sales and profits (and, hence, their own salaries and bonuses, which are tied to those sales and profits) with a stroke of a pen—and without risking a cent of their own personal money. If a firm's own economic crop of new or cheaper products were homegrown, the crop probably wouldn't ripen before the incumbent manager retired. Rome could not be built in a day, but in the 1980s its economic equivalent could be bought in a single day.

Those who rise to the top from finance, a large fraction of American CEOs, may in fact know far more about fighting the financial wars than they know about running their own companies. It is what they are good at. It is what they have been trained to do. Attack or be attacked! Some managers will, of course, lose in the takeover games, but those on the losing side have the solace of multimillion-dollar golden parachutes.

Financial takeovers are always justified on the grounds that they will enhance productivity and competitiveness, but the promised leaner and meaner corporations do not seem to emerge. No one can know for sure how today's mergers will be performing fifteen years from now, but we do know that the last conglomerate merger wave in the late 1960s and early 1970s did not lead to firms with superior performance. The whole process looked much like a random walk—some winners, some losers—on average, average.

The short-run results of the current wave of financial activities are only too clear. Productivity growth is lower at the end of the decade than it was at the beginning of the decade. Firms ended up loaded with too much debt, having too few free funds to invest in new products, new processes, or research and development. With all of that debt, they became more risk-averse—less willing to bet on new activities. In many cases they simply could not bet on the future, since the company had effectively already been bet.

Firms become financially weaker and more vulnerable to collapse in recessions. The 1991 recession was the first big test of the merger wave of the 1980s. Would the firms that were affected by those activities be able to survive a downturn in revenue, given their needs to make huge interest payments? Until a recovery is well under way, we won't know the exact extent of the damage, but midway through the process, for too many the answer is already no. A 1991 list of the firms in bankruptcy that in the 1980s participated in the merger wars would go on for many pages.

Those who argue for the virtues of the takeover movement do so on the basis that it enriches the shareholders and that firms exist *solely* to serve the interests of the shareholders. There is no doubt that the enrichment part of the argument is true, but the question remains whether firms exist solely to serve the interests of the shareholders. Shareholders' rights are not in fact paramount.

In the dicta of Adam Smith, the individual search for profits would always promote the nation's economic growth. But in practice a problem developed. Too often, Adam Smith's "invisible hand" became the hand of a pickpocket. Free unfettered markets had a habit of discovering very profitable but nonproductive activities. Practical experience taught that profit maximizing did not necessarily lead to output maximizing.

In the midnineteenth century, the railroads used their monopoly over the means of transportation to divert the fruits of other's productive energies to themselves by setting transportation prices that extracted monopoly rents. The railroad barons were profit maximizers, but their profit maximizing did not lead to a larger economic pie. Quite the reverse; it led to a smaller economic pie. There was simply more money to be made extracting monopoly rents than there was to be made in operating better transportation systems. In response, the United States created the Interstate Commerce Commission to refocus the attention of railroad entrepreneurs on running better railroads rather than on economically raping the rest of society.

Later, the robber barons in steel, oil, and copper discovered that man-made monopolies were as good as those made by technology. Establishing monopolies and raising prices were far more profitable than increasing efficiency and production. In engaging in these activities, the corporation was fulfilling its private obligation to maximize profits and shareholder wealth, but it was not meeting its social obligation of being a vehicle for maximizing national growth and a higher standard of living for everyone. Again, society refocused the profit-making ambitions of the robber barons with the Sherman Antitrust Act of 1890 and the Clayton Antitrust Act of 1914. The new laws were designed to insure that the name of the game was not simply to make money, but to make money by building a better or cheaper product.

Present laws are often the equivalent of shooting oneself in the foot. General Motors, for example, is permitted to engage in a joint venture with Toyota that will effectively attack Ford and Chrysler, whereas it would not be permitted to engage in a joint venture with Ford to repel the Japanese auto invasion. Antitrust limitations that apply to two American firms do not apply to an American and a Japanese firm, although there is now a world, not an American, market for cars.

Private firms exist in our society because Americans have collectively decided that private firms are in general the best way to promote economic growth and to expand the output available to everyone—shareholder and nonshareholder alike. If private firms fail to serve this social function, they will be redirected, as they have been in the past, with new sets of rules and regulations that will hopefully once again set them off on productive paths.

What has to be done, however, is not simply to deregulate or to make minor changes in antitrust laws. The entire regulatory framework governing finance and industry must be altered so that the biggest profits and highest incomes are paid to those who expand productivity and output rather than to those who rejiggle financial assets. The financial Vikings, today's counterpart to yesterday's robber barons, need to be reined in so as to refocus their attention on production, just as those earlier robber barons needed to refocus on production rather than monopoly profits.

In the 1970s and 1980s the United States had a good record when it came to new start-ups, but new start-ups do not substitute for giant corporations that retain their vitality. The new start-ups most needed are precisely those that eventually become giant corporations. A small business that remains small is of limited value. It is also possible to have too much entrepreneurship. New firms cannot grow big because they are always hemorrhaging their most talented people, who in going off to become entrepreneurs themselves, prevent both the new and the new-new firms from gaining critical mass.[53] Occasionally, brilliant entrepreneurs will come to the fore and nurture a corporation into one of America's largest, but within one or two generations, that corporation, like the rest of American industry, will be without a dominant shareholder.

To put real capitalists back into American capitalism, today's short-term financial traders must be remade into tomorrow's long-term capitalistic builders. Once there, they then have to be boxed in so that their profit-making energies are focused on activities that raise productivity and output. To do so, the legal limits that now prevent financial institutions from acquiring a dominant or majority shareholding position in industrial firms should be removed. Instead of preventing these institutions from becoming real capitalists, they should be encouraged to buy controlling interests, to sit on the board of directors of companies in which they invest, to actively hire and fire the firms' managers, and to worry about the strategies and investments that will make their companies successful.

Instead of legally being forced to be short-term, speculative share traders, financial institutions should be encouraged to become real institutional capitalists whose success or failure is based on their ability to grow healthy industrial corporations. Instead of being encouraged to remain liquid with many small investments in widely scattered firms, they should be encouraged to get into financial situations from which they cannot extract themselves, except by making the corporations in which they have invested successful. Instead of maintaining an arms-length separation between finance and industry, they should be encouraged to become so entwined that their destinies cannot be separated.

Essentially, American finance should be put in an institutional straitjacket where it cannot succeed unless American

industry succeeds. Key to this is changing the financial regulations (mostly found in the Glass-Steagall Act of 1933 and in
the antitrust laws) that prevent American banks and other financial institutions from becoming merchant banks—financial
institutions that own and control industrial corporations or are
owned by them.

Allowing America's financial institutions to take stakes in
industrial companies (or the reverse) will, over time, lead to
the formation of business groups that are the equivalent of
those that now exist in Japan or Germany—or that used to
exist in the United States prior to the Great Depression. These
groups are simply necessary to compete in today's world.[54]
What is needed is a framework of mutual support where raiding is difficult (ownership of each other's shares makes it hard
to acquire a majority interest), but where directors have real
clout to fire bad managers, since they represent real owners.

Some of what were once America's most successful companies—General Electric, U.S. Steel, International Harvester—
were founded by merchant bankers before that financial species was outlawed during the Great Depression. Others, such
as AT&T and Kodak, would not have become successful without such help.[55] In recent years, small-scale merchant bankers
have reappeared in the guise of venture capitalists. They play
a vital role in helping companies get started, but when the
companies become middle-sized and offer their shares for sale
to the public, the venture capitalist usually sells his stock and
starts over again with a new company. Venture capital is not
a substitute for large-scale merchant banks.

Outside directors who own few if any shares are no substitution for directors who represent a controlling block of
shares. The former are controlled by management, except in
time of crisis; the latter control management at all times. Outside directors who own only a few shares in the company simply cannot play the role they should play.

In reformulating banking and antitrust laws, conglomerate
groups or vertical supplier-customer groups such as those that
exist in Japan should be permitted.[56] What should be prohibited is the single industry groups that J. P. Morgan sometimes
organized, where much of the entire steel industry would be
organized into one company. The latter leads to monopoly;
the former leads to more competition.

Given that they will have access to inside information, the new laws should see to it that all dominant shareholders, institutional or individual, are locked into their investments. While the ownership of a large block of shares constitutes a substantial lock-in (it is difficult to sell a substantial number of shares without depressing one's own stock price), this natural lock should be buttressed. Those who own a dominant position in any company—say 20 percent or more—should be forced to give the public one day's advance notice of their intention to sell any of their shares. Unless this announced sale can be explained to the satisfaction of the investing public on grounds other than expected future failure, any such notice will inevitably trigger a general rush to sell that stock before the major investor can sell, leaving the big investor to sell at much reduced prices. Locked-in institutional investors will think long and hard before trying to bail out of a company if it is having trouble. Instead, they have a major incentive to minister to their sick company, designing the strategies necessary to return it to health.

To reinforce the distinction between traders and investors, the voting rights of equity shares should rise over time. Major investors subject to the 20 percent rule would become instant owners, but others would gain full voting rights only over some substantial period of time. No voting rights would be given to those who have owned shares less than two years, with full voting rights gradually restored over the next three years—in year three, one third of a vote for each share held; in year four, two thirds of a vote for each share held; and in year five, a full vote for each share held. Stock traders could still be traders who get rich by buying and selling shares, but those who want to be short-term traders would be separated from those that want to be long-term owners.

While the tyranny of the quarterly profit statement is probably exaggerated as a deterrent to good management, it should be repealed as a symbolic measure. Japan has gradually moved from quarterly to half-year to annual profit reports. Nothing has been lost. The same should be done in the United States. Managers should not be placed in a position where if they incur expenses this quarter to make future prospects better, they will be penalized by falling stock prices. While this may not happen very often, too many managers believe that it will.

Today's laws also draw too sharp a distinction between loans and equity. To avoid the appearance of a conflict of interest, executives from banks, insurance companies, and other lenders are not supposed to be financially involved participants. They are supposed to have an arms-length relationship with their customers. But that flies in the face of reason. It is precisely the institutions that provide major long-term loans to companies that should be taking an active role in the strategic direction of these companies. They should be interested directors rather than outsiders wondering what is going on. To bring this about, long-term loans should carry voting rights. A one-hundred-million-dollar long-term loan might, for example, entitle a lender to half the voting rights of a one-hundred-million-dollar long-term equity investment. Major lenders, like equity investors, should not be allowed to be absentee landlords.

In today's world economy, where American firms must match up against the business groups of Germany of Japan, American firms need to be able to form the same strategic alliances, the same self-help societies, and the same joint strategies for conquering world markets. They must have an equal arsenal of weapons. To give them the necessary weapons, America's laws and regulations must be drastically overhauled.

In any reformulation of the rules governing America's industrial structure, one central goal must be kept in mind. Put real capitalists back in the driver's seat of the American corporation. Then box them in so that they have no choice but to improve their firms and, hence, the nation's productivity and competitiveness if they want to be personally successful. Only patient, locked-in, long-term owners have long time horizons.

National Strategies

It is the official American position that it does not need to worry about the national strategies of other countries. Foreign national strategies simply won't work. But this is a belief that looks increasingly untenable if one looks at the industries that have been lost, such as robots, or industries under threat, such as aircraft manufacturing. It also confronts a world of man-made comparative advantage where the brainpower industries of the future will exist in those places where institutions organize to capture them.

The rest of the world is not cheating when it employs national strategies. That is just the way those nations play economic football. Americans can respond in one of three ways:

1. True believers in the American way can argue that we Americans have got it right and that the Germans and the Japanese have got it wrong. In the end their national strategies will hurt them more than they help. Keep the faith!

2. The agnostics can argue for changing American laws to permit American firms to get together if they wish. Try a few experiments with national industrial policies. Let a thousand flowers bloom!

3. The converts (heretics?) can argue for an aggressive American effort to counter foreign national strategies with American strategies. Fight fire with fire!

Bench marking reveals a variety of foreign models. The Japanese Ministry of International Trade and Industry (MITI) orchestrates the development of a game plan in Japan. In Germany the large industrial banks, among them, the Deutsche Bank, are the conductors of the economic orchestra. Government-owned firms play a key role in France. But none of these foreign systems could easily be grafted onto the U.S. system. America is going to have to find a uniquely American way to develop a game plan.

The nature of the problems are neatly encapsulated in America's experience with amorphous metals—metals made by rapidly quenching alloys of iron, boron, and silicon to give them a glasslike consistency that has exceptional electrical and magnetic properties. Amorphous metals were developed by Allied-Signal, a New Jersey–based firm, in the early 1970s.[57] Much of the market for the products it makes is in Japan. If Japanese engineers had used amorphous metals, they would

have saved one billion dollars per year in electricity costs
alone. But Japanese officials intervened to delay patent approval for eleven years, which left very little time to use the
products before the original patents expired. Japanese companies were also persuaded not to use amorphous metals until
the American patents expired. As the end of the patents ap-
proached (1993), MITI announced a catch-up program involv-
ing thirty-four Japanese companies in an effort to learn how
to make amorphous metals themselves so that no time would
be lost when the patents expired. What should have been a
market of over one hundred million dollars per year has never
been a market of more than a few million.

What should Americans do when other nations target an
industry where they have a technical lead? Screams and protests do very little good. After intensive negotiations with the
American trade representative, the Japanese agreed to buy
thirty-two thousand amorphous-metal transformers (0.5 percent of the market) before the patents run out in 1993—essentially nothing. Allied-Signal has been accused by security
analysts of having spent too much money on research and
development. If it cannot make its R&D pay off by selling its
products, it should do no R&D. On one level, the stock-market analysts are right. If products cannot be sold, they should
not have been invented.

To be successful, American firms have to be able to build
dominant market shares when they have technological leadership. If this is prohibited by foreign industrial policies, others
will effectively compete in the U.S. market when they have
technical superiority, but American firms will not be able to
compete effectively in foreign markets when Americans have
technological superiority.

The key difference between the United States and the rest
of the industrial world is not the existence of protection.
About 25 percent of all U.S. imports, double the amount of
two decades ago, are now affected by nontariff trade barriers.[58] International businessmen see Japan as the world's most
unfair trading nation, but they see the United States as the
third most unfair after Korea and Japan.[59] The European Community has published a book listing hundreds of American
violations of free trade.[60]

If industrial policies are defined as trade protection, American industrial policies are as extensive as those in either Germany or Japan. But as the Japanese say, it as a "loser-driven" industrial policy—the product of random political lobbying power to gain protection for dying industries.[61, 62] The rest of the world's industrial policies involve strategic thinking and are "winner-driven." The Japanese protect amorphous metals; the Americans protect low-tech steel. While Americans are afraid to use the term *industrial policy*,[63] the Europeans are proudly designing pan-European industrial policies.[64]

The results show. Although a big decline in the value of the dollar succeeded in reducing the Japanese-U.S. trade deficit, the high-tech, high-wage part of the trade deficit is expanding.[65] America is increasingly depending upon low-wage, low-tech commodity exports to balance its trading accounts. Any country can be competitive as a low-wage country. Any country can reduce its wage level by reducing the value of its currency. The issue is not balancing trading accounts but being competitive while paying high wages.

At some point Washington will have to come to grips with foreign industrial policies. What does one do when other nations target an industry? The American solution to Airbus is to try to stop European funds from going into Airbus Industries by getting GATT to rule their activities illegal. As in amorphous metals, America will fail. It does not have the power to force the rest of the world to abandon national strategies. Airbus subsidies won't be ruled illegal by GATT; if ruled illegal, that ruling would simply be ignored by the Europeans.

In 1989 and 1990 the Bush administration was engaged in an internal intellectual debate revolving around high-definition television (HDTV): Should the Defense Department subsidize research on HDTV? Sadly, the debate remained an abstract ideological debate about the merits of government interference in the market rather than a real debate over whether HDTV was the place to jump back into consumer electronics, and if so, how? The ideological crusaders in the White House, a troika composed of John Sununu, Richard Darman and Michael Boskin, beat the advocates of government research subsidies in the Commerce and Defense departments, but it is also clear that their victory was temporary. The issue will continue to reappear.

It is of course possible to argue that the American system is uniquely unsuited to formulating strategic policies. A recent article by Pietro S. Nivola in the *Brookings Review* provides a good example of the argument. In outline, the argument is as follows:

1. America has a "closet industrial policy" hidden in its Defense Department.
2. Target industries in the rest of the world haven't earned high or even normal rates of return.
   a. Scholars argue over whether Japanese industrial policies have helped or hurt.
3. Industry-led industrial policies could become self-serving to the firms that participated.
   a. It is hard to figure out "who is us" when American firms manufacture abroad and foreign firms manufacture in the United States.
   b. Lemon socialism might result.
4. Americans would not be very good in defensive "tit-for-tat" industrial policies, since American government institutions aren't very flexible.
   a. Random interventions aren't always bad.[66]

Because of our own incompetence, we may be able to do nothing better than do nothing. No one can prove with complete certainty that this argument is wrong. But what we do know for certain is that the American system as it is now formulated isn't working. That is what falling real wages, stagnant productivity growth, and a growing high-wage trade deficit mean. America may try something new, and it may fail, but nothing will have been lost—the old ways aren't working anyway.

In the real world of the twenty-first century, defensive industrial policies are unavoidable. To have any chance, America's corporations at least need a defensive strategic-trade policy in the United States.[67] Such a policy is not designed to help American corporations (there is the problem of who is us), it is simply part of a general strategic-growth policy designed to help the American people. Public investments made to gain sustainable advantages should be limited to investments that will stay in America, such as investments in skills or domestic infrastructure.

Beyond such home investments, the search for strategic advantage abroad now revolves around process R&D investments. In Japan, MITI has shifted from the foreign-exchange and capital-allocations strategies of earlier decades to a strategy of pushing key technologies. The Europeans have set up an alphabet soup of cooperative R&D projects—Esprit, Jessi, Eureka—designed to do the same for European firms. While the details differ as to how it is done on the other sides of the Atlantic and Pacific oceans, the basic organizational structures are similar.

As George Lodge, a Harvard Business School professor, has described in detail in his recent book, *Perestroika for America*, strategies are industry-led when groups of companies, not government civil servants, propose the technologies that should be pushed.[68] Governments never provide more than 50 percent of the total funding. If companies don't think that projects are worth risking some of their own money, the projects simply aren't done. Companies have to put together consortia, so that the government is not subsidizing a special favorite. More than one company has to think that the technology is important. In Europe the consortia have to come from more than one country. In the United States they could be required to come from more than one region. The idea is to magnify private funds with public funds, not to publicly finance research and development. The projects must have finite lifetimes with clearly stated objectives. No project is publicly funded forever. The purpose of a project must never be to advance knowledge for the sake of advancing knowledge. Other institutions, such as the National Science Foundation, have that task. The bureaucracy that makes the funding decisions can be very small, since business firms are making the basic go–no-go decisions when they decide whether they are willing to risk their own money.

Economic analysis shows that there are gains to be made with strategic trade policies, especially in industries with increasing returns, and this advantage will get bigger in a world of man-made comparative advantage and trading blocks.[69] If government aid drives technology faster, everyone is a winner in the long run. More funds go into important areas that will raise long-run living standards, and no region of the world is going to be able to keep any key technology secret for more than a short period of time. A twenty-first-century civilian R&D race for supremacy among the economic superpowers is far better than the twentieth-century military R&D race for supremacy among the military superpowers.

Ideally, a new GATT for quasi trading blocks would limit government aid to R&D subsidies. But in a world without clearly defined rules that determine what governments can permissibly do to aid their strategic industries, America's game plan has to go beyond an R&D policy.[70] Like American companies that advertise they will not knowingly be undersold, the United States should announce that it will duplicate any policies put in place in the rest of the world. Foreign industrial policies in wealthy countries will be matched dollar for dollar. Any subsidy going to Airbus Industries in Europe will be matched by an equivalent subsidy to the American airframe-manufacturing industry. Any delay in permitting an American telecommunication device to be used abroad, such as the delays Motorola experienced in Japan with its cellular telephones, will be matched with delays for advanced Japanese equipment in the United States. Americans are no longer in a position to force the rest of the world to play the economic game by its rules, but Americans can play the game by their rules. If they want to play hardball, we'll play hardball.

Change is blowing in the winds. Listen to the words of two prominent economists that used to argue regularly against industrial policies:

> Unlike the United States, both Japan and Europe have had extensive programs aimed at improving commercial performance. . . . As long as Japan and other nations helped companies that produced goods that the United States imported, such as textiles and steel, the United States was likely to gain. But the United States was hurt as countries started to subsidize products that competed with U.S. exports, such as aircraft, satellites, and computers. Targeting by foreign coun-

tries must be taken more seriously as they become competitive with the United States.

—Robert Lawrence, Brookings economist[71]

My own proposal is that we adopt an explicit, but limited, US industrial policy. That is, the US government should make a decision to frankly subsidize a few sectors, especially in the high technology area, that may plausibly be described as "strategic." . . . One of the main purposes of this proposal is precisely to provide an alternative to managed trade. . . . Viewed from the right perspective, then, limited US industrial policies could be a relatively cheap way to cope with the stresses produced by the relative US decline and the special problem of dealing with Japan.

—Paul Krugman, MIT economist[72]

Even in a conservative Republican administration, there are now rumblings. While it is not politically correct for members of the Bush administration to talk about industrial policies, it is permissible for Bush's appointees to argue for government aid to support precompetitive, generic, enabling technologies.

AN EMPIRICAL EXPERIMENT

A decade ago it was possible to argue that instead of experimenting with strategic-growth policies to stimulate investments (physical and human), business groups, and national strategic planning, America could solve its problems by moving to a more vigorous form of traditional Anglo-Saxon capitalism. Both Mrs. Thatcher in Great Britain and Mr. Reagan in the United States were elected on such platforms. Both advocated a return to "ancient virtues"—that is, they emphasized the role of the individual in economic performance, the stress on the Anglo-Saxon *I*. Government enterprises were privatized in Great Britain. American personal income taxes were dramatically lowered. Both experiments are now more than a decade old. Neither succeeded.

In the United Kingdom unemployment is higher than it was when Mrs. Thatcher came into office (7.3 percent versus 5.8 percent), and the UK continues its slow drift down the list of the world's richest countries.[73] In the United States productivity growth was negative in the two years before Reagan took office and in the two years after he left office.[74] What was a small trade surplus became a large trade deficit.

Empirical experimentation revealed that a return to ancient Anglo-Saxon virtues is not the answer.

BOTTOM-LINE BENCHMARKING

Japan and Germany, the countries that are outperforming America in international trade, do not have less government or more motivated individuals. They are countries noted for their careful organization of teams—teams that involve workers and managers, teams that involve suppliers and customers, teams that involve government and business.

There is nothing antithetical in American history, culture, or traditions to teamwork. Teams were important in America's history—wagon trains conquered the West, men working together on the assembly line in American industry conquered the world, a successful national strategy and a lot of teamwork put an American on the moon first (and thus far, last). But American mythology extols only the individual—the Lone Ranger or Rambo. In America, halls of fame exist for almost every conceivable activity, but nowhere do Americans raise monuments in praise of teamwork. Only national mythology stands between Americans and the construction of successful economic teams. To say this is not, however, to say that change is easy. History is littered with the wrecks of countries whose mythologies were more important than reality.

Systematic bench marking reveals that the United States does not have to undergo a period of blood, sweat, and tears to regain its productive edge. Much of what has to be done, such as improving the K–12 education system, would make America a better place to live. With clear goals, schools would be more fun—not less. If spread out over time, even changes that would require a reduction in short-term American standards of living, such as a shift from consumption to investment, would be barely noticeable. Consumption, both public and private, just has to grow more slowly than the GNP. It doesn't have to fall.

While the necessary solutions would impose small burdens on the present, the failure to adopt these small solutions will impose major burdens on the future. We and our children will not have a world-class standard of living, and some of the chances for the good things of life that Americans have come to expect, such as heading major corporations, will diminish. Not doing anything is far worse than doing something.

The American problem does not lie in the severity of the necessary solutions. America's tough problem is realizing that there are problems that must be solved. Without that realization, nothing can be done. Minor problems that remain unsolvable in the present will create major problems that are difficult to solve in the future.

NOTES

CHAPTER 1

1. CIA Directorate of Intelligence, *Handbook of Economic Statistics* (Washington, D.C., 1986), p. 65. Council of Economic Advisers, *Economic Report of the President, 1986* (Washington, D.C.: GPO, 1986), p. 254.
2. Francis Fukuyama, "The End of History," *National Interest,* Summer 1989, p. 4.
3. Richard McKenzie and Dwight Lee, *Should 'The End of History' Have Ever Been in Doubt?* CSAB Working Paper no. 135, October 1990 (Washington, D.C.: Center for the Study of American Business, 1990), p. 1.
4. International Monetary Fund, *International Financial Statistics, Yearbook 1990,* (Washington, D.C., IMF, 1990), pp. 162–163. International Monetary Fund, *World Economic Outlook,* May 1991: 4.
5. Stephen Labaton, "The Bailout Agency Becomes a Highly Motivated Seller," *New York Times,* March 31, 1991, p. E4.
6. Keith Bradsher, "Airline Woes May Damage Pension Unit," *The New York Times,* March 23, 1991, p. 29. Karen Ball, "U.S. Seizes Pan Am Pensions," *The Tennessean,* July 25, 1991, p. E-1.
7. Richard W. Stevenson, "California Seizes Insurer Burdened with 'Junk Bonds,'" *The New York Times,* April 12, 1991, pp. A1, D5.
8. Masahito Ishizuka, "End This Laissez-faire Relationship with U.S.," *The Japan Economic Journal,* March 16, 1991, p. 9.
9. Shintaro Ishihara, *The Japan That Can Say No: Why Japan Will Be First Among Equals* (New York: Simon & Schuster, 1991), p. 31.
10. Deutsche Bank Economics Department, *The Peace Dividend: How To Pin It Down?* (Frankfurt: Deutsche Bank, 1991), p. 1.
11. Lester C. Thurow, *The World at a Turning Point,* Zahid Husain Memorial Lecture, no. 8, July 1985 (Karachi, Pakistan: State Bank of Pakistan, 1985) p. 1.

CHAPTER 2

1. "She Makes Her Stand," *The Economist*, June 29, 1991, p. 27.
2. "Ivon Dawnay Looks at How the Opposition Plans to Keep London Ahead of Frankfurt," *Financial Times*, April 26, 1991, p. 10.
3. *The Economist*, July 28, 1990, p. 83.
4. *The Economist*, October 15, 1988, p. 127.
5. Government and Private Fringe Benefits Are Much More Extensive in Germany Than They Are in the United States, *The Economist*, August 6, 1988, p. 81.
6. "Cutting the Workweek," *Journal of Japanese Trade & Industry*, no. 1: 49.
7. Robert Summers and Alan Heston, "The Penn World Table: An Expanded Set of International Comparisons, 1950–1988," *The Quarterly Journal of Economics*, May 1991: 327.
8. "Industry Brief," *The Economist*, May 16, 1987, p. 76.
9. *The Brookings Review*, Summer 1990: 20
10. *The Economist*. July 27, 1991, p. 90.
11. *Fortune*, August 26, 1991, p. 171.
12. Nomura Research Institute of America, *New Directions in Corporate Management and the Capital Market* (New York: The Institute, 1990), p. 1.
13. Shintaro Ishihara, *The Japan That Can Say No: Why Japan Will Be First Among Equals* (New York: Simon & Schuster, 1991), p. 50.
14. Nomura Research Institute, *Japan Can Say No*, p. 1.
15. "Kohl to Reassure Soviets on Unification," *The Boston Globe*, February 9, 1990, p. 2.
16. "France's New Prime Minister a Socialist Battler," Toronto Globe and Mail, May 16, 1991, p. A16.
17. Gianni De Michelis, "Europe: A Golden Opportunity Not to Be Missed," *International Herald Tribune*, March 26, 1990, p. 2.
18. George C. Lodge, *Perestroika for America* (Boston: Harvard Business School Press, 1991), p. 15–16.
19. H. Brest, *The New Competition* (Cambridge, Mass.: Harvard University Press, 1990). Robert Kuttner, "Atlas Unburdened: America's Economic Interests in a New World Era," *The American Prospect*, Summer 1990: 90.
20. "Graduates Take Rites of Passage into Japanese Corporate Life," *Financial Times*, April 8, 1991, p. 4.
21. Masaru Yoshitomi, "Keiretsu: An Insider's Guide to Japan's Conglomerates," *International Economic Insights*, Sept/Oct 1990: 10.
22. "Inside the Charmed Circle," *The Economist*, January 5, 1991, p. 54.

23. Carla Rapoport, "Why Japan Keeps Winning," *Fortune*, July 15, 1991, p. 77.
24. John Dornberg, "The Spreading Might of Deutsche Bank," *New York Times Business World*, September 23, 1990, p. 28.
25. "The Old Bank Network," *The Economist*, March 14, 1987, p. 64.
26. *The Japan Economic Journal*, March 17, 1990, p. 1. "A Tokyo Stuttgart Axis?" *The Economist*, March 10, 1990, p. 72.
27. Steven Greenhouse, "There's No Stopping Europe's Airbus Now," *The New York Times*, June 23, 1991, p. F1.
28. Simon Beavis and Jule Wolf, "Europe Sets Its Sights on Lead in New TV Market," *Europe*, June 26, 1990, p. 10.
29. Hans Dieter Weger, ed., *Strategies and Options for the Future of Europe: Aims and Contours of a Project* (Frankfurt: Bertelsmann Foundation, 1989), p.1.
30. Robert Ford and Wim Suyker, "Industrial Subsidies in the OECD Countries," *OECD Economic Studies*, no. 15 (Autumn 1990): 37.
31. "State Still Accounts for Half of GDP," *Financial Times*, March 15, 1991, Spain, p. 4.
32. "Sell by 1992," *The Economist*, March 20, 1991, p. 14.
33. W. O. Henderson, *The Rise of German Industrial Power, 1834–1914* (Berkeley: University of California Press, 1955), p. 71.
34. Gavin Wright, "The Origins of American Industrial Success, 1879–1940," *The American Economic Review*, September 1990: 651.
35. U.S. Department of Labor, *Employment and Earnings*, February 1990: 33–34.
36. Council of Economic Advisers, *Economic Report of the President, 1990* (Washington, D.C.: GPO, 1990) p. 296. U.S. Department of Commerce, *Survey of Current Business*, June 1990: S-25. U.S. Department of Commerce, *Business Statistics*, 1982 (Washington, D.C.: GPO, 1982) p. 104.
37. International Monetary Fund, *Primary Commodities: Market Development and Outlook*, July 1990: 26.
38. Tamin Bayoumi, *Savings-Investment Correlations* IMF Working Paper 89/66, August 1989 (Washington, D.C.: IMF, 1989), p. 1.
39. International Monetary Fund, *International Financial Statistics*, July 1990: 312, 542.
40. *Financial Times*, June 1, 1990, p. 5.
41. Margo Thorning, *Update on the U.S. Cost of Capital*, Special Report, January 1990 (Washington, D.C.: American Council for Capital Formation Center for Policy Research), p. 1.
42. Milan Brahmhatt, "Japan Confronts Expensive Capital," *DRI/McGraw-Hill Review of the U.S. Economy*, December 1990: 21.

43. Joint Economic Committee of Congress, Testimony of Edwin Mansfield, 99th Cong., 1st sess., December 2, 1986, p. 4.
44. Michael L. Dertouzos, Richard Lester, and Robert Solow, *Made in America: Regaining the Productive Edge* (Cambridge, Mass.: MIT Press, 1989), p. 72. Edwin Mansfield, p. 6.
45. Dertouzos, Lester, and Solow, *Made in America*, p. 6.
46. Ibid.
47. U.S. Congress, Mansfield Testimony, p. 1.
48. "High Hopes, High Costs for Wall Street's High Technology," *The Economist*, February 2, 1991, p. 77.
49. Lester C. Thurow, "The End of the Post-Industrial Era," *Business in the Contemporary World*, Winter 1990: 21.
50. Lester C. Thurow, *Toward a High-Wage, High-Productivity Service Sector* (Washington, D.C.: Economic Policy Institute, 1989).
51. "Kasparov," *The New York Times Magazine*, October 7, 1990, p. 62.
52. Walter Russell Mead, *The Low Wage Challenge to Global Growth.* (Washington, D.C.: Economic Policy Institute, 1990), p. 1.
53. "Labor Costs a Burden," *Korean Business World*, December 1990, p. 20.
54. Brendan Murphy, "Factor Price Changes and Imported Intermediate Goods," *International Economic Journal*, Winter 1989: 19.
55. Council of Economic Advisers, *Economic Report of the President 1991* (Washington, D.C.: GPO, 1991), p. 36.
56. Chris Tilly, *Short Hours, Short Shift* (Washington, D.C.: Economic Policy Institute, 1990), p. 1.
57. L. F. Katz and G. W. Loveman "An International Comparison of Changes in the Structure of Wages," as reported in "Wage Inequality and the Rising Demand for Skills," *Financial Times*, July, 8, 1991, p. 4.
58. Dertouzos, Lester, and Solow, *Made in America*, p. 81.
59. William E. Nothdurft, "Reinventing Public Schools to Create the Workforce of the Future," German Marshall Fund, as summarized in *Transatlantic Perspectives*, Autumn 1989: 11.
60. This section is an adaptation of an article written earlier with Laura Tyson. Laura Tyson and Lester C. Thurow, "The Economic Black Hole," *Foreign Policy*, Summer 1987: 3.
61. Walter Russell Mead, *The United States and the World Economy.* Walter Russell Mead, "From Bretton Woods to the Bush Team," *World Policy Journal*, Summer 1989: 3, 10, 26.
62. International Monetary Fund, *International Financial Statistics*, April 1991: 1.
63. William Dudley, ed., *Trade Opposing Views* (San Diego: Greenhaven Press, 1991), p. 1.

64. Council of Economic Advisers, *Economic Report of the President, 1991* (Washington, D.C.: GPO, 1991), p. 402.
65. U.S. Congress, *Prospects for Development of a U.S. HDTV Industry: Hearings before Committee on Government Affairs, United States Senate,* 101st Congress, 1st sess., August 1989.
66. "Mercantilists in Houston," *The Economist,* July 7, 1990, p. 13.
67. Andrew Fisher, "Home Thoughts Rather Than Abroad," *Financial Times,* July 26, 1991, p. 13.
68. "Helping the NICs Help the World Economy," *Journal of Japanese Trade & Industry,* 1988 no. 4: 11.
69. World Bank, *Handbook of International Trade and Development Statistics* (Washington, D.C.: The Bank, 1989), p. A36–A37.
70. "Nothing to Lose but Its Chains," *The Economist,* September 22, 1990. p. 5.
71. Ibid, p. 30.
72. Ibid, p. 36.
73. Allen Sinai and Zaharo Sofianou, "U.S. Service Exports: 'Who Buys What?'" *The Service Economy,* April 1991 (Washington, D.C.: Coalition of Service Industries, 1991), p. 13.
74. Louise Kehoe, "Chip Pact Gives Letter to the Spirit of US Hopes," *Financial Times,* June 6, 1991, p. 5.
75. David Goodhard, "Germany Raises Child Care Leave to 3 Years," *Financial Times,* August 15, 1991, p. 2.
76. Ferdinand Protzman, "Greetings from Fortress Germany," *The New York Times,* August 18, 1991, p. F6.

CHAPTER 3

1. U.S. Congress, Joint Economic Committee, *Bibliography on Europe in 1992,* ed. Hunter Monroe, April 26, 1989 (Washington, D.C.: GPO, 1989), p. 1.
2. EC Delegation to the United States, *A Guide to the European Community* (Brussels: EC, 1991).
3. Michael Emerson, *The Economics of 1992: The EC Commission's Assessment of the Economic Effects of Completing the Internal Market* (Oxford: Oxford University Press, 1988), p. 1.
4. "Playing As One?" *The Economist,* June 29, 1991, p. 9.
5. Merton J. Peck, "Industrial Organization and the Gains from Europe in 1992," *Brookings Papers on Economic Activity,* 1989, no. 2: 296.
6. Vittorio Grilli, "Financial Markets and 1992," *The Brookings Papers on Economic Activity,* 1989, no. 2: 322.

7. Bertelsmann Foundation, *European Deficits, European Perspectives: Taking Stock of Tomorrow* (Gütersloh, Germany: The Foundation, 1989), p. 1.

8. "Headlong to GEMU," *The Economist*, February 17, 1990, p. 85.

9. Deutsche Bank, *The New German Federal States* (Frankfurt: DB, 1990), p. 1.

10. David Marsh, "Germany Records Trade Deficit As Imports Surge," *Financial Times*, June 11, 1991, p. 1.

11. "Will Germany Tow Europe into Trouble?" *The Economist*, August 31, 1991, p. 53.

12. Walter Russell Mead, "Coming to Terms with the New Germany," *World Policy Journal*, Fall 1990: 593.

13. "The Other Fortress Europe," *The Economist*, June 1, 1991, p. 45.

14. "A Survey of Business in Europe," *The Economist*, June 8, 1991, p. 11.

15. "Gatt and Services: Closer, Closer," *The Economist*, July 14, 1990, p. 68.

16. "Battlefield of the 1990s: The Japanese Gear Up for European Production," *Financial Times*, December 15, 1990, p. 13.

17. "Europe Gears Up for Car Wars," *Financial Times*, April 4, 1991, p. 12.

18. "New Kid on the Dock," *Time*, September 17, 1990, p. 63.

19. Umberto Agnelli, "Thinking Big as Frontiers Tumble," *The Times Higher Education Supplement*, p. 25.

20. Sumihiko Nonoici, "Japan's Exports to EC 'Made in US,'" *The Nikkei Weekly*, August 10, 1991, p. 9.

21. *The Asian Wall Street Journal*, August 1, 1991, p. 2.

22. Ferdinand Protzman, "Greeting from Fortress Germany," *The New York Times*, August 18, 1991, p. F1.

23. "Brussels' Unreal Dominion," *The Economist*, May 4, 1991, p. 19.

24. Steve Lohr, "British M.P.s See 'Fortress Europe,'" *The New York Times*, November 12, 1989, p. 35.

25. "Poor Marks for EC External Trade Practices," *Financial Times*, April 17, 1991, p. 6.

26. Paolo Cecchini, *The European Challenge, 1992: The Benefits of a Single Market* (Aldershot, England: Gower, 1988), pp. xix–xx.

27. Lucy Kellaway, "Brussels to Press Non-EC Countries Over Bank Curbs," *Financial Times*, February 6, 1990, p. 1.

28. Steven Greenhouse, "The Fighter of France," *The New York Times*, May 16, 1991, p. 3.

29. Colin Nickerson, "Japan's l'affaire Cresson," *The Boston Globe*, May 1, 1991, p. 2.

30. Kenjiro Ishikawa, "Protectionist Plans for Europe's Single Market," *Economic Eye*, Autumn 1990: 23.

31. Toshiro Tanaka, "European Community and Japan: Countdown to 1992," *Japan Review of International Affairs*, Fall/Winter 1989: 219.

32. Robert Kuttner, *Managed Trade and Economic Sovereignty* (Washington, D.C.: Economic Policy Institute, 1989), p. 1. Richard N. Cooper, "Europe Without Borders," *Brookings Papers on Economic Activity*, 1989, no. 2: 331.

33. Peter Morici, *Trade Talks with Mexico: A Time for Realism* (Washington, D.C.: National Planning Association, 1991), p. 1.

34. Kazuo Ogawa, "Japan Sea Rim: Catalyst for Growth," *Journal of Industry*, 1991, no. 3: 17.

35. Tomio Shida, "Powerful Asian Economic Bloc Emerging," *The Japan Economic Journal*, November 12, 1988, p. 3.

36. Janos Kornai, *The Road to a Free Economy: Shifting from a Socialist System: The Example of Hungary* (New York: Norton, 1990), p. 1. Deutsche Bank Economics Department, *Rebuilding Eastern Europe*, March 1991 (Frankfurt: Deutsche Bank, 1991), p. 1.

37. "Eastern Europe's Economies: What Is to Be Done?" *The Economist*, January 13, 1990, p. 21.

38. Peter Passell, "A Centerless Soviet Economy May Not Be So Bad, Western Experts Say," *The New York Times*, September 5, 1991, p. A13.

39. "Grossly Deceptive Product," *The Economist*, March 10, 1990, p. 71.

40. "Perestroika's Pantry," *The New York Times*, December 5, 1990, p. A10.

41. Deutsche Bank, *New German Federal States*, p. 1.

42. International Monetary Fund, "Economic Reform in Eastern Europe and the USSR," chap. 5 in *World Economic Outlook May 1990* (Washington, D.C.: IMF, 1990), p. 64.

43. Ferdinand Protzman, "East Germany's Economy Far Sicker Than Expected," *The New York Times*, September 20, 1990, p. D6.

44. Quentin Peel, "Two Sides of a Coin to German Monetary Union," *Financial Times*, July 26, 1991, p. 2.

45. Deutsche Bank Economics Department, *Unification Issues: Growth Forecast for 1991 Revised Downward* (Frankfurt: Deutsche Bank, 1991), p. 1.

46. Ernst Helmstader, "Mistaken Assumptions About Revitalising New Lander" *The German Tribune*, May 5, 1991, p. 6. Fides Krause Brewer, "Amid the Gloom, Some Signs That an Upswing Is Beginning in the East," *The German Tribune*, May 5, 1991, p. 7.

47. Stephen Engelberg, "For Poles, Road to Capitalism is Rough," *The New York Times*, July 29, 1990, p. 1.
48. "A Survey of Business in Eastern Europe," *The Economist*, September 12, 1991, p. 19.
49. Craig R. Whitney, "East Europe Joins the Market and Gets a Preview of the Pain," *The New York Times*, January 7, 1990, p. E3.
50. John Wyles, "Punishing Price of Perestroika," *Financial Times*, January 29, 1990, p. 19.
51. "A Random Walk Around Red Square," *The Economist*, August 24, 1991, p. 12. "The Soviet Economy Still Bust," *The Economist*, August 24, 1991, p. 21.
52. German Information Center, *Treaty Between the Federal Republic of Germany and the German Democratic Republic Establishing a Monetary, Economic and Social Union* (Bonn: The Center, 1990), p. 1.
53. "A Survey of the New Germany," *The Economist*, June 30, 1990, p. 3.
54. Horst Siebert, "The Economic Integration of Germany," *Kieler Diskussionbeitrage*, May 1990, p. 1.
55. Donald Shanor, "Calculating the Costs of German Unity," *The New Leader*, July 9, 1990, p. 6.
56. "Upgrading Seen in '91 in East German Phones," Agence France Presse wire-service article in *International Herald Tribune*, July 4, 1990, p. 13.
57. Deutsche Bank Economics Department, *German Economic and Monetary Union*, April 1990 (Frankfurt: Deutsche Bank, 1990), p. 1.
58. David March, "Germany Plans Subsidy Cuts," *Financial Times*, July 11, 1991, p. 2.
59. Ferdinand Protzman, "What Price Reunion?" *The New York Times*, September 24, 1990, p. A6.
60. "The Costs of Unity Keep On Mounting," *Financial Times*, November 13, 1990, p. 24.
61. Protzman, "What Price?" p. A6.
62. "Don't Mention the Wall," *The Economist*, April 6, 1991, p. 67.
63. Geoffrey A. Hosking, "The Paradox of Perestroika," *The Atlantic*, February 1990, p. 20.
64. Armand Clesse and Lothar Ruhl, *Beyond East-West Confrontation: Searching for a New Security Structure in Europe* (Baden-Baden: Nomos Verlagsgesellschaft for The Institute for European and International Studies, Luxembourg, 1990), p. 1.
65. Chuck Sudetic, "Ethnic Rivalries Push Yugoslavia to Edge," *The New York Times*, September 24, 1990, p. A6.

66. "And Now for the Hard Part," *The Economist*, April 28, 1990, p. 3.

67. Deutsche Bank, *The Soviet Union at the Crossroads: Facts and Figures on the Soviet Republics* (Frankfurt: DB, 1990), p. 1.

68. David White, "Russia Likely to Become New Nuclear Superpower," *Financial Times*, August 28, 1991, p. 2.

69. *The Economist*, July 13, 1991, p. 110.

70. John Lloyd, "Triple Panic That Sparked Kremlin Putsch," *Financial Times*, August 21, 1991, p. 3.

71. "Book Ends for the Cold War," *The Boston Globe*, July 8, 1990, p. 10.

72. "New Zealand, Return to Rogernomics," *The Economist*, March 23, 1991, p. 79.

73. Amitai Etzioni, "Eastern Europe: The Wealth of Lessons," *Challenge*, July/Aug. 1991: 4.

74. John Michael Montias, "Eastern Bloc Faces Obstacles to Free-Market Economy," *The Boston Globe*, February 4, 1990, p. A23.

75. "Combines Forever," *The Economist*. December 22, 1990, p. 21.

76. Ibid, p. 24.

77. William C. Rhoden, "The Roads Are Potholed and the Luxuries Few, Yet Many People Find They're Better Off," *The New York Times*, August 18, 1991, p. 1.

78. Robert Taylor, "States 'Fail to Understand Free Market,'" *Financial Times*, August 27, 1991, p. 3.

79. Steven Greenhouse, "Eastern Europe Awaits the Storm," *The New York Times*, December 17, 1989, p. 4.

80. Nicholas Denton, "Discontent Threatens Hungary's Fragile Stability," *Financial Times*, April 17, 1991, p. 2.

81. "Polls Show People in 3 Republics Want Continued Soviet Control," *The Japan Times*, July 29, 1991, p. 14.

82. Michael R. Kagay, "Americans Share Soviet Economic Pessimism," *The New York Times*, July 10, 1991, p. 1. Gabreille Glaser, "Audis, Champagne and Liposuction: Capitalism Arrives for Many Poles," *The New York Times*, October 15, 1991, p. A2.

83. Boris Rumer, "New Capitalists in the USSR," *Challenge*, May/June 1991, p. 21.

84. Federal Reserve Bank of Kansas City, *Central Banking Issues in Emerging Market-Orientated Economies* (Kansas City: Federal Reserve Bank, 1990), p. 1.

85. William D. Nordhaus, "Soviet Economic Reform: The Longest Road," *Brookings Papers on Economic Activity*, 1990, no. 1: 303.

86. Francis X. Clines, "The Next Revolution: A Gold Rush in Apartments," *The New York Times*, October 15, 1991, p. A4.

87. Vito Tanzi, *Tax Reform in Economies in Transition: A Brief Introduction to the Main Issues*, IMF Working Paper, March 1991 (Washington, D.C.: IMF, 1991), p. 3.

88. John Lloyd, *Soviet Economy Still Bust*, IMF Working Paper, March 1991 (Washington, D.C.: IMF, 1991), p. 3.

89. Bruce Stokes, "Germany's Turbulent Unification," *Trans-atlantic Perspectives*, Summer 1991: 14.

90. J. P. Morgan, *World Financial Markets*, February 14, 1990, p. 13.

91. "Soviet Debt, What Is to Be Done?" *The Economist*, August 24, 1991, p. 66.

92. Stephen Fidler, "Governments Could Be Main Creditors," *Financial Times*, September 5, 1991, p. 2.

93. "Soviet Debt," *The Economist*, August 24, 1991, p. 66.

94. Joshua E. Green and Peter Isard, *Currency Convertibility and the Transformation of Centrally Planned Economies*, IMF Occasional Paper, no. 81 (Washington, D.C.: International Monetary Fund, 1991), p. 1.

95. David Lipton and Jeffrey Sachs, "Privatization in Eastern Europe: The Case of Poland," *Brookings Papers on Economic Activity*, 1990, no. 2: 293.

96. Deutsche Bank Economics Department, *Unification Issues: The State of Privatization* (Frankfurt: Deutsche Bank, 1990), p. 1.

97. "Time to Sort Out Who Owns What," *Financial Times*, April 16, 1991, p. 16.

98. Frau Heuwagen, "Claims and Counter Claims and Inadequate Records," *The German Tribune*, April 14, 1991, p. 14. Gunther Gescke, "In the Pending Tray," *The German Tribune*, September 15, 1991, p. 6.

99. Siebert, "Economic Integration, p. 8.

100. Quentin Peel, "Soviet Factories Face Standstill over Lack of Supplies," *Financial Times*, July 20, 1990, p. 8.

101. Blue Ribbon Commission, Project Hungary, "Action Program for Hungary in Transformation to Freedom and Prosperity," April 1990 (Budapest), p. 1.

102. Name withheld.

CHAPTER 4

1. David E. Sanger, "Japanese Cars Stronger in Weak U.S. Economy," *The New York Times*, September 4, 1991, p. D1.

2. "Toyota Motor Buckles Down to Overtake GM," *Tokyo Business Today*, February 1991, p. 32.

3. "Big Three Computer Makers Ready to Tackle 'Big Blue,'" *Japan Economic Journal*, August 18, 1990, p. 1.
4. David E. Sanger, "IBM Losing Ground in Japan," *The New York Times*, June 3, 1991, p. D1.
5. Dominic Salvatore, *The Japanese Trade Challenge and the U.S. Response* (Washington, D.C.: Economic Policy Institute, 1990), p. 20.
6. Ibid, pp. 10–11.
7. Yuro Mizuno, "Trade Surplus Up 26.3 Percent—Exports to EC Swell," *The Nikkei Weekly*, July 20, 1991, p. 3.
8. Ibid, p. 17.
9. Ibid, p. 18.
10. Ibid.
11. R.C.O. Matthews, "Animal Spirits," Keynes Lecture in Economics, June 1984, *Proceedings of the British Academy 1985* (Oxford: Oxford University Press, 1985), p. 1.
12. Karel van Wolferen, *The Enigma of Japanese Power* (New York: Knopf, 1989), p. 1.
13. Yoshi Tsurume and Hiroki Tsurumi, "Value Added Maximizing Behavior of Japanese Firms and Roles of Corporate Investment Finance," *The Columbia Journal of World Business*, Spring 1985: 20.
14. Ronald Dore, *Taking Japan Seriously* (Palo Alto: Stanford University Press, 1987), p. 13.
15. Lester C. Thurow, "Producer Economics," in *IRRA 41st Annual Proceedings* (New York: Industrial Relations Research Association, 1989), p. 9. J. L. Baxter, *Social and Psychological Foundations of Economic Analysis* (New York: Harvester/Wheatsheaf of Simon & Schuster, 1988), p. 1.
16. "Chairman of Jaguar Plans to Retire in June," *The New York Times*, March 28, 1990, p. D3.
17. "As Losses Mount, Saab Aims to Change Gears," *International Herald Tribune*, November 14, 1990, p. 13.
18. Susan Moffat, "Should You Work for the Japanese," *Fortune*, December 3, 1990, p. 107.
19. Vladimir Pucik, "American Managers, Japanese Bosses," *Journal of Japanese Trade & Industry*, 1990, no. 6: 40.
20. Kenneth B. Noble, "American Executives Finding Out About Japanese Management as Employees," *The New York Times*, January 24, 1988, p. D1.
21. Joseph J. Fucini and Suzy Fucini, *Working for the Japanese* (New York: Free Press, 1990), p. 1.
22. "Culture Shock at Home: Working for a Foreign Boss," *Business Week*, December 17, 1990, p. 81.

23. Alice H. Amsden, "East Asia's Challenge to Standard Economics," *The American Prospect*, Summer 1990: 71.
24. "Wages Rise Slower Than Productivity," *The Japan Economic Journal*, May 30, 1987, p. 3.
25. "A Survey of International Finance," *The Economist*, April 27, 1991, p. 39.
26. Council of Economic Advisers, *Economic Report of the President, 1991* (Washington, D.C.: GPO, 1991) p. 387.
27. *The Economist*, February 16, 1991, p. 75.
28. *The JAMA Forum*, 6, no. 2 (1986): 19. *Weekly Tokyo Keizi*, November 11, 1989.
29. "Study Finds That Japanese Consumers Pay the Price," *Financial Times*, May 21, 1991, p. 7.
30. "Japan Ranks Highest in Quality of Life," *Journal of Japanese Trade and Industry*, 1991, no. 2, p. 6.
31. Japan Statistical Bureau, "Principle Interest Rates on Postal Savings," in *Japan Statistical Yearbook, 1986* (Tokyo: The Bureau, 1986), p. 418.
32. *Fortune*, July 30, 1990, p. 109.
33. *Financial Times*, June 1, 1990, p. 3.
34. U.S. Department of Commerce, *Survey of Current Business*, January 1991: 10.
35. James Fallows, *The JAMA Forum*, 6, no. 1 (1986): 6.
36. Edwin Mansfield, *Technological Change in Robotics: Japan and the United States*, University of Pennsylvania Working Paper (Philadelphia: The University, 1985), p. 12.
37. George N. Hatsopoulos, Paul R. Krugman, and Lawrence H. Summers, "U.S. Competitiveness: Beyond the Trade Deficit," *Science*, July 1988: 303.
38. Alex Taylor III, "Nissan's Bold Bid for Market Share," *Fortune*, January 1, 1990, p. 100.
39. Katsusada Hirose, "Corporate Thinking in Japan and the US," *Journal of Japanese Trade & Industry*, 1989, no. 4: 40.
40. *Moody's Industrial Manual*, vol. 2, 1971–1990 (New York: Moody's Financial Information Services).
41. "The Best Companies," *The Economist*, September 7, 1991, p. 22.
42. Hirose, "Corporate Thinking," p. 41.
43. Shinichi Yamamoto, "Japan's Trade Lead: Blame Profit-Hungry American Firms," *The Brookings Review*, Winter 1989/90, p. 14.
44. Chikao Tuskuda, "Closing the Investment Gap," *Journal of Japanese Trade & Industry*, 1990, no. 6: 8.
45. Paul Healy and Don Lessard, Singapore MIT-NYU Symposium on Global Economy, Nam Yang University, Singapore, July 1991.

46. "Top 300 Foreign Owned Companies in Japan, 1990," *Tokyo Business Today*, August 1991, p. 54.
47. Statistical Bureau, *Japan Statistical Yearbook, 1986*, p. 427. "The Art of Not Learning from Experience," *The Economist*, March 2, 1991, p. 73.
48. "The Decline of U.S. Consumer Electronics," in vol. 1 of *The Working Papers of the MIT Commission on Industrial Productivity* (Cambridge, Mass.: MIT Press, 1989), p. 9.
49. Yamamoto, "Japan's Trade Lead," p. 14. Hiroki Tsurumi, "Value Added Maximization Behavior of Firms and the Japanese Semiconductor Industry," *Managerial and Decision Economics* 12: p. 123.
50. Gregory Clark, "Understanding Differences: Why Western Models Can't Comprehend Japan," *The JAMA Forum*, May 1991: 6.
51. Carla Rapoport, "Why Japan Keeps on Winning," *Fortune*, July 15, 1991, p.85.
52. *The Economist*, February 16, 1991, p. 75.
53. "The Giants That Refuse to Die," an article, attributed to Tom Hill of SG Warburg, in *The Economist*, June 1, 1991, p. 72.
54. David E. Sanger, "Some Lessons from a Failed Assault on a Japan Inc. Fortress," *The New York Times*, May 5, 1991, p. 2.
55. Rapoport, "Japan Keeps Winning," p. 80.
56. "Japanese Takeovers: The Global Contest for Corporate Control," *The Economist*, February 2, 1991 p. 63.
57. J. Bradford De Long, *Did J. P. Morgan's Men Add Value? A Historical Perspective on Financial Capitalism*, Working Paper (Cambridge, Mass.: National Bureau of Economic Research and Harvard Economics Department, 1989), p. 1.
58. New York Stock Exchange *Institutional Investor Fact Book* (New York: NYSE, 1991), pp. 28–41.
59. John Markoff, "IBM's Chief Criticizes Staff Again," *The New York Times*, June 19, 1991, p. D1.
60. Masakazu Yamazaki, "The Impact of Japanese Culture on Management," in *The Management Challenge: Japanese Views*, ed. Lester C. Thurow (Cambridge, Mass.: MIT Press, 1986), p. 31.
61. W. Karl Kester, *Japanese Takeovers: The Global Contest for Corporate Control* (Boston: Harvard Business School Press, 1991), pp. 21, 79.
62. James C. Abegglen and George Stalk, Jr., *Kaisha, The Japanese Corporation: How Marketing Money and Manpower Strategy, Not Management Style, Make the Japanese World Pace-setters* (New York: Basic Books, 1984).
63. Ronald Dore, *British Factory–Japanese Factory* (Berkeley: University of California Press, 1989), p. 201.

64. *Financial Times,* June 8, 1990, p. 1.
65. Lawrence Mishel and David M. Frankel, *The State of Working America* (Washington, D.C.: Economic Policy Institute, 1990), p. 121.
66. Thomas A. Stewart, "Where We Stand," in *The New American Century, Fortune,* Special Issue, 1991, p. 15.
67. "How Countries Rank Business Functions," *Financial Times,* May 31, 1991, p. 1.
68. Hirose, "Corporate Thinking," p. 41.
69. D. Eleanor Westney, "Sociological Approaches to the Pacific Region," in *The Pacific Region: Challenges to Policy and Theory* (Cambridge, Mass.: American Academy of Political and Social Science, 1989), p. 27.
70. U.S. Department of Labor, *Handbook of Labor Statistics,* Bulletin 2175 (Washington, D.C.: GPO, n.d.), p. 180.
71. "Economic Cost of the Human Factor," *Financial Times,* February 20, 1991, p. 8.
72. Dore, *British Factory–Japanese Factory,* p. 139.
73. Emiko Terazono, "Graduates Take Rites of Passage into Japanese Corporate Life," *Financial Times,* April 8, 1991, p. 4.
74. "Japanese Students Favor Big Company Stability," *Tokyo Business Today,* April 1991, p. 21.
75. Keizai Koho Center, *Japan: An International Comparison, 1991* (Tokyo: The Center, 1991), p. 71, 73.
76. Michael Dertouzos, Richard Lester, and Robert Solow, *Made in America: Regaining the Productive Edge* (Cambridge, Mass.: MIT Press, 1989), p. 81.
77. National Science Foundation, *R&D Expenditures* (Washington, D.C.: GPO, 1990), pp. 1–20.
78. "Corporate Governance in Germany," *The Economist,* February 23, 1991, p. 66.
79. Bryan Burrough and John Helyar, *Barbarians at the Gates* (New York: Harper & Row, 1990), p. 1.
80. Dore, *British Factory–Japanese Factory,* pp. 37, 146.
81. *Fortune,* July 30, 1990, p. 269.
82. "The 100 Largest Diversified Service Companies," August 26, 1991, *Fortune,* p. 171.
83. *The Economist,* April 7, 1990, p. 61.
84. Ichiro Fujiwara, "Forced Changes," *Business Tokyo,* April 1987, p. 28.
85. "Managing MITI: Inside the Policy Process," April 1987, *Business Tokyo,* p. 22.
86. Rapoport, "Japan Keeps Winning," p. 85.

87. Yuko Inque, "CNN Blockage in Japan Stirring Criticism," *The Japan Economic Journal*, May 11, 1991, p. 1.
88. Neil W. Davis, "Government Agency Aims To Help Nation Develop Basic Research," *The Japan Economic Journal*, June 17, 1991, p. 3.
89. "MITI's Vision for the 1990s," *Journal of Japanese Trade & Industry*, 1990, no. 5: p. 6.
90. Louise Kehoe, "Japanese Refuse to Sell Machines to U.S.," *Financial Times*, May 17, 1991, p. 20.
91. Ronald Dore, *Flexible Rigidities* (London: Athlone Press, 1986), p. 1.

CHAPTER 5

1. International Monetary Fund, *International Financial Statistics*, July-Dec. 1952: pp. 124, 125, 129.
2. Alfred D. Chandler, Jr., *Scale and Scope: The Dynamics of Industrial Capitalism.* (Cambridge, Mass.: Harvard University Press, 1990), p. 1.
3. International Monetary Fund, *International Financial Statistics*, August 1952: pp. 20, 161.
4. John Taft, *American Power* (New York: Harper & Row, 1989), p. 1.
5. Keizai Koho Center, *Japan: An International Comparison, 1991* (Tokyo: The Center, 1991), p. 12.
6. Michael Dertouzos, Richard Lester, and Robert Solow, *Made in America: Regaining the Productive Edge* (Cambridge, Mass.: MIT Press, 1989), p. 1.
7. *The Japan Economic Journal*, April 30, 1985, p. 1.
8. David Sanger, "Sony, Apple Negotiating Laptop Deal," *The New York Times*. October 1, 1990, page D1.
9. Robert B. Cohen, *Countdown on Military Research and Development: A Briefing Book* (Washington, D.C.: Ploughshares Fund, 1990), p. 10.
10. World Economic Forum, *The World Competitiveness Report, 1990* (Geneva: WEF,1990), p. 10–15. Ibid., *The World Competitiveness Report, 1991* (Geneva, WEF, 1991), pp. 11–16.
11. U.S. Department of Labor, *The Impact of Research and Development on Productivity Growth*, Bulletin 2331, September 1989 (Washington, D.C.: GPO, 1989).
12. Thomas A. Stewart, "Where We Stand," in *The New American Century, Fortune*, Special Issue, 1991, p. 17.

13. William J. Broad, "In the Realm of Technology, Japan Looms Ever Larger," *The New York Times*, May 28, 1991, p. C1.
14. Leonard L. Lederman, "Science and Technology Policies and Priorities: A Comparative Analysis," *Science*, September 1987: p. 1125.
15. Thomas D. Cabot, "Is American Education Competitive?" *Harvard Magazine*, Spring 1986, p. 14.
16. "The Big Test: How to Translate Talk of School Reform into Action?" *The New York Times*, March 24, 1991, p. E4.
17. Michael J. Barrett, "The Case for More School Days," *The Atlantic*, November 1990, p. 80.
18. "Do U.S. Schools Make the Grade," *Fortune*, Special Issue, Spring 1990, p. 50.
19. "Why We Should Invest in Human Capital," *Business Week*, December 17, 1990, p. 89.
20. "Personal Savings Rise," *The Japan Economic Journal*, September 15, 1990, p. 3. Council of Economic Advisers, *Economic Indicators*, August 1990: 6. Dean et al., "Savings Trends and Behavior in OECD Countries," *OECD Economic Studies*, Spring 1990: 14.
21. "The Squirrel's Curse," *The Economist*, February 9, 1991, p. 69.
22. "Economists," *San Francisco Chronicle*, November 12, 1990, p. A-18.
23. "It's Peacefully Smooth Riding the French Rails at 186 MPH," *The Boston Globe*, Travel Section, September 30, 1990.
24. Heinz Bluthmann, "New Super Train Ready to Show Its Paces," *The German Tribune*, March 10, 1991, p. 7.
25. David Alan Aschauer, *Public Investment and Private Sector Growth* (Washington, D.C.: Economic Policy Institute, 1990), p. 9.
26. Ibid., p. 17.
27. David Alan Aschauer, "Infrastcuture: America's Third Deficit," *Challenge*, March/April 1991: 42.
28. Michael L. Dertouzos, "Building the Information Market Place," *Technology Review*, January 1991: 29.
29. K. Tsipis, "Proposal for Funding of the Project on Research Resources Redeployment," MIT Working Paper (Cambridge, Mass.: MIT, 1990), p. 5.
30. World Economic Forum, *World Competitiveness Report*, 1990, pp. 10–15., Ibid., 1991, pp.11–16.
31. Hideyki Shishido, "Poll Shows Koreans Rate Japan over US in Goods, Services," *The Japan Economic Journal*, May 23, 1990, p. 1.
32. *The Japan Economic Journal*, November 12, 1988, p. 8.
33. NBC News, "April National Poll," April 1987.

34. Robert Kuttner, *The End of Laissez-Faire* (New York: Knopf, 1991).
35. Shintaro Ishihara, "Advice for an Ailing Giant," *The International Economy*, Oct./Nov. 1990: 65.
36. "Wage Costs," *The Economist*, October 13, 1990, p. 111.
37. "Labour Costs in Manufacturing," *The Economist*, May 11, 1991, p. 99.
38. *The Economist*, August 6, 1988, p. 81.
39. U.S. Department of Commerce, Bureau of the Census, *Current Population Reports, Consumer Income*, ser. P-60, no. 123 (Washington, D.C.: 1979), pp. 248, 252. Ibid., no. 166 (Washington, D.C., 1989), pp. 42, 53.
40. Economic Policy Institute, "The State of Work America," News Release, Washington, D.C., September 1990, p. 2.
41. "Job Training: Missing Bridge," *The Economist*, February 9, 1991, p. 30.
42. Robert Pear, "U.S. Reports Poverty Is Down but Inequality is Up," *The New York Times*, September 23, 1990, p. 1.
43. Council of Economic Advisers, *Economic Report of the President, 1991* (Washington, D.C.: GPO, 1991), p. 338.
44. Ibid.
45. *National Institute Economic Review*, November 1989, p. 98.
46. Keizai Koho Center, *Japan: A Comparison, 1991*, p. 70.
47. *Book of Vital World Statistics* (London: The Economist Books, 1990), p. 72.
48. National Coalition for Advanced Manufacturing, "Industrial Modernization: An American Imperative," October 1990 (Washington, D.C.: Thomas Magazine Group, 1990) p. 8.
49. *Science*, July 15, 1988, p. 311.
50. Economic Policy Institute, *Manufacturing Numbers: How Inaccurate Statistics Conceal U.S. Industrial Decline* (Washington, D.C., The Institute, 1988), p. 3.
51. Edwin Mansfield, *The Speed and Cost of Industrial Innovation in Japan and the United States*, University of Pennsylvanna Working Paper (Philadelphia: The University, 1985), p. 3.
52. American Council on Capital Formation, *US Investment Trends: Impact on Productivity, Competitiveness, and Growth*, (Washington, D.C.: The Council, 1991), p. 1.
53. Jeffrey G. Williamson, "Productivity and American Leadership," *Journal of Economic Literature*, March 1991: 51.
54. Lester C. Thurow, *Towards a High-Wage Service Sector* (Washington, D.C.: Economic Policy Institute, 1989), p. 1.
55. Lester C. Thurow, "The End of the Post-Industrial Era," *Business in the Contemporary World*, Winter 1990: p. 21.

56. U.S. Department of Labor, *Employment and Earnings,* January 1981: 12. Ibid., January 1991: 10.

57. "The Japanese Advantage in Autos," *The New York Times,* April 1, 1983, p. A12.

58. When Matsushita took over the Quasar Motorola facilities it was able to reduce white collar overheads by 25 percent. "The Japanese Way at Quasar," *The New York Times,* October 16, 1982, p. D1.

59. Carol J. Loomis, "Harold Geneen's Money Making Machine Is Still Humming," *Fortune,* September 1972, p. 88.

60. "Harold Geneen's Tribulations," *Business Week,* August 11, 1973, p. 102.

61. Loomis, "Geneen's Money Making Machine," p. 218.

62. Geoffrey Colun, "The De-Geneening of ITT," *Fortune,* January 11, 1982, p. 36.

63. Ibid.

64. "Geneen's Tribulations," p. 104.

65. Ibid., p. 110.

66. "Harold Geneen Rests His Case," *Forbes,* June 15, 1977, p. 42.

67. U.S. Department of Commerce, *Employment and Earnings,* January 1979: 172. Ibid., January 1986, 178.

68. John Simmons and William Mares, *Working Together,* (New York: Knopf, 1983), p. 194.

69. Bill Saporito, "The Revolt Against 'Working Smarter,'" *Fortune,* July 21, 1986, pp. 59, 60.

70. Harley Shaiken, "The Automated Factory: The View from the Shop Floor," *Technology Review,* January 1985: p. 21.

71. Lester C. Thurow, ed., *The Management Challenge: Japanese Views* (Cambridge, Mass.: MIT Press, 1985), pp. 8, 9.

72. Dertouzos, Lester and Solow, *Made In America.,* pp. 15.

73. Michael Skapinker, Robert Thomson and Louise Kehoe, "Onward March of the Japanese," *Financial Times,* March 19, 1991, p. 17.

74. National Advisory Committee on Semiconductors, *A Strategic Industry at Risk,* November 1989 (Washington, D.C.: The Committee, 1989). p. 1.

75. Louise Kehoe, "Failure of Chip Venture 'Bodes Ill for US Industry,'" *Financial Times,* January 17, 1990, p. 24. "Motorola Plans Sendai Chip Plant," *The Japan Economic Journal,* December 15, 1990, p. 12.

76. "Big Three Computer Makers Ready to Tackle 'Big Blue,'" *The Japan Economic Journal,* August 18, 1990, p. 1.

77. Mike Cusumano, *Japan's Software Factories* (New York: Oxford University Press, 1991), p. 1.
78. Artemis March, "The Future of the US Aircraft Industry," *Technology Review*, January 1990: p. 7.
79. "The Clouds Close in on Boeing," *Financial Times*, February 19, 1990, p. 14.
80. *The Economist*, September 8, 1990, p. 69. Eduardo Lachica, *The Wall Street Journal*, September 10, 1990, p. A4.
81. David E. Sanger, "Goldstar's Stake in Zenith Involves Widespread Links," *The New York Times*, March 26, 1991, pp. D1, D10.
82. Elisabeth Rosenthal, "For More Drugs, First Test Is Abroad," *The New York Times*, August 7, 1990, p. C1.
83. "Auto Makers Plan to Slash Output 14%," *The Wall Street Journal*, March 8, 1991, p. 2.
84. James P. Womack, Daniel T. Jones and Daniel Roos, *The Machine That Changed the World*, (New York: Rawson Associates, 1990), p. 1.
85. Robert Meier, "A Car Is Rated Most Trouble-Free, but How Good Is That?" *The New York Times*, October 13, 1990, p. 31.
86. Robert E. Cole, "US Quality Improvement in the Auto Industry: Close but NO Cigar," *California Management Review*, Summer 1990: p. 77.
87. David J. Collis, "The Machine Tool Industry and Industrial Policy, 1955–82," *International Competitiveness*, ed. Michael Spence and Heather Hazard (Cambridge, Mass.: Ballinger, 1988), p. 77. Andrew Baxter, "US Drops out of World Machine Tool Top Five," *Financial Times*, February 12, 1991, p. 4.
88. "America's Last Robot," *The New York Times*, September 29, 1990, p. 14.
89. Robert B. Reich, *The Work of Nations* (New York: Knopf, 1991), p. 1.
90. DeAnne Julius, *Global Companies and Public Policy* (London: Royal Institute for International Affairs, 1990).
91. Daniel E. Bob, *Japanese Companies in American Communities* (New York: Japan Society, 1990), p. 1.
92. Ibid., p. 143.
93. Paul Krugman, *The Age of Diminished Expectations* (Cambridge, Mass.: MIT Press, 1990), p. 127.
94. "Bridgestone to Bounce Foreign Workers," *The Nikkei Weekly*, August 10, 1991, p. 8.

CHAPTER 6

1. Thelma Liesner, *One Hundred Years of Progress* (London: The Economist Publications, 1989), p. 76.
2. John Ridding, "South Korea to Allow Foreign Share Ownership," *Financial Times*, June 17, 1991, p. 1.
3. International Monetary Fund, *China: Economic Reform and Macroeconomic Management*, January 1991 (Washington, D.C.: IMF, 1991). "They Couldn't Keep It Down," *The Economist*, June 1, 1991, p. 15.
4. International Monetary Fund, *International Financial Statistics, Yearbook 1990* (Washington, D.C.: IMF, 1990), pp. 287, 289.
5. Robert Wade, *Governing the Market: Economic Theory and the Role of Government in East Asian Industrialization* (Princeton, N.J.: Princeton University Press, 1990), p. 1.
6. "A Survey of Hong Kong: Weighing the Odds," *The Economist*, June 3, 1989, p. 5.
7. Edwin A. Winckler and Susan Greenhalgh, eds., *Contending Approaches to the Political Economy of Taiwan* (New York: Columbia University; Armonk, N.Y., M. E. Sharpe; 1988).
8. 1988 Report Council for Economic Planning & Development (Taiwan Republic of China: Economic Development Commission, 1988), p. 1.
9. Singapore Productivity Board, *Productivity: The Key to Higher Standard of Living* (Singapore: Government of Singapore, 1990), p. 1. *The Next Lap* (Singapore: Government of Singapore, 1991), p. 1.
10. "The Incredible Shrinking Deficit," *The Economist*, August 25, 1990, p. 57.
11. "A Survey of the Yen Block: Together Under the Sun," *The Economist*, June 15, 1991, p. 5. Takashi Noguchi, "Shaping and Sharing Pacific Dynamism," in *The Pacific Region: Challenges to Policy and Theory* (Cambridge, Mass.: American Academy of Political and Social Science, September 1989), p. 48.
12. "Asian Tigers Discover Japan Is Still King of the Jungle," *Financial Times*, March 15, 1991, p. 6.
13. "Too Tough on Knitwear," *The Japan Economic Journal*, November 13, 1990, p. 10.
14. George W. Landau, Julio Feo, and Akio Hosono, *Latin America at a Crossroads*, Trilateral Commission Report no. 39, August 1990 (New York: The Commission, 1990), p. 1.
15. Albert Fishlow, "Latin American Failure Against the Backdrop of Asian Success," in *The Pacific Region*, p. 117.

16. Laurance Whitehead, "Tigers in Latin America," in *The Pacific Region*, p. 142.
17. Fernando Fajnzylber, "Growth and Equity via Austerity and Competitiveness," in *The Pacific Region*, p. 80.
18. Benjamin J. Cohen, "What Ever Happened to the LDC Debt Crisis?" *Challenge*, May/June 1990: p. 47.

CHAPTER 7

1. Walter Russell Mead, "The United States and the World Economy: New Directions for International Policy," *World Policy Journal*, Summer 1989: p. 425.
2. American Council for Capital Formation, *Environmental Policy & the Cost of Capital* (Washington, D.C.: The Council, 1990), p. 1.
3. Leonard Silk, "A Global Program for the Environment," *The New York Times*, April 17, 1990, D2.
4. Jim MacNeill, Peter Winsemius, and Taizo Yakushiji, *Beyond Interdependence: The Meshing of the World's Economy and the Earth's Ecology* (New York: Trilateral Commission, 1990), p. 1.
5. *Managing Planet Earth, Scientific American*, Special Issue, September 1990.
6. S. Fred Singer, "Global Warming: Do We Know Enough to Act?" Center for the Study of American Business, March 1991 (Washington, D.C.: The Center, 1991), p. 1.
7. D. Brooks, "Journalists and Others for Saving the Planet," *The Wall Street Journal*, October 5, 1989, p. 1.
8. *The Economist*, December 15, 1990, p. 100.
9. *DRI/McGraw Hill Review of the U.S. Economy*, October 1990: 13.
10. Keith Bradsher, "U.S. Gap in World Investing," *The New York Times*, June 10, 1991, p. D1.
11. Martin Tolchin and Susan Tolchin, *Buying into America* (New York: Times Books/Random House 1988). p. 1.
12. Alexandre Lamfalussy, "The Credit Crunch is Real," *World Link*, no. 3: 1991, p. 10.

CHAPTER 8

1. "The Nation State," *The Economist*, December 22, 1990, p. 46.
2. Michael Silva and Bertil S. Jogren, *Europe 1992 and The New World Power Game* (New York: Wiley, 1990), p. 1.
3. *OECD Main Economic Indicators*, July 1991: p. 102.
4. *The Banker*, June 1971, p. 663. *American Banker*, July 26, 1991, p. 16A.

5. *Automotive News*, January 11, 1971, p. 4. Automotive News, *Automotive News 1991 Market Data Book*, (Detroit: AN, 1991), entry for May 24, 1991, p. 20.
6. Council of Economic Advisers, *Economic Report of the President 1991* (Washington, D.C.: GPO, 1991), p. 411.
7. *Fortune*, July 30, 1990, p. 109.
8. Ibid.
9. DeAnne Julius, *Global Companies and Public Policy* (London: Royal Institute of International Affairs, 1990), p. 1.

CHAPTER 9

1. John Naisbitt, *Megatrends 2000* (New York: Morrow, 1990), p. 1.
2. Jacques Attali, *Millennium: Winners and Losers in the Coming Order* (New York: Random House/Times Books, 1991) p. 40.
3. Council on Competitiveness, *Competitiveness Index* (Washington, D.C.: The Council, 1988), p. 1.
4. Council of Economic Advisers, *Economic Report of the President, 1991* (Washington, D.C.: GPO 1991), pp. 286, 316.
5. Phil Davis, *The Development of Pension Funds: An International Comparison*, Bank of England Working Paper, May 1991 (London: The Bank, 1991). p.7
6. Council of Economic Advisers, *Economic Report of the President, 1991*, p. 316.
7. U.S. Department of Commerce, *Survey of Current Business*, May 1991: p. 14. Ibid., July 1982: 53.
8. Council of Economic Advisors, *Economic Report of the President, 1990* (Washington, D.C., GPO, 1990), p. 326.
9. *The Economist*, August 11, 1990, p. 98.
10. U.S. Department of Commerce, *Survey of Current Business*, May 1991: 13. Ibid., July 1982: 47.
11. Ibid.
12. Lester C. Thurow, "An Establishment or an Oligarchy?" *National Tax Journal*, December 1989: 405.
13. Kevin Quinn, *False Promises* (Washington, D.C.: Economic Policy Institute, 1990), p. 27.
14. Jeff Faux and Max Sawicky, "Deficit Reduction for Growth and Fairness" (Washington, D.C.: Economic Policy Institute, 1990).
15. *The Economist*, September 20, 1989, p. 105.
16. Rob Norton, "What Ought to Be Done About Taxes," *Fortune*, March 25, 1991, p. 99.
17. Gunther M. Wiedemann, "Uncertainty as Armed Forces Are Cut Back," *The German Tribune*, August 18, 1991, p. 3.

18. "Health Care Survey," *The Economist,* July 16, 1991, p. 5.
19. Committee on America's Future, *An 'Investment Economics' for the Year 2000* (Washington, D.C.: Rebuild America Coalition, 1988).
20. Lester C. Thurow, "VAT: The Least Bad of Taxes," *Newsday,* March, 9, 1986, p. 3.
21. Lester C. Thurow, *The Zero-Sum Solution* (New York: Simon & Schuster, 1985), p. 207.
22. *The Economist,* March 23, 1991, p. 112.
23. John Immerwahr, "Saving: Good or Bad?" (New York: Public Agenda Foundation, 1989), p. 11.
24. Daniel Yankelovich, "The Competitiveness Conundrum," *The American Enterprise,* Sept/Oct 1990: p. 43, 45. Public Agenda Foundation, "Public Misperceptions," Working Paper (New York: The Foundation 1990), Chart A.
25. Martin Gilbert, *Winston S. Churchill* (Boston: Houghton Mifflin, 1983), p. 566.
26. Commission on Workforce Quality and Labor Market Efficiency, *Investing in People,* September 1989 (Washington, D.C.: The Commission, 1989), p. 1. Contains more than five thousand pages of briefing papers on educational problems.
27. Commission on the Skills of the Work Force, *America's Choice: High Skills or Low Wages!* chap. 5 (Washington, D.C.: The Commission, 1990), p. 1.
28. "Job Training: Missing Bridge," *The Economist,* February 9, 1991, p. 30.
29. U.S. Department of Commerce, *Survey of Current Business,* July 1989: 64.
30. Nancy J. Perry, "More Spinoffs From Defense," in *The Next American Century, Fortune,* Special Issue, 1991, p. 72.
31. David Charncross and Ronald Dore, "Employee Training in Japan," Office of Technology Assessment Report (Washington, D.C.: GPO, 1991) p. 23.
32. "A Winning European Formula: Schools + Industry = Work Readiness," *Transatlantic Perspectives,* Spring 1990: 6.
33. Commission on Work Force Skills, *America's Choice,* Chap. 9.
34. "The Next Ages of Man," *The Economist,* December 24, 1988, p. 12.
35. *Education 1990, Fortune,* Special Issue, p. 54.
36. Workforce Quality and Labor Market Efficiency Commission, *Investing in People,* p. 51.
37. "US Sets Priorities," *International Herald Tribune,* February 17, 1988, p. 9.
38. "Role Models Galore," *The Economist,* March 9, 1991, p. 58.

39. John Bishop, *Why the Americans Learn Less Than the Dutch in Secondary School* (Ithaca, N.Y.: Center for Advanced Human Resource Study, Cornell University, 1990), p. 1.
40. M. Edith Rasell and Lawrence Mishel, *Shortchanging Education* (Washington, D.C.: *Economic Policy Institute*, 1990), p. 1.
41. John Bishop, "Incentives for Learning," in *Investing in People*, vol. 1, p. 1.
42. Bishop, "Why Americans Learn Less," in *Investing in People*, vol. 1, p. 41.
43. Commission on Work Force Skills, *America's Choice*, chap. 6, p. 120.
44. Michael L. Dertouzos, Richard Lester, and Robert Solow, *Made in America: Regaining the Productive Edge* (Cambridge, Mass.: MIT Press, 1989), p. 81.
45. U.S. Department of Commerce, *Survey of Current Business*, July 1989: 65.
46. Lester C. Thurow, "A System of Lifetime Voluntary Social Insurance for Education and Training," MIT Working Paper (Cambridge, Mass.: MIT, 1987), p. 1.
47. World Economic Forum, *The World Competitiveness Report, 1990* (Geneva: The Forum, 1991), pp. 10–15.
48. "Keeping America Competitive," *Electronic Business*, January 15, 1988, p. 53.
49. Peter Nulty, "Small Payoffs from Big Deals," *Fortune*, December 7, 1987, p. 137.
50. Robert Taylor, "Ericsson Unveils Record Results (and Stock Price Falls by 11 Percent)," *Financial Times*, February 8, 1991, p. 17.
51. J. Bradford De Long, *Did J. P. Morgan's Men Add Value? A Historical Perspective on Financial Capitalism*, Working Paper (Cambridge, Mass.: Harvard Economics Department, 1989). "The Great American Universal Banking Experiment," *The International Economy*, Jan/Feb 1991: 68.
52. Rob Norton, "Who Owns This Company, Anyhow?" *Fortune*, July 29, 1991, p.131.
53. Gordon B. Baty, "Entrepreneurship: Too Much of a Good Thing?" *MIT Management*, Winter 1988: 17.
54. "Keiretsu: What They Are Doing, Where They Are Heading," *Tokyo Business Today*, September 1990: 26. "Mitsubishi and Daimler-Benz Start Collaboration," *Tokyo Business Today*, November 1990: 8.
55. *The Economist*, August 6, 1988, p. 81.
56. George Bittlingmayer, *The Stock Market and Early Antitrust Enforcement*, FTC Working Paper (Washington, D.C.: Federal Trade Commission, 1990), p. 1.

57. "Low Tricks in High Tech," *The Economist*, September 29, 1990, p. 78.

58. "Mercantilists in Houston," *The Economist*, July 7, 1990, p. 13.

59. William Dullforce, "Japan Viewed As World's Most Unfair Trading Nation," *Financial Times*, March 13, 1990, p. 20.

60. European Community, *Report on United States Trade Barriers and Unfair Practices 1991: Problems of Doing Business with the US* (Washington, D.C.: The Community 1991), p. 1.

61. *Journal of Japanese Trade & Industry*, 1988, no. 4: 15.

62. Rebuild America Coalition, *Fiddling While US Industry Burns*, February 1990 (Washington, D.C.: The Coalition, 1990), p. 1.

63. Chalmers Johnson, "Who's Afraid of Industrial Policy?" *The New York Times*, September 16, 1990, p. C11.

64. Walter Grunsteidle, "An Industrial Policy for Europe," *European Affairs*, Autumn 1990: 14.

65. Clyde H. Farnsworth, "US is Asked to Review Japan Trade," *The New York Times*, March 25, 1991, p. D1.

66. Petro S. Nivola, "More Like Them? The Political Feasibility of Strategic Trade Policy," *The Brookings Review*, Spring 1991: 14.

67. Jeffrey A. Hart and Laura Tyson, "Responding to the Challenge of HDTV," *California Management Review*, Summer 1989: 1.

68. George C. Lodge, *Perestroika for America* (Boston: Harvard Business School Press, 1990), p. 1.

69. Kenneth Froot and David B. Yoffie, *Strategic Trade Policies in a Tripolar World*, HBS Working Paper 11/17/90 (Boston: Harvard Business School, 1990), p. 1. Alfred D. Chandler, Jr., *Scale and Scope: The Dynamics of Industrial Capitalism* (Cambridge, Mass.: Harvard University Press, 1990), p. 1.

70. Lucy Gorham, "No Longer Leading: A Score Card on US Economic Performance and the Role of the Public Sector Compared with Japan, West Germany and Sweden" (Washington, D.C.: Economic Policy Institute, 1988), p. 1.

71. Robert Z. Lawrence, "Innovation and Trade: Meeting the Foreign Challenge," *Setting National Priorities: Policy for the Nineties*, ed. Charles Schultz (Washington, D.C.: Brookings Institution, 1990), pp. 149, 162.

72. Paul Krugman, "Japan is Not Our Nemesis," *NPQ*, Summer 1990, p. 45.

73. National Institute of Economic and Social Research, *National Institute Economic Review*, no. 90 (November 1979): 23. Ibid., no. 132 (May 1991): 23.

74. Council of Economic Advisers, *Economic Report of the President, 1991*, p. 339.

INDEX